The
Police Function
in Canada

Contributors

J. A. Blake
John Braithwaite
William J. Brown
James W. Cooley
H. S. Cooper
Ian V. Dubienski
Golden Leeson
Clare Lewis
Antoine Lussier
William T. McGrath
R. J. Marin
Michael P. Mitchell
Royal Canadian Mounted Police
B. J. Saxton
Clifford D. Shearing
Arn Snyder
Victor Szyrynski
Eric L. Teed

The Police Function in Canada

Edited by

William T. McGrath
Executive Director,
Canadian Criminology and
Corrections Association

and

Michael P. Mitchell
Ministry of the Solicitor
General of Ontario

 **Methuen**

Toronto New York London
Sydney Auckland

Copyright © 1981 by Methuen Publications
A division of the Carswell Company Limited

Canadian Cataloguing in Publication Data

Main entry under title:

The Police function in Canada

Includes index.
ISBN 0-458-93920-X

1. Police – Canada. 2. Law enforcement – Canada.
I. McGrath, William T., 1917–   II. Mitchell,
Michael P., 1949–

HV8157.P65   363.2'3'0971   C80-094068-7

Cover: Patrick Rowan

Printed and bound in Canada
1 2 3 4 5   81   85 84 83 82

Contents

Introduction

In recent years, the function of Canadian police forces has broadened beyond the traditional law enforcement role to encompass problems of a non-criminal origin. As this has evolved, it has become more difficult for police to operate in isolation from the other segments of the criminal justice system.

In *The Police Function in Canada* we have provided an overview of the varied dimensions of the contemporary police function, a historical perspective, and in-depth studies of several specific issues currently confronting private and public police. In this manner, it is hoped that it will be possible to determine what goals police agencies will pursue in the 1980s.

The Police Function in Canada was written primarily as an aid for police training. It should fill a void in the limited literature on Canadian policing by discussing inter-relationships between police and other agencies and by addressing topics which are not discussed in other books. In particular, we have attempted to locate the police role within the context of the entire criminal justice system. It is our hope that this work will provide a starting point for discussion about the police function at present and in the coming decade and will prove valuable to law enforcement officers, trainees and also to readers outside police agencies.

Chapter 1

Crime and the Concept of Justice
W. T. McGrath

Whenever a group of people live and work together, conflicts of interest arise. They arise in small, temporary groups and in the large semi-permanent societies defined by political boundaries. It is essential to orderly living that each society establish rules of conduct and procedures to enforce them.

Some of these rules are informal and are enforced through social pressure. The individual's desire for group approval and his need for friendship will suffice in many instances to ensure his compliance. In highly structured, closed societies extreme pressure can be applied to the individual through ostracism, and in primitive societies little further is needed. It is more difficult to bring social pressure to bear on individuals in our modern urban society.

Behaviour considered too serious or too complex to be dealt with through informal control only is defined in legislation, along with the formal control procedures. *Health and welfare legislation* provides one form of statutory control. People suffering from some illnesses may have their freedom curtailed; those who fail to fulfill their parental duties may find their children removed from their care. No punishment is provided in such legislation.

Civil law settles disputes between individuals or groups where it is considered society has no direct interest beyond ensuring that the dispute is settled fairly and without violence. If, for instance, two parties sign a contract and one party fails to abide by its terms, the aggrieved party may sue under civil law and ask the court to enforce the contract. No punishment is levied against the defaulter, although he may be ordered to pay financial compensation to the aggrieved party and his assets may be seized to ensure payment.

Criminal law is invoked in relation to behaviour considered threatening to the whole community. The conflict is between the offender and the state rather than between the offender and the person he has injured or whose property he has damaged. There is provision for punishment and if the penalty is financial (a fine) it is paid to the state, not to the victim of the crime.

W. T. McGrath is the Executive Director of the Canadian Criminology and Corrections Association.

The distinctions between health, welfare, civil and criminal legislation are not absolute and depend on the interpretation placed on a particular form of behaviour at any given time. Child neglect may lead only to the removal of the child from parental authority, or in more serious cases to a charge under the Criminal Code. At what point a dispute passes from civil to criminal jurisdiction is a matter of judgement. *Diversion* practices, whereby an effort is made to reach an agreement between the offender and his victim that will not involve a court hearing, tend to blur further the distinction between civil and criminal law.

An Arbitrary Definition

Criminal law may be defined as any legislation that forbids any specific act or demands the performance of any specific duty (such as paying income tax) and provides a penalty for non-compliance. A crime is any act that violates the provisions of criminal legislation.

In Canada there is a constitutional limitation on the use of this generally accepted definition of criminal law. The British North America Act places criminal law under the exclusive prerogative of the government of Canada. This means that no provincial statute may be classed as criminal. However, the distinction is a formal one and many provincial statutes function exactly like criminal legislation and would be classified as criminal in other countries. These include laws controlling traffic, liquor, hunting and trading in securities.

Two factors must be present in the commission of a crime: an act by some person or persons and a legal prohibition of that act. The incidence of crime can therefore be increased or decreased by either influencing the behaviour of members of the public or changing the legislation.

Criminal law is established and enforced by political power, and its provisions do not always coincide with abstract notions of justice. In an oligarchy, the law reflects the interests of the ruling class and may be quite opposed to the interests of the majority of citizens. Such undemocratic regimes as South Africa and Zimbabwe Rhodesia are maintained by their criminal law. The will of a conquering power is imposed on the defeated through the law.

The interests of the people as a whole are more to the fore in a democracy, but even under this system criminal law and its enforcement are politically determined and thus subject to the power structure that bears on political decisions. The use of criminal law in recent history to suppress the growth of trade unionism in Britain, the United States and Canada is revealing. The advantage of a democracy is that the people have some recourse against unfair laws. Unfortunately, Canadians are not sufficiently interested or informed about criminal law and the agencies of justice to use their political power effectively.

However, the oft-heard claim that our system of criminal justice is entirely based on political expediency is unsubstantiated. Many politicians and public officials, past and present, have devoted their careers to the furthering of objective principles of justice, and we have the protection of a long tradition that cannot be abandoned without public outcry. At the same time, political reality must be faced.[1]

Changing Patterns of Crime

Patterns of crime are constantly changing as social and technological conditions change. In the past, crime was largely a personal matter between the offender and his victim. Today, new challenges are appearing and traditional concepts, policies and procedures must be adjusted to meet them. Among these new challenges are the following:

(a) *Corporate crime,* which has become particularly acute as criminal syndicates have moved into what were formerly legitimate businesses;
(b) *Invasion of privacy* by electronic eavesdropping and computerized files on individuals held by such groups as credit organizations;
(c) *Ecological defence,* covering the whole range of environmental protection, including false advertising, automobile safety, pollution, noise control, and the destruction of wildlife and parklands;
(d) *Mass demonstrations,* including protests that get out of control and rock festivals where drugs are widely used and sold.

The Aims and Purposes of Criminal Justice

In 1969 the Canadian Committee on Corrections laid down eight principles as appropriate in defining the proper scope and functions of criminal justice.[2] In 1973 the Canadian Criminology and Corrections Association (now the Canadian Association for the Prevention of Crime) issued the following edited version of those eight principles.[3]

1. *The basic purpose of criminal justice is to protect all members of society from seriously harmful and dangerous conduct.*
The emphasis here on protecting the individuals who make up society rather than the structure of society is important. It avoids any implication that the criminal law should be used to protect entrenched privilege beyond the protection offered all citizens.

The rejection of the theory advanced by the Law Reform Commission of Canada that the purpose of the criminal law is to protect so-called community values is also important.[4] Protecting these hard-to-define values sometimes means imposing the will of the majority or of the influential in regard to matters that pose no real danger.

2. *The basic purposes of the criminal law should be carried out with no more interference with the freedom of individuals than is necessary.*
In commenting on this principle, the Canadian Committee on Corrections said:

> Society should receive the maximum protection from criminals that is consistent with the freedom of those to be protected, at the same time inflicting no more harm on the offender than is necessary.
> To accomplish this, the number of laws must be limited to what is essential, since too many laws invite public rejection and increase the scope of state interference while reducing its effectiveness. Police and court procedures must ensure that the process of enforcement will be carried on effectively but with a minimum of interference with the individual. . . .

The criminal law should interfere with social innovation only when necessary. Without innovation, society stagnates.

3. *Recognition of the rights and dignity of all those involved in the criminal justice process, including witnesses, suspects, accused (innocent or guilty), victims and officials, must be assured by proper protection at all stages of the criminal process.*
The need to protect the rights of these people is obvious. Less obvious is the need to protect their dignity. The agencies of justice are not always considerate. The police may speak roughly to a citizen or keep him waiting for attention. Witnesses and accused may be kept waiting in uncomfortable surroundings for long periods prior to court appearances and may be exposed to abuse and ridicule on the witness stand. Law enforcement officers may be subjected to insulting language from members of the public. None of this enhances the dignity or fairness of our criminal justice system.

4. *No conduct should be defined as criminal unless it represents a serious threat to members of society, and unless the act cannot be dealt with through other social or legal means.*

5. *The criminal justice process can operate to prevent crime and protect members of society only by way of:*
  (i) the deterrent effect, both general and particular, of criminal prohibitions and sanctions;

(ii) the educative effect, guiding and alerting members of the public;

(iii) a range of sanctions including prohibitive, custodial and corrective measures, aimed at the rehabilitation of the offender, where possible, and including control and detention under such conditions and for such periods of time as are deemed appropriate within the law and with special consideration to offenders found to constitute a grave threat to the safety and welfare of others;

(iv) compensation and restitution to victims of crime.

The Canadian Committee on Corrections makes this comment:

> The Committee believes that the rehabilitation of the individual offender offers the best long-term protection for society, since that ends the risk of a continuing criminal career. However, the offender must be protected against rehabilitative measures that go beyond the bounds of the concept of justice. Some modern correctional methods, such as probation, suspended sentences and medical treatment are part of the arsenal of sanctions but are not conceived as punishments. Their purpose is rehabilitative. Whatever their purpose, however, it cannot be assumed that such treatment methods are necessarily more humane and more effective in practice than moderate penalties. Treatment is not more humane than punishment if it imposes more pain, restricts freedom for longer periods, or produces no results regarded as desirable by the individual concerned.

6. *The law enforcement, judicial and correctional processes should form an interrelated sequence.*

About this principle, the Canadian Committee on Corrections said:

> There must be consistency in philosophy from the moment the offender has his first contact with the police to the time of his final discharge. In the past, there has been some conflict in aims among the different processes. The aim of corrections has been rehabilitative while the aims claimed for the criminal law have included retribution, deterrence, segregation, denunciation of evil and declaration of moral principles. However, in recent years it is being increasingly recognized that the law enforcement, judicial and correctional processes all share a common overriding aim: the protection of society from criminal activity. Once this is fully recognized the necessity for the three processes to work in harmony will be accepted.

7. *Discretion in the application of the criminal law should be allowed at each step in the process: arrest, prosecution, conviction, sentence and corrections, but such discretion should be controlled within guidelines and applied without unfair discrimination or prejudice.*

Such discretion is already exercised by the authorities, most frequently in connection with minor offences. If charges were laid in every possible instance, the criminal justice system would not be able to handle the workload. A great deal of attention is now being given to the possibility of developing more formal procedures for dealing with adult offenders outside the criminal justice system, as we have been doing with juveniles for many years. These procedures, known under the general term *diversion*, include taking no action at all, but they also include such experiments as getting the offender and his victim to co-operate in working out a solution acceptable to both without a court hearing. A danger in the more formal diversion practices is that an innocent person might be coerced into admitting responsibility for an offence to avoid a trial. Such practices also frequently backfire and result in more people being charged in court because the police avoid the risk of criticism in diverting cases when there is a structured agency to take the responsibility.

8. *The criminal process, including the correctional process, must be such as to command the respect and support of the public according to basic concepts of fairness and justice; the process should also, as far as possible, be such as to command the respect of the offender.*

Protection of Individual Rights
The criminal law performs a vital function in protecting the individual citizen against the arbitrary use of power. The Magna Carta, considered to be one of the pillars of our legal system, is not concerned with protecting society from crime. Its purpose is to set limits on the power of the king and his officials. Three clauses will illustrate its spirit:

> No bailiff shall for the future put any man to trial upon his simple accusation without producing creditable witnesses to the truth thereof. (38)

> No freeman shall be taken, imprisoned, disseised [dispossessed of land], outlawed, banished, or in any way destroyed, nor will we proceed against or prosecute him except by lawful judgement of his peers [equals] or the law of the land. (39)

> To no one will we sell, to none will we deny or defer, right or justice. (40)

The principle that the sovereign is subject to the law is extremely important to the police who function in the sovereign's name: if she is subject to the law, so are the police. It is important that the police set an example of scrupulous observance of the law.

By setting out exactly what actions are legal, the law protects the citizen against an artificial charge being laid against him by the authorities or by an enemy. By setting out the procedures required in dealing with a person charged with an offence, the law protects the citizen against conviction and sentence for an offence he did not commit.

It is not too extreme to say that our democratic way of life itself depends on the protection afforded by the criminal law. Our right to speak out against government policies, to a free vote, and to the other essentials of democracy would be in jeopardy without that protection.

Punishment

Historically, punishment has occupied a central place in criminal justice. It was assumed that human beings are rationally motivated and respond to the threat of punishment in direct proportion to its severity. Modern psychology and sociology have taught us that the sources of human conduct are much too complicated for such simple manipulation.

Three theoretical positions have been developed to guide our dealings with convicted criminals. The *retribution* theory is closely related to the religious principle of atonement and purification through suffering. It expresses the belief that the criminal should suffer for the harm he has done.

To put this theory into practice, a way must be found to assess the degree of guilt so a punishment fitting the crime may be ordered. When all the offender's characteristics are considered—the kind of upbringing he has received, his mental and emotional capacities, the experiences he has lived through—this becomes an impossible task. Retribution comes down to a policy of vengeance, and vengeance is unacceptable as the basis of our justice system.

Many people would maintain that the above is an unfair representation of the theory of retribution. They would argue that its aim is not revenge, but to instill an instinctive abhorrence of crime. However, it would be most difficult to demonstrate that the public's view of any particular crime bears much relationship to the judicial punishment traditionally meted out for it.

The theory of *deterrence* is based on the belief that, when others see the suffering of the condemned person, they will refrain from committing the same or a similar offence. It is impossible in the present state of our knowledge to establish the extent of deterrence generated by the criminal justice system or the conditions under which it operates. While we have been naive in our past reliance on deterrence, it seems reasonable to assume that some deterrent effect does apply. If there were no criminal laws and no prospect of punishment, violent and unscrupulous people would be more active in infringing the rights of others. This was well illustrated by the outbreak of crime during the recent police strikes in Fredericton, Montreal and Regina. Indeed, if the criminal justice system has no deterrent effect, there is no basis for its existence.

Possibly deterrence operates more effectively in relation to some crimes than to others.

There are two groups to be considered in this question of deterrence. The first is people who have never been in trouble with the law, who have secure family, business and other community ties. If the fear of disgrace before friends and business associates and the fear of making his innocent family suffer will not restrain the person who belongs to this group, then neither will the threat of judicial punishment, especially if he believes that the chances of not getting caught are excellent.

The second group consists of those who have already been in trouble with the law and have no reputation to lose. They have relatively little fear of the judicial process and simply hope to avoid being caught. The deterrent effect of punishment is demonstrably weak with this group. It appears, then, that the main deterrent value lies in the probability of arrest and conviction rather than the kind or amount of punishment that might follow.

The third theory of punishment is *reformation*, which is based on the belief that the best protection for members of society lies in the reform of the individual criminal. The pragmatic and humanitarian advantages to this approach are obvious. However, our efforts to develop techniques for "treating" convicted criminals have proved most disappointing and suggest that perhaps the best we can do is avoid the damage to the individual criminal that would arise from excessive punishment or undue interference with his normal way of life. Certainly, any policy of giving a longer or more restrictive sentence on the grounds that the criminal will receive treatment is untenable.

Another function performed by the criminal justice process is the *segregation* of the dangerous offender so he cannot repeat his violent actions. The aim is not punishment or to make the criminal suffer, but simply public protection by prevention. There seems to be a growing acceptance that some violent offenders must be incarcerated for life, with proper review procedures to ensure their release when "cured." This policy would not only protect the public but might relieve public apprehension and permit more experimental approaches to the non-dangerous offender. The difficulty lies in identifying the dangerous offender. Predicting how any individual will behave in the future is a dubious process and it is particularly uncertain in connection with those who have committed violent crimes.

Restitution

The terms *restitution* and *compensation* are often confused. Compensation refers to payments to the victim of a crime or his dependants, by the state if necessary; restitution refers to the contribution to this end by the criminal.

The potential of restitution by the criminal to his victim has never been exploited in Canada. The aim should be to restore as far as possible the situation that existed before the commission of the crime, taking into consideration the victim as well as the criminal.

Restitution may help an offender's rehabilitation by making him feel he has done his best to make amends and can go forward with a clearer conscience. Also, being forced to look at his victim as a person rather than as the faceless target of his crime may help him comprehend the full import of his action.

This theory is in contrast to the effect of imprisonment. It is said that a person who has served a prison term "has paid his debt to society." However, the debt may not be to society but to the person who suffered as a result of the crime. Society gains as much economically when stolen money is spent by the thief as if it were spent by the rightful owner; from society's view, only a redistribution of wealth has occurred. A fine is of benefit to the state but does not help the victim.

Provincial schemes to compensate victims of violent crime are now widespread in Canada. Neither our criminal law nor the practice of our courts stresses restitution by the offender.

The first requirement when a person is convicted of a crime where either physical injury or property loss is involved should be an examination of whether restitution applies and, if so, how it can be implemented. Generally, restitution takes the form of money payments, and many offenders have no resources to make such payments. Restitution should always be related to the offender's ability to pay; loading him with a large debt he cannot discharge would hinder his rehabilitation. Payments on time or even token payments may apply in some cases.

A system whereby the state pays compensation and then receives whatever restitution is available from the criminal is preferable in most instances to having the criminal pay restitution directly to the victim. There are cases, however, especially with juveniles or young adult offenders, where restitution in forms other than cash, and in some instances paid directly to the victim, can have a salutary effect.

There is a public gain when restitution is paid, since the state is relieved of responsibility for compensation to the extent of the restitution. There is also a probable gain in terms of general deterrence. The best way to deter financial crimes may be to ensure that the criminal makes no profit from his crime. Crimes involving environmental damage might also be less frequent if the polluter were required to pay the full cost of the damage he has done. There should be provision for a prison sentence in lieu of payment of restitution.

Restitution should apply not only to individual criminals, but to corporations as well. There are advantages in restitution as applied to corporations, since the alternative of imprisonment is not as readily applicable. A procedure similar to bankruptcy whereby all assets of a major offender, individual or corporate, would be seizable to pay restitution should be introduced.

The fact that a criminal pays restitution does not rule out the possibility of additional penalties.

Some Practical Considerations

The aim is not to control crime as such, since crime exists only as we define it. The aim is to protect members of society against what is seen as dangerous or undesirable behaviour. Just how far we go in providing protection depends on such practical considerations as financial cost and the amount of surveillance the public will tolerate. Oversurveillance is self-defeating. As historian Arthur M. Lower has said, "Democracy is not compatible with too much order and safety."[5]

A distinction should be made between law and order, although the two are often joined in political slogans. Order may be maintained by arbitrary and excessive force, with no regard to law.

There are very few, if any, fully law-abiding citizens. Estimates of undetected adult crime are exceedingly high.[6] Many relatively honest citizens indulge in smuggling.[7] Industrial theft, much of it by employees, is common,[8] and many businesses budget routinely to cover such loss. University bookstores and libraries are particularly vulnerable to theft. Few motorists obey all the rules. Liquor laws are frequently broken. This tendency to crime seems to be greater during youth.

If all dangerous and undesirable behaviour now defined as crime were eradicated, society would find new definitions. As Emile Durkheim pointed out, even in a society of saints, there would be rules and rule breaking.[9]

Some theorists see crime as necessary to a stable society. They maintain that crime performs three useful social functions:

1. *General integration.* Identifying criminal acts permits a harmless channelling of aggression, while reinforcing group solidarity;
2. *Norm reinforcement.* Each public denouncement of a criminal act reminds the public of the norm behind the law and its importance;
3. *Innovation.* Innovation is necessary to any society's survival. Deviant acts serve to stimulate innovation.[10]

Professor J. D. Morton likens the criminal justice process to a morality play.[11] He suggests that the aim is not to identify and punish all criminals, but to select from their numbers a limited group whose public trial and condemnation exerts a beneficial influence on public attitudes toward crime.

This argument may have had more validity in the rural communities of the past, but it probably does not apply in modern urban Canada. In rural areas everyone knows when an individual is charged with a crime, and they follow his trial with interest. They also know his sentence if he is convicted. Who knows what goes on in the courts of a modern city? Not one case in five hundred is mentioned in the press. Even serious offences like armed robbery get little or no coverage unless there is something unique about the crime. In what way is today's citizen impressed by the solemnity of court proceedings or deterred by the punishments meted out?

If the proposition that we all have tendencies toward illegal behaviour and that crime is a necessary ingredient of society is accepted, a number of interesting conclusions follow:

1. Two categories of crime must be recognized. The first includes the type of crime most, if not all, citizens get involved in or would if they had the opportunity. Those convicted of this kind of crime usually cannot be classed as "abnormal" or "sick," although there are exceptions. The second category is more limited and consists of the types of crime, often involving violence, the average citizen seldom commits, although he may do so in an extreme situation. Those who commit this category of crime can probably be classed as "abnormal," although not necessarily insane.
2. There is nothing to "treat" in those who indulge in "normal" crime, although they may need practical assistance in getting reestablished. Some of those who commit "abnormal" crimes do need treatment.
3. The search for causes of crime based on statistical analysis of psychological or social characteristics is futile, although the etiology of "abnormal" crime is pertinent. Greater stress should be put on the study of crime rather than criminals, and on the process that selects a few of the many offenders for condemnation.
4. The elimination of crime is an unattainable dream. We can, however, reduce its incidence. Reducing major crime may be more feasible than reducing minor crime.
5. The "we-they" approach to crime control is invalid. There is probably no fully law-abiding segment of society.
6. Too high a crime rate indicates that society is failing to provide sufficient opportunities for its members. Too quiescent a society may indicate stagnation.

Economic Theories of Crime

The newest theories related to crime and its control come from the science of economics.[12] These theories are gaining in popularity because they stress deterrence and are in tune with the backlash against what is seen as laxity in crime control. They are also attractive because they deal with concrete matters and offer simple, if expensive, solutions.

The economists maintain that society is motivated by economic factors, but they recognize that other factors, some based on reason and some on emotion, enter in. They do not try to predict the behaviour of people as individuals, but focus only on the aggregate. These theories do not require an explanation of how an individual's preferences have come about. What matters is what he wants today. The individual's preferences cannot be measured directly, but they are reflected in behaviour that can be measured in economic terms; i.e., what he is willing to give up to satisfy his preference. For instance, the size of the fine an individual is willing to pay to avoid imprisonment is a measure of how much he values his freedom.

Criminal behaviour can be reduced in society if its economic rewards are reduced. There are two ways in which these economic rewards can be curtailed:

1. The perceived economic disparities among members of society can be lessened or eliminated. The term "perceived" is important here: the individual is influenced by comparisons between what he has and what others have, rather than by absolute measures of poverty. The supporters of this approach have suggested such extreme actions as the elimination of inheritance and a high-level guaranteed income. It has even been suggested that the criminal justice system be eliminated and the money used to equalize economic opportunity.
2. The criminal should be required to make good the economic cost of his crime.

There are three major weaknesses in these theories:

(a) They assume a dollar has the same value for everyone, which is obviously not true. The millionaire may be willing to pay a higher fine than the poor man because he can afford it, not because he values his freedom more highly;

(b) They give no recognition to moral considerations, only economic. If a thief could show greater economic return from what he has stolen than the original owner could, his theft would be considered acceptable;

(c) They fail to take into account the fact that only a minority of criminals are caught, and the threat of economic reprisals is reduced accordingly. The cost of raising law enforcement to the point where a substantial majority of criminals would be caught would be prohibitive.

Criterion of Right

There is a lack of agreement as to the proper basis for determining what actions should be defined as crime and what procedures are acceptable as fair and just. There are, in the writer's opinion, only three possible criteria: divine revelation, the opinion of experts, and public opinion.

Divine revelation has exerted a very great influence on the criminal law. It was even maintained that many of the earlier codes were dictated directly by some deity. This was true of Mosaic law, which has had such influence on those countries that adhere to Christianity. However, belief in divine revelation is not as widespread today, and to ask the public, and perhaps particularly youth, to accept it as the basis for the criminal law is no longer feasible. Another obvious difficulty is that the various religions have had different revelations, and in a multi-religion country such as Canada these differences are hard to reconcile.

The opinion of experts is equally unacceptable. Experts, by their very nature, deal in limited areas, and the more expert they become in their own field, the less they know about other matters. A narrow approach based on expertise is particularly dangerous in relation to a topic like criminal justice which affects every facet of life. There is also the problem of choosing which experts on whom to rely. Some people would say this is a task for the lawyers, others for the sociologists, psychologists or theologians.

If, then, divine revelation and the opinion of experts are rejected as the measure of what is right and what is wrong in criminal law, only public opinion is left.

This is a crucial point. As long as we maintain that there is some eternal, divine or objective principle or set of principles underlying our criminal law, our system of justice will continue to be out of touch with reality on many important issues. If, instead, we recognize the criminal law for what it is, a pragmatic, necessarily imperfect attempt to reach a difficult goal, then greater realism should characterize our efforts.

The difficulty, or perhaps impossibility, of getting a full picture of what the public wants on a topic as complicated as the criminal law must be recognized. It is obvious that the criminal law cannot be in a constant state of flux to reflect temporary changes in public opinion; some permanence is necessary to provide stability of application. Also, we must remember the lessons of history. Many of the principles on which our criminal law is based were established after centuries of bitter experience, and we would be foolish to abandon them without most careful consideration. Nevertheless, despite all these difficulties, in the long run there can be no criterion in this matter except public opinion.

Putting such a tenet into practice would require regular and organized efforts to test public opinion on matters related to criminal justice. It would also require a continuing and concentrated program to inform the public on these matters.

One change that is necessary if the public is to understand our criminal law, and be in a position to influence its provisions, is to abandon the unnecessarily complicated and technical language in which our legislation is written. The practice here is in sharp contrast to that in Europe, where criminal laws are usually brief and written in clear, non-technical language. We seem to believe that every possible eventuality should be spelled out fully in written form. The Europeans are content to set out principles, leaving the details to established practice and the courts.

The Adversary Concept

The Canadian citizen probably sees a criminal trial not as an objective effort to get at the truth, but as a game which employs very peculiar rules and where the best equipped team wins. If he is charged with a criminal offence, he believes that a lawyer competent in playing the game can get him off.

This view stems from our adversary system of criminal proceedings. Our trials are presided over by a judge who knows nothing about the case except what is told him in court. He plays a passive role in the trial, except for seeing that the rules of judicial procedure are followed. He may know that important information is being kept from him, but his decision must be based only on what is presented in court. The two sides—prosecution and defence—take turns presenting their side of the case from frankly biased positions. This is where the term "adversary system" comes from. The same procedures hold if there is a jury.

In theory, the Crown is expected to be neutral and to present only unbiased information to the court but, although there are limits placed on the Crown's freedom, in most cases the responsibility for bringing out evidence that favours the accused rests with the defence.

The critics of our adversary system give many examples of what they see as its shortcomings. They point to limitations on the power of the judge to play more than a passive role in the trial, even when he knows important information has not been placed before him. They point to the right of the accused to remain silent, the freeing of accused persons on technicalities, the confusion over expert witnesses (especially psychiatric witnesses), the policy in preliminary hearings to produce only enough evidence to establish a *prima facie* case (sufficient justification to send the accused to trial) rather than full disclosure, and to the ban on hearsay evidence.

These criticisms are not necessarily justified, and they cannot all be debated in this short space. The question of full disclosure at the preliminary hearing will serve as an illustration of what seems just criticism. At present, only such evidence is presented by the prosecution at the preliminary hearing to establish that there are sufficient grounds for sending the accused to trial. The defence is not required to disclose any of its evidence whatever. This means both parties may come to trial with little knowledge of what evidence will be presented by the opposition, and both parties are in a position to spring surprises, not very helpful in establishing the truth. If full disclosure were required of both parties, they would come to the trial fully prepared, and an accurate picture of the true situation should be easier to obtain.[13]

Conclusion

Criminal justice is going through a period of upheaval. Traditional policies and practices are being challenged on sound grounds. Major changes will occur, but it is far from clear what those changes will be. Those employed in the field must be prepared to adapt to these changes and should play a part in determining what the new policies and practices are to be. Working under such conditions will be difficult, but there will be compensation in helping develop a better system.

NOTES
1. Guy Tardif, *Police et politique au Québec.* Montreal: L'Aurore, 1974.
2. Canada. Department of the Solicitor General, *Toward Unity: Criminal Justice and Corrections.* Report of the Canadian Committee on Corrections. Ottawa: 1973, chapter 2.
3. Canadian Criminology and Corrections Association, *Toward a New Criminal Law for Canada.* Ottawa: 1973.
4. Law Reform Commission of Canada, *Working Paper 3: The Principles of Sentencing and Dispositions.* Ottawa: 1974.
5. Arthur M. Lower. "Two Ways of Life: The Spirit of Our Institutions," *The Canadian Century.* Toronto: Gage Educational Publishing, 1933, p. 170.
6. See, for instance, United States of America, President's Commission on Law Enforcement and Administration of Justice, *Task Force Report: Crime and Its Impact—an Assessment.* Washington: U.S. Government Printing Office, 1967, pp. 7-19.
7. "Few People Come Through Customs Without Trying to Cheat a Little," Toronto *Globe and Mail,* 12 August 1974, p. 5.
8. Canadian Association of Chiefs of Police, *Report of the Crime in Industry Committee.* Ottawa: Journal of Proceedings, August 27–September 1, 1972, pp. 41–45.

9. Emile Durkheim. *Rules of Sociological Method.* Glencoe, Ill.: Free Press, 1950.
10. Patrik Tornudd. "The Futility of Searching for Causes of Crime," *Scandinavian Studies in Criminology,* Volume 3. Oslo: Universitetsforlaget, 1971.
11. J. D. Morton. *The Foundation of Criminal Law in 1962.* Toronto: Canadian Broadcasting Corporation, 1962.
12. Richard F. Sullivan. "The Economics of Crime: An Introduction to the Literature," *Crime and Delinquency,* April 1973.
13. Law Reform Commission of Canada, *Working Paper 4: Criminal Procedure, Discovery.* Ottawa: 1974.

FURTHER READINGS

Allen, Francis A. *The Crime of Politics.* Chicago: University of Chicago Press, 1974.
Andenaes, Johannes. *Punishment and Deterrence.* Ann Arbor: University of Michigan Press, 1974.
Canada. Department of the Solicitor General. *Toward Unity: Criminal Justice and Corrections.* Ottawa: Information Canada, 1969.
Canadian Criminology and Corrections Association. *The Child Offender and the Law.* Ottawa: 1963.
_____. *Toward a New Criminal Law for Canada.* Ottawa: 1973.
Doleschal, Eugene and Nora Klapmuts. "Toward a New Criminology," *Crime and Delinquency Literature.* Hackensack: National Council on Crime and Deliquency, Vol. 5, No. 4 (December, 1973).
Evans, Robert. *Developing Policies for Public Security and Criminal Justice.* Ottawa: Economic Council of Canada, 1973.
Lower, Arthur M. "Two Ways of Life: the Spirit of Our Constitutions," in A. J. M. Smith, *The Canadian Century.* Toronto: Gage Educational Publishing, 1973.
McGrath, W. T. *Youth and the Law.* Toronto: Gage Educational Publishing, 1973.
_____. *Crime and Its Treatment in Canada.* Toronto: Macmillan Company of Canada, 1975.
McRuer, J. C. *The Evolution of the Judicial Process.* Toronto: Clarke, Irwin and Co., 1957.
Morton, J. D. *The Foundation of Criminal Law in 1962.* Toronto: Canadian Broadcasting Corporation, 1962.
Reasons, Charles E. *The Criminologist: Crime and the Criminal.* Pacific Palisades: Goodyear Publishing Company, 1974.
Scandinavian Research Council for Criminology. *Scandinavian Studies in Criminology,* Vol. 3. Oslo: Universitetsforlaget, 1971.

Chapter 2

The Living Law
R. J. Marin

Are we well served by our criminal law? Are we subservient to it? Is crime reaching crisis proportions? Are the courts beset by the worst backlog of cases in our history?

On all of these topics, opinion is divided. Some claim that we are facing a major crisis, while others point to history, suggesting that it inevitably repeats itself. In criminal justice, answers are seldom definite and rarely either totally correct or totally wrong. An examination of the history of law enforcement does, however, provide an interesting dimension to the problem; a close examination of our statistics on crime perhaps suggests a less alarming situation than we have been led to believe. While the legislative process is considered slow, and painfully so at times, it is equally prudent to ensure that we do not overreact legislatively to all apprehended wrongdoing, imagined or real, merely because it is different conduct, which may offend some but harm no one.

Crime and Crime Control; A Historical Overview

Concern about crime, law enforcement and the means available to control antisocial behaviour is not new. Before the Norman Conquest of England, the headman and the members of each settlement were responsible for each other's conduct under the law, and the internal peace of each locality. Unless excused, every adult male was enrolled in a group of ten families, known as a tithing, headed by a tithing-man. If any member of the group committed a crime, the others had to produce him for trial. Failure to do so resulted in the payment of compensation. In turn, these groups of ten were incorporated into groups of one hundred, and the head man of that group, known as the hundred-man, exercised judicial control within his jurisdiction. His powers were both judicial and administrative. He, in turn, was responsible to a sheriff, who was directly answerable to the king for keeping the peace in a predefined area. The sheriff could muster a

Judge Marin is a County and District Court Judge and was formerly with the Law Reform Commission of Canada. He was Chairman of an Inquiry into Public Complaints, Internal Discipline and Grievance Procedure within the RCMP.

"posse" in case of emergency. In addition, anyone in the community could expect to be called upon to join in pursuing a "felon" if a "hue and cry" were raised.

When England became united in one kingdom, the king, in return for the loyalty of his subjects, accepted the obligation to keep the king's peace. The Norman Conquest changed nothing: the sheriff's functions, however, were not only retained but increased. Local barons also developed their own local courts. It is only in the thirteenth century that the word "constable" first appeared in English. Originally the "parish constable" inquired into offences, served summonses and executed warrants; he also organized the "hue and cry" and took charge of prisoners. Despite the additional powers given to the first justice of the peace appointed in 1361, the duty to keep the peace remained the responsibility of every citizen.

The system of law enforcement and the assistance provided by ill-paid and often ignorant men appointed as substitutes for the appointed unpaid constables precluded proper enforcement and did little to suppress crime. This led to public concern about whether or not the law could be enforced to the satisfaction of the public.

Much reliance was placed on the harshness of the criminal law to deter citizens from committing crime. Punishment was usually swift and certain; until the mid-nineteenth century, there were almost three hundred crimes in England punishable by a corporal punishment similar to or appropriate to the offence committed. More than two hundred crimes were subject to capital punishment; in 1785 there were ninety-seven executions, but only one of these was for a conviction of murder, the others were mostly for theft or other property offences.

The harshness of the criminal law was such that Blackstone in his *Commentaries* noted that:

> ... among the variety of actions which men are daily liable to commit, no less than 160 have been declared by act of Parliament to be felonies without the benefit of clergy: or in other words to be worthy of instant death. So dreadful a list instead of diminishing, increase the number of offenders ...[1]

The overriding consideration was the belief that behaviour could be controlled by fear. It was popularly believed that punishment would deter the offender and prevent others from committing the same offence. However, despite the harshness of punishment, disorder flourished in the eighteenth century, especially in large metropolitan areas, as villagers decided to settle into urban areas and crowded into slums to seek work in factories.

In 1748 Henry Fielding became chief magistrate at Bow Street and his concern about the corrupt state of justice and the amount of unpunished crime in London did much to arouse public concern. He and his brother, John, were instrumental in organizing a full-time body of uniformed men to patrol the streets of London and to apprehend criminals. However there was a reluctance by many to sacrifice freedom of action; it was generally felt that policing might do just that. Policing, according to John Fielding, was to be merely preventive. He is reported to have said: "It is much better to prevent even one man from being a rogue than apprehending and bringing forty to justice."[2]

Organized Law Enforcement

Two events acted as catalysts and served to prepare the population of London for organized policing. The Gordon Riots of 1780 alarmed the public. A large part of London had been set on fire by an anti-Catholic mob. The London population was aroused—but not sufficiently to take action towards the establishment of a police force. In 1786, while England was still discussing the idea, the City of Dublin set up a full-time police force. Likewise, in 1800, in an effort to combat crime in the Port of London, the Thames River Police Force was established.

Then, in 1811, two entire families in London's East End were silently exterminated in macabre circumstances, and the event left London in the grip of public panic. Hesitation concerning the need for an organized police force vanished almost instantly. Armed patrols were formed and the culprit was arrested. The suspect, however, committed suicide by hanging himself in his cell, prior to being brought to justice. The home secretary, because of public concern as to whether or not the suspect had escaped or committed suicide, authorized the body to be displayed in a high, open cart, which was driven slowly along the crowded streets of London.

Sir Robert Peel, then home secretary, sought to introduce a bill to establish a full-time police force but a select committee of the House of Commons rejected the idea as being inconsistent with political freedom.

Some critics felt that the establishment of a full-time police force would adversely affect the freedom of action that was essential to British society.

This idea was not new. Jeremy Bentham (1748–1832), a man of great influence in many branches of public affairs, widely circulated the works of Italian Marquis Beccaria, whose "Essay on Crime and Punishment" was translated to English. The essay advocated that:

> It is better to prevent crimes than to punish them. This is the chief aim of every good system of legislation, which is the art of leading men to the greatest possible happiness or to the least possible misery, according to calculation of all the goods and evils of life.[3]

The similar views of Voltaire also had equal prominence.

While some worked to control crime and have the laws respected through the establishment of an organized police force, others assumed the role of criminal law reformers, attempting "to purify the criminal code from its medieval barbarity." Eventually it appears that both groups merged in support of Bentham's proposed Constitutional Code, advocating a centralized preventive police system under the control of the government. His support and that of a lawyer, Edwin Chadwick, helped Peel succeed in his idea of establishing a police force in London in 1829. He introduced the Metropolitan Police Act, which he described in Parliament as a project for a vigorous preventive police force consistent with the "free principles of our free constitution."

One of the first orders of the Metropolitan Police stated:

> It should be understood, at the outset, that the principal object to be attained is the prevention of crime. To this goal, every effort of the police is to be directed. The security of person and property, the preservation of public tranquillity and all the other objects of a Police Establishment will thus be better effected than by the detection and punishment of the offender, after he has succeeded in committing the crime.[4]

Thus, it came to pass that the concern for controlling crime and having the laws enforced was passed to an organized police force, but not without some misgivings and many subsequent aborted attempts to abolish the new police force.

As a footnote to history, it must be remembered that while Sir Robert Peel was instrumental in the establishment of the first police force in England, he was equally active in purifying the Criminal Code of some of its medieval barbarity. As home secretary, he introduced and supervised legislation abolishing capital punishment for almost one hundred offences.

Is the Rate of Criminality Beyond Control?

It is necessary at the outset to reaffirm that society's ultimate goal is to be free of crime. However, it appears that we see more and hear more about crime today than ever before, and one has to wonder whether or not we are in the middle of a new crime wave of proportions yet undetermined.

An examination of events preceding the formation of organized police forces in England leaves no room for doubt that there was indeed very serious crime as early as the thirteenth century. Crime also appeared to rise in direct proportion to the urbanization of certain areas. It is equally important to remember that all was not well in the field of law enforcement even after the creation of the first police force. There were, as early as 1918, police strikes. In 1918, six thousand members of the Metropolitan London Police went on strike to draw attention to poor working conditions and inadequate pay. A committee appointed under Lord Desborough recommended higher pay and better working conditions. Discontent, however, did not abate and before the recommendation contained in Desborough's report could be acted upon, a second strike was called in August 1919. This time the issue was recognition of a police union. The union was never recognized, its members were fired and it was made an offence for policemen on the Metropolitan Police Force to join a trade union or to go on strike.

Here in Canada, and indeed throughout North America, crime and violence were present throughout the eighteenth and nineteenth centuries. The exploration of the American West was accompanied by violence and coercion; indeed, it was the violence that resulted in the massacre of a party of Assiniboine Indians at Cypress Hill by Americans in 1873 that led directly to the creation of the Northwest Mounted Police. While its establishment had been discussed before, it appeared crystallized in part by the desire to extend law enforcement to the West.

In Montreal in 1849 the Parliament buildings were set on fire by the English-speaking citizens of that city to protest the signing of the Rebellion Losses Bill: the governor general, Lord Elgin, was stoned in the same incident.[5] In 1853 the Gavazzi Riots resulted in the death of several soldiers and eleven citizens who themselves were attempting to attack anti-Catholic lecturer Alessandro Gavazzi.

The development of our West and the discovery of gold in the Yukon were both accompanied by violence and serious crimes. Some of our most notable strikes have seen not only violence but a high degree of bloodshed and criminality: the coal miners' strike at Estevan, Saskatchewan; the Winnipeg general strike; the Quebec asbestos workers' strike and the Newfoundland woodworkers' strike are but a few examples that should serve to remind us that violence did not begin in this or in the last decade.

It is, of course, impossible to determine how much crime has been prevented by the presence of organized police forces, but it should be observed that the original goal of Peel to control crime by prevention has been elusive as a concept of crime control or as a concept of law enforcement. To suggest, however, that crime has risen to an unprecedented level is to ignore facts of historical relevance.

Let us examine the long-term statistics extracted from *The Criminal in Canadian Society*, a 1973 publication of the Department of the Solicitor-General.[6]

44981

Year	Indictable Offences per 100,000 population
1891	112.5.
1911	238.00
1930–1960	500 to 550
1960	600 to 635

The interpretation of statistics is always hazardous; one has to use a great deal of care not to give to statistical data a dimension that is neither desired nor supportive of the facts.

Several figures on crime trends only show an increase in crimes without the necessary and indispensable correlation to population increase, or clarification as to whether it is a crime charged or conviction recorded. The necessity in some cases of charging an individual with more than one offence arising out of one set of circumstances must be appreciated and should properly be reflected in statistical data.

Some statistics give the reader little assistance. For example, the 1975 *Report of the Solicitor General for Canada*[7] contains figures with respect to crime trends in the area of policing by the RCMP. These read as follows:

Crime Trends (All Offences)
Calendar Years

Offences	1973	1974	Percent Increase
Person	29,087	31,785	9.3
Property	137,749	164,402	19.4
Criminal Code Traffic	54,655	61,489	12.5
Total Criminal Code	354,077	387,218	9.4
Federal (Other)	41,090	42,236	2.8
Drugs	29,146	30,476	4.6
Total Federal	70,236	72,712	3.5
Provincial	141,759	150,585	6.2
Provincial Traffic	357,109	381,975	7.0
Municipal	13,606	17,862	31.3
Total Offences	936,787	1,010,352	7.9

A close examination of these figures reveals the highest increases in property, Criminal Code traffic and municipal offences. The increase in municipal offences, however, does not reflect an increase in serious crimes of violence, as these offences are of a comparatively minor nature.

Statistics on crime are largely dependent on improvements in policing and statistical reporting. Likewise, the endless list of new offences on our books has certainly had an impact on property and municipal offence statistics. Again, one has to consider the increase in the number of motor vehicle-related offences, which have multiplied each year at an alarming rate. The automobile hardly had an impact on our criminal law in 1930. One also has to examine property offences in light of the insistence of some retailing outlets in displaying their wares in a most vulnerable way. This increases the number of thefts. To this, one must also add the variable of the more open availability of cash in banking institutions and the fact that often preventive measures by banking institutions to protect their vulnerability are sometimes haphazard. The Stockholm Police Force succeeded in reducing the rate of armed robbery from banks in the City of Stockholm in one year by almost 30 percent through proper preventive measures exercised by the banks, but legislated by the central government.

One also has to consider the increased ability of provinces to enact legislation and create new offences of a quasi-criminal nature. In 1969, 1.4 million convictions out of 1.8 million recorded related directly to provincially enacted offences. The Law Reform Commission noted that there were seven hundred Criminal Code offences in Canada, plus 20,000 federal offences of a criminal nature, and 20,000 offences created by provincial law, in addition to a multitude of municipal by-law offences, all of them of a quasi-criminal nature.

Surely there has been an increase in criminality and no amount of eloquence can avoid that reality. The increase, however, should neither be exaggerated nor used to exert pressure against fundamental rights asserted in the Canadian Bill of Rights.

Many look to the backlog in our courts and suggest that the volume of crime can best be illustrated by the sheer accumulation of cases awaiting trial by jury. This suggestion can also be misleading. J. Peter Rickaby, Q.C., Crown Attorney for the Judicial District of York, in an address delivered on 9 April 1976 to the Advocates' Society on the theme "Crises in the Criminal Court—Justice or Chaos," said:

> In 1961 there were four magistrates courts operating at the Old City Hall and about five courts in the suburbs which operated about three days a week each. The courts at the Hall ran five days a week but rarely sat in the afternoon. There were two county courts, one for sessions cases and one for CCJCC cases. About thirty cases per sessions were heard by a grand jury at the beginning of each session, and these cases were generally completed by the end of that session with some time to spare. That year there appeared to be 134 jury trials, thirteen of which were drug cases taken by special prosecutors appointed by the federal

Department of Justice. Also that year there were approximately 125 CCJCC cases heard. Life in the Crown Attorney's Office was pleasant and unhurried; there was time and time enough; there was lots of time to prepare for anything unusual in the otherwise very manageable court lists. Legal Aid consisted of one man, Jack Weisdorf whose salary was paid by the Law Society and who was provided with part-time secretarial services.

Let me make it clear that there is no artifice to my figures or to my selection of 1961 as an unusual year; the number of cases tried in the county court is about the same for any of the four years on either side of 1961.

Compare that with the scene today. In 1976 there are fifteen provincial criminal courts operating at the Old City Hall, five days a week, morning and afternoon. In the Metro suburbs there are still only six courts but some are so badly overloaded (with cases being set for trial five or six months hence) that in two of them I have had to provide two Crowns to handle one court. There are an additional two provincial courts north of Metro. There are eight county courts running ten months of the year with one or two operating in July and August, which last year, heard over 1,600 cases and to which over 2,000 cases were committed for trial; the difference being part of a steadily growing backlog. These county courts, of course, process jury and non-jury trials indiscriminately. The cost of criminal legal aid for York County for the year ending March 1975 was $4.8 million. It is interesting that there appear to be almost exactly four times as many courts operating here as there were in 1961. This factor of four also appears in the police disposition rate, which in 1961 was about 27,000 and in 1975 was [about] 100,000. I will explain what "disposition" is in a minute.

So what's happened over the last fifteen years? We can't blame it on a huge population increase; the County of York population has risen only about a third, from 1.7 million in 1961 to about 2.3 million in 1974, the latest figures available, let's say, 2.4 million now. *What about a monster crime wave? No, that won't do, I still feel safe on the streets of Toronto.* Ah, you will say, we remember or have heard about those dark ages before legal aid, described recently in a letter to the *Globe* as being "a stain on the history of the administration of justice," this by a lawyer who at the time would be still wet behind the ears; we know that accused pleaded guilty without benefit of legal advice, often because he couldn't raise the bail or didn't know the professional bondsmen, or the coppers coaxed him into it; we know that only those that could afford it or who could steal the money could retain a lawyer to take the case "upstairs" to a jury where they stood a better chance of acquittal. Surely Rickaby must understand that the huge increase in the election of trial by jury is a demonstration that, by providing legal aid to the poor, the scales of justice have been balanced and we are now witnessing the selection of a forum, the county court, that was only available to the well-off before.

Well, I don't want to disillusion you, but here comes that paradox. *Taking into account the population increase, there are fewer jury trials now than there were in 1961.* Fewer jury trials. . . . In 1961 there were 134 jury trials, of which thirteen were drug cases. In 1975 there were 181 jury trials, of which about fifty were drug cases. This leaves about 130 cases under the Criminal Code—hardly a significant increase from 120 in 1961.[8]

The words of J. Peter Rickaby should remind us that the crisis in our courts is not such as to cause undue alarm or curtail trials by jury for some offences. While they do not suggest that matters will resolve themselves automatically, neither should it be suggested that rash action should be undertaken, nor that basic and fundamental rights should be curtailed to meet an immediate or forthcoming crisis. Those who advocate more laws and a creation of more offences as a measure of control should perhaps consider the next move with much care.

Dynamics of the Legislative Process

All federal legislation must receive parliamentary approval: in actuality, all legislative proposals of general importance are first introduced and passed in the House of Commons. The Senate's occasional resistance may be regarded as a conditional impediment rather than a positive menace to the power of the Commons, so that in effect the House of Commons initiates all federal legislation. Usually a minister will initiate legislative changes after consultation with his Cabinet colleagues. The minister, before bringing his proposed bill to the consideration of his Cabinet confrères, will have had an opportunity to examine the proposal carefully with his senior departmental advisers. Once the proposed bill has received the blessing of Cabinet, the caucus is assessed of the proposed law before it is tabled in the House of Commons. The tabling constitutes a first reading, which is usually followed by a close examination, clause by clause, of the proposed law by a committee of the House chosen for that purpose. The appropriate committee is representative of the government and opposition parties: to these members fall the task of a detailed discussion of the most important bills and the investigation of matters related to them.

It is unfortunate that so little publicity is given to this important stage of parliamentary proceedings. Two bills in recent years deserve comment because of the excellence of the discussion held at the committee stage. These are the Bail Reform Act and the Protection of Privacy Act, both of which were discussed at length by the Justice and Legal Affairs Committee of the House of Commons. Both of these bills were thoroughly examined and witnesses were heard in support of and against these proposals. This type of participation is available to all sectors of the public, but unfortunately is seldom used.

Once the bill has gone through committee, it is referred or returned to the House of Commons for second reading and approval in principle, with any changes suggested by the committee. The third reading and vote are in many cases a matter of routine, although it became much less routine in 1976, when the bill to abolish capital punishment was returned to the House for a third reading and vote.

The bill is then sent to the Senate and the process is repeated; after final reading and vote in the Senate the bill becomes law upon receiving royal assent, given by the governor general or his appointee, who is usually the chief justice of Canada or another judge of that court acting as "persona designata." Some laws come into effect on a date to be proclaimed; others on receiving royal assent.

The legislative process in the provincial legislative assembly is identical, with the exception that the provincial legislature does not have an upper house or senate.

Many have expressed some disenchantment with the legislative process and the heavy machinery of government that must be invoked each time it is sought to amend, enact or repeal a law. Often it is suggested that the legislative process does not keep up with the times and that the government hardly has time to be innovative in the field of criminal law given all the other more urgent priorities that inevitably confront it in its day-to-day administration. Accordingly, it is suggested that government has little or no time to involve itself in law reform.

In England this realization led to the creation of a law reform commission in 1965. Lord Scarman, the chairman of that commission, on the occasion of the Lindsay Memorial Lecture delivered at the University of Keele in November 1967, said:

> The government and Parliament have recognized reform as a responsibility of the legislature. They have established an advisory legal body, institutional in character, to plan the course of reform, and to formulate detailed reform proposals for their consideration and, also, for the consideration of the public. Nevertheless, it is intended to keep law reform out of politics. In this endeavour reliance will be placed both upon the character of the Commission, divorced as it is from the executive and Parliament, and upon the very process it is called upon to operate, i.e., the independent planning and formulation of proposals—both to be carried out in the full glare of publicity before submission to the government or Parliament. The idea is that this independent specialist body should engage in a process which is itself designed to produce proposals that, by the time they are submitted to Parliament, will enjoy a substantial consensus of opinion, both in the legal profession and amongst the lay interests affected.[9]

England's lead was followed in Canada in 1970 when Minister of Justice John N. Turner tabled in Parliament the Law Reform Commission Act (R.S.C. 1970, C.23, 1st Supp.). It is significant that his predecessor, Pierre Trudeau, had conceived of such a commission as early as 1966.

The objects of the Law Reform Commission are contained in Section 11 of the Act and read as follows:

11.   The objects of the Commission are to study and keep under review on a continuing and systematic basis the statutes and other laws comprising the laws of Canada with a view to making recommendations for their improvement, modernization and reform, including, without limiting the generality of the foregoing:

(a) the removal of anachronisms and anomalies in the law;

(b) the reflection in and by the law of the distinctive concepts and institutions of the common law and civil law legal systems in Canada, and the reconciliation of differences and discrepancies in the expression and application of the law arising out of differences in those concepts and institutions;

(c) the elimination of obsolete laws; and

(d) the development of new approaches to and new concepts of the law in keeping with and responsive to the changing needs of modern Canadian society and of individual members of that society.

The Minister of Justice outlined his "Manifesto for Law Reform in the '70s" in a speech given in Montreal, when he said:

The faith that must move us, then, is the creative and even revolutionary role that law can play in the building and restructuring of a new society. For law is not just a "technical body of rules"; it is the organizing principle for the reconfiguration of society. Law is not just an agency of social control; it articulates the values by which men seek to live. The business of government, then, is the making of laws, and the process of law reform goes to the core of defining the kind of society we will have as a Canadian people and the kind of rights which we will enjoy as individuals.
  . . . It is somewhat commonplace to say that legislatures are continually engaged in law reform; indeed, the very business of government is the making of laws. However, such law-making tends to be organized around reports of Parliamentary committees, task forces or royal commission reports and bills which have come forward as a result of work in government departments. What is needed, however, is an institution uniquely dedicated to the process of law reform.[10]

The first chairman of the Law Reform Commission, the Honourable E. P. Hartt, put it this way when addressing the Canadian Association of Chiefs of Police, in Edmonton, in August of 1970:

What our law has lacked in the past has been an institution uniquely dedicated to the process of systematic law reform in order to give institutional expression to this double function of the law. The Law Reform Commission fills this gap. It is basically a balancing institution which, hopefully, will place the traditional stress on conservatism within its proper perspective. . . .
  . . . Parliament, on the other hand, does not have the time or the desire to become deeply involved in law reform. Its cumbersome procedures are already overburdened with the mass of social legislation which the government of the day presses for enactment. Its

greatest institutional limitation, therefore, resides in the demands made upon the Parliamentary timetable. More fundamentally, however, law reform should not be a partisan endeavour. Yet, ultimately, if the efforts of a Law Reform Commission are not to be wasted, its work must be conducted in such a way that it will eventually be reflected, with a minimum of wrecking amendment, in legislation. It is of great importance, then, that the activities of the Commission be related to the parliamentary process.

The National Law Reform Commission is a new legal institution specifically fashioned to complement Parliament and the courts and thus increase the capacity of our legal system to meet the urgent challenges of our rapidly changing world. It is the creation of an Act of Parliament and can be abolished only by an Act of Parliament. Its function is described in the Act as nothing less than the studying and keeping under review of all the laws of Canada with a view to making recommendations for their improvement, modernization and reform. The really significant innovation embodied in the Commission is that the initiative for law reform has been institutionalized. It has been carefully structured so that this initiative will be sustained and directed towards action. . . .

. . . The independent status and specialist standing of the Commission are vital to the success of its program. If the originating body is one which enjoys the confidence of Parliament, the legal profession and the public at large, then the process of enacting the legislation is likely to be that much smoother and less protracted. It is important, in this regard, that the Commission is directed, "to the extent that it deems it practicable to do so in the course of formulating its recommendations," to consult with the minister of justice, associations of members of the judiciary and of the bar, institutions and persons engaged in the teaching of or research into the law, and other interested bodies and persons likely to be concerned with or affected by its recommendations. This is the key to an understanding of how the Commission will perform its work. The process of law reform is too important to be left to the lawyers alone. Law touches the lives of everyone; it is therefore the business of everyone. The functioning of a legal system depends upon a co-operative effort between the citizen and his government, an effort which should begin with the very process of making law. The public must therefore be actively engaged in a dialogue with the Commission concerning the revision of the law and the formulation of new laws. The procedure of circulating working papers to get feed back on proposals for reform and to encourage consultation at every step has been employed with success by law reform commissions and will constitute an important tool in the functioning of this Commission.[11]

The Commission under E. P. Hartt decided to bring in a new dimension to law reform via a consultative approach. This was in direct contrast to other law reform commissions established by various provinces. One notable example was the Province of Ontario, whose approach was not one of consultation but rather of drafting legislation for consideration of the minister and possible enactment by the provincial legislative assembly. In contrast the Law Reform Commission of Canada encouraged interest groups to comment on working papers and study papers, then examine the submissions and comments received before preparing a report to be placed in the hands of the minister of justice.

Many have suggested that such an approach cannot succeed; other criticism directed at the commission was the time taken by such consultative process. The Law Reform Commission could very well have countered by suggesting that not only was the attempt unique but that the Canadian public and interest groups had their first opportunity ever for input prior to legislation being enacted, and that the response was not only minimal but almost discouraging. True, certain interest groups did examine the papers and made extensive comments. These groups included the judiciary and Crown Attorneys' Association; however, members of the Canadian Bar Association and other groups made little or no effort to examine the proposals seriously. While there is some indication that this is about to change, it is too early yet to predict whether the outlook of the profession has improved.

The fact remains that throughout the tenure of the Honourable E. P. Hartt as chairman of the commission a genuine effort was made to keep the commission sensitive to all views expressed. Regrettably, impact of the Law Reform Commission of Canada on criminal law has not been to date impressive, if one measures impact or success by actual amendments to the Criminal Code or to the criminal law. But then the broad question is: "What is law reform?" and whether or not law reform always equates change.

The Honourable Mr. Justice Jean Beetz, in an article in 1972 in the *University of Toronto Law Journal*, said: "Reform does not necessarily mean change. It even implies some degree of conservation, since to reform presupposes the preservation of that which is being reformed, the modernization and the restoration of old systems with a view to saving them by adapting them to new situations."[12]

While leaving to history and to others with more impartial views the task to assess the federal Law Reform Commission, its role in the dynamics of legislative process and its responsibility in keeping our laws current, one matter cannot pass without comment: the instrumentality of the Law Reform Commission in bringing about a new awareness. We may have become over-legislated and the commission has crystallized the views of many with respect to approach to our criminal law in the future. This in itself is not only a healthy but a necessary and vital process.

Are We Over-Legislated?

The empirical research of the Law Reform Commission has been fruitful in many ways. In discovering the living laws that really govern the Canadian people, it discovered how laws can multiply quickly. The commission concluded that:

> ... criminal law is not the only means of bolstering values. Nor is it necessarily always the best means. The fact is, criminal law is a blunt and costly instrument—blunt because it cannot have the human sensitivity of institutions like the family, the school, the church or the community, and costly since it imposes suffering, loss of liberty and great expense.
>
> So criminal law must be an instrument of last resort. It must be used as little as possible. The message must not be diluted by overkill—too many laws and offences and charges and trials and prison sentences. Society's ultimate weapon must stay sheathed as long as possible. The watchword is restraint—restraint applying to the scope of criminal law, to the meaning of criminal guilt, to the use of the criminal trial and to the criminal sentence.
>
> In reaffirming values, criminal law denounces acts considered wrong. Accordingly, it has to stick to really wrongful acts. It must not overextend itself and make crimes out of things most people reckon not really wrong or, if wrong, merely trivial. Only those acts thought seriously wrong by our society should count as crimes.
>
> Not all such acts, however, should be crimes. Wrongfulness is a necessary, not a sufficient condition of criminality. Before an act should count as a crime, three further conditions must be fulfilled. First, it must cause harm—to other people, to society or, in special cases, to those needing to be protected from themselves. Second, it must cause harm that is serious both in nature and degree. And third, it must cause harm that is best dealt with through the mechanism of the criminal law. These conditions would confine the criminal law to crimes of violence, dishonesty and other offences traditionally in the centre of the stage. Any other offences, not really wrong but penalty-prohibited because this is the most convenient way of dealing with them, must stay outside the Criminal Code and qualify merely as quasi-crimes or violations.[13]

Many of our laws, especially some at the provincial or the municipal level, could hardly survive the test of relevancy as expounded by the Law Reform Commission in its report. In many cases the criminal law has been used as a blunt instrument of behaviour control, which may have caused certain citizens to challenge society, when such confrontation could have been avoided. Consider recent provincial legislation on seat belts or municipal anti-smoking bylaws, and a host of others, which seem to antagonize and invite defiance despite their possible desirability. A law that invites disrespect, because of the impossibility of enforcing it, or because it appears to unnecessarily curtail freedom, weakens the social fabric and belief in our criminal justice system. The Criminal Justice and Corrections Committee, otherwise known as the Ouimet Committee, on page 11 of its Report states:

> ... the number of laws must be limited to what is essential, since too many laws invite public rejection and increase the scope of state inter-

ference while reducing its effectiveness. Police and court procedures must ensure that the process of enforcement will be carried on effectively but with a minimum of interference with the individual. . . .

Likewise, at page 12, the Committee suggests:

> It would appear to the Committee that there are some matters which are at the moment designated as crimes and yet which are in general agreement not appropriate to be dealt with by the criminal law. To apply the criminal process to such matters is to impose an intolerable burden upon the whole process of correction.

The Committee adopts the following criteria as properly indicating the scope of criminal law:

1. No act should be criminally proscribed unless its incidence, actual or potential, is substantially damaging to society.
2. No act should be criminally prohibited where its incidence may adequately be controlled by social forces other than the criminal process. Public opinion may be enough to curtail certain kinds of behaviour. Other kinds of behaviour may be more appropriately dealt with by non-criminal legal processes, e.g. by legislation relating to mental health or social and economic condition.
3. No law should give rise to social or personal damage greater than that it was designed to prevent.

To designate certain conduct as criminal in an attempt to control antisocial behaviour should be a last step. Criminal law traditionally, and perhaps inherently, has involved the imposition of a sanction. This sanction, whether in the form of arrest, summons, trial, conviction, punishment or publicity is, in the view of the Committee, to be employed only as an unavoidable necessity.[14]

Legislation that encourages contestation and confrontation by otherwise peaceful and law-abiding citizens is only made less effective when the police attempt to enforce these laws. The offence may appear to be minimal, but the individual is treated as if the matter were of a serious criminal nature. In most cases the breach gives rise to apprehension, a court appearance, a full trial with the adversary process—and in many cases, conviction and sentence. While the sentence may only be a fine, many prefer to go to jail instead of paying the fine; often a citizen is left bitter and unhappy about the entire administration of justice because of his confrontation with it over an issue that might have been settled administratively.

To these difficulties experienced by the police in dealing with the endless list of quasi-crimes is added yet another demand. Our police forces deal daily with persistent social problems. Fully 80 percent of their time is spent on non-criminal matters such as family disputes, disturbances and other problems such as alcoholism, depression and attempted suicide. The police inherited this role by default, since no one else is prepared to intervene and, after all, the policeman is available twenty-four hours a day. This unwanted role gives rise to further potential police alienation, and more dissatisfaction and disrespect by citizens toward authority as symbolized by the police. The police have shown a remarkable degree of adaptation to the new demands visited upon them: the formation of crisis intervention units is one of several worthwhile efforts. Can they expect from society the support they are entitled to?

Law and Justice: A Quest for a Proper Balance

The tendency of legislators to enact a law and expect the police to assume its enforcement, whether it is the violation of a building bylaw or an offence of murder, must cease, or we should accept the real limitations of the criminal justice system, recognize the inordinately high demand placed upon it and adjust our expectations accordingly. Ways must be found to use the civil process to enforce the laws, if indeed these laws must be enforced.

One case in point is the high number of arrests for default of payment of fines incurred as a result of convictions for driving offences. The thousands of arrests across this country for non-payment of fines, followed by subsequent incarceration, could well be avoided through an imaginative licence-issuing process that would require a yearly check on applicants seeking to renew licences or purchase licence plates. Certainly with the advent of computer technology and more advanced data processing, the screening of applicants could reveal those with delinquent accounts for unpaid fines, which could then be settled.

The thousands who parade through court for driving offences where no injuries are sustained could well remain at work and administrative action regarding their licence could be taken. If those adversely affected by administrative action wish to contest such action, then a hearing could be scheduled—but its character should be administrative and not judicial. The deterrent effect of having to appear in a court of law for serious offences all but disappears because of the abuse it has suffered from countless thousands of persons who have attended for minor offences.

While we must learn to respect and accept laws, the present surfeit of laws often invites the opposite reaction. Before enacting further laws with enforcement based on our criminal justice system, we should re-examine the laws we already have and get down to the task of removing anachronistic laws from our books.

There should also be a genuine attempt made to divert from our criminal courts certain minor and quasi-criminal offences.

In that regard, Working Paper No. 7 of the Law Reform Commission suggests that the following situations might well be screened for diversion rather than dealt with by charge:

(a) incidents involving juveniles or the elderly;
(b) family disputes;
(c) misuse of alcohol or drugs;
(d) incidents involving mental illness or physical disability;
(e) nuisance-type incidents.

Criteria to be considered in deciding that a charge should or should not be laid might include:

(a) The offence is not so serious that the public interest demands a trial.
(b) The resources necessary to deal with the case by screening out are reasonably available in the community.
(c) Alternative means of dealing with the incident would likely be effective in preventing further incidents by the offender in the light of his record and other evidence.
(d) The impact of arrest or prosecution on the accused or his family is likely to be excessive in relation to the harm done.
(e) There was a pre-existing relationship between the victim and offender and both are agreeable to a settlement.[15]

Public Attitudes and the Law

Canadians should develop a deeper respect for others; intolerance for those whose lifestyle may offend because it is different does not result in respect for justice. Accordingly, for many justice will remain illusory as long as our expectation of justice and the law is either thwarted or unbalanced.

Justice is hard to define; like a prism suddenly crossed by a ray of light, it takes on many colours and is viewed differently by those who claim its protection, those who seek redress and those who administer it.

Many claim that justice is freedom from the constraint and interference of all laws. In an age characterized by turmoil, economic or otherwise, opposing claims often obscure the image of justice and the relationship between law and liberty that must exist before justice is attainable. Yet, the law exists so that we can enjoy liberty.

In fact, no one is free unless there is a legal order that requires other persons to abstain from interfering with that freedom. Liberty cannot be absolute; it must involve restraints imposed in order that others may enjoy freedom. Freedoms that must be protected by the legal order are the rights to be free from arbitrary interference, from abuse of power and from interference that lacks a reasonable justification.

Those who view justice as capable of protecting them from all interference and allowing them unbridled freedom will be visited with disappointment and will soon find that clamouring for justice can afford little comfort. Their own behaviour interferes with the freedom of others and justice cannot countenance such behaviour.

The quest for balance must not confuse mere nonconformity in opinion, lifestyle, clothing or otherwise with socially harmful conduct, to be suppressed for the protection of society, which includes the offender himself. It must be remembered that one of the characteristics of a true democracy is its ability to tolerate dissent and nonconformity in matters that do not pose a real threat to general security.

The quest for balance must not ignore the victim of a criminal offence. We have expressed a great deal of concern for the accused in the past, and quite rightly so; I suggest, however, that prolonged and continued ignorance of victims of crimes may indeed be interpreted as a denial of justice. The establishment of boards to compensate victims of crimes is a poor substitute for the concern they deserve. We must rededicate ourselves to showing more concern for victims, not at the cost of depriving the accused of due process but in order to guarantee to all parties involved in the criminal trial fairness and equity. Justice demands no less.

Change must be accepted. While many of us find it uncomfortable to confront change in our day-to-day attitudes and in our expectations, history has revealed that many who have repudiated change were themselves short-sighted and later proven wrong. Over a hundred years ago, the commissioner of patents in the United States sent his resignation to President Lincoln because he felt that everything worthwhile had already been invented and he wanted to take up a new occupation to provide for his old age.

Those of us associated with the criminal justice system cannot ignore social or judicial change. Indeed, our ability to change is perhaps the best assurance that justice can be preserved.

The law and its administration can remain relevant only if public participation is invited: likewise, interest groups, including the police, must have an input into the formulation of laws.

Public participation is already significant in such areas of law enforcement as crime prevention and, to a limited extent, in volunteer probation. The police must make a real effort to stress prevention and enlist public support in that endeavour.

Regrettably, in the past we have measured police success or failure by crime solution or increases in the crime rate. As one writer put it:

> The result has been that the end product of detective activity, expressed in a ratio of crime cleared up to crime which is reported to the police, has, for many people, become a gauge of police success or failure, and public opinion about the police tends to rise or fall with the result of this calculation.[16]

Every citizen has a duty to take sensible, basic precautions to prevent the commission of crime, and the failure to do so is not only the rejection of a clear social duty but also makes the citizen a passive and involuntary participant in crime. The police must persuade citizens of their role in this regard. The police should also take steps to measure their success in the field of crime prevention and set aside a reasonable percentage of their annual budget to that area of responsibility.

The public should be encouraged to participate in community projects, such as volunteer probation programs, and could in many ways contribute to various diversion systems. Without more public input, the strain on the criminal justice system will increase and become unbearable.

The failure of organized groups to express their views on law reform has dismayed law reformers and government alike. The former chairman of the Law Reform Commission, the Honourable E. P. Hartt, has often commented on this failure. Likewise, when the Standing Committee of the House of Commons on Justice and Legal Affairs is debating an important bill that will affect a large sector of the population, it would welcome witnesses, expert or otherwise, to appear, testify, challenge or support any area of the proposed law. The police have rarely taken the opportunity to let our nation's representatives hear about problems of enforcement and differing views with respect to changes in the law. All interested groups must realize that unless they express their opinions clearly to the proper authorities before a proposal becomes law, then society is deprived of the potential good that could have resulted from the criticism, and the advantages of open and free discussion.

Our laws are alive and well. In fact, the debate presently taking place is not only healthy but very necessary. We must benefit from history and be realistic enough to appreciate the limitations faced by our criminal justice system, limitations that are both real and inevitable, if we insist in adding to the already heavy burden placed upon it. If we lower our expectations, assist in preventing unnecessary offences, assist and believe in diversion while at the same time showing some tolerance for others who are merely acting differently and not criminally, we shall not only improve our system of justice but we shall be far more successful in enforcing our criminal law.

NOTES

1. *Commentaries on the Law of England*, William Blackstone, Vol. 4, p. 8. New York: Oceana Publications, 1966.
2. T. A. Critchley. *A History of Police in England and Wales*, 2nd. ed. London: Constable and Company, 1972.

3. "Essay on Crime and Punishment," by Marquis Beccaria, 1767, quoted by Professor Radzinowicz in *History of English Criminal Law*. London: Stevens and Sons Ltd., 1949, p. 426.
4. Charles Wegg Prosser. *The Police and the Law*. London: Oyez Publishing Ltd., 1973, p. 24.
5. Quoted by J. M. S. Careless in the *Unions of Canada: The Growth of Canadian Institutions—1841-1857* (1967) and reproduced in *Colombo's Canadian Quotations*. Edmonton: Hurtig Publishers, p. 181.
6. *The Criminal in Canadian Society*. Department of the Solicitor-General. Ottawa: Information Canada, 1973.
7. Report of the Solicitor-General for Canada. 1975.
8. Remarks to The Advocates' Society by J. Peter Rickaby, Crown Attorney for the Judicial District of York, April 9, 1976, entitled: "Crisis in the Criminal Court—Justice or Chaos," reproduced in the Crown Attorney's Newsletter, August 1976.
9. Lindsay Memorial Lecture, Lord Scarman, Law Reform Commission of England. London: Routledge Kegan Paul Ltd., 1968, p. 14-15.
10. Remarks to Convocation, McGill University, May 1970.
11. Honourable E. P. Hartt to the Canadian Association of Chiefs of Police, Edmonton, Alberta, August 1970, pp. 1, 3, and 9.
12. Jean Beetz, "Reflections on Continuity and Change in Law Reform," *University of Toronto Law Journal*, vol. 22, 1972, pp. 138-39.
13. *Our Criminal Law*. Report to the Minister, March 16, 1976. Law Reform Commission of Canada, pp. 27-28. Department of Supply and Services, Ottawa.
14. Report of the Canadian Committee on Corrections, Queen's Printer, Ottawa, 1969, pp. 11-13.
15. Law Reform Commission of Canada. Working Paper 7. "Diversion." Information Canada, January 1975, p. 7.
16. Honourable Emmett E. Hall, Q.C. Remarks to Convocation, Law Society of Upper Canada, 21 March 1975.

Chapter 3

The Evolution of Canadian Police
H. S. Cooper

Police forces as we know them today are a relatively modern development. Generally speaking, they appeared first in the western world in the nineteenth century. Police inherited the title "constable" and it is of interest to examine briefly the history of that title, as it forms part of the story of the development of police forces.

According to the *Encyclopaedia Britannica*, the Byzantine *Comes Stabuli* was originally the head of the Imperial stables and an important official. The Frankish kings adopted the title for an official of similar position and rank. As time went on the importance of the position increased and the constable also became an important figure in the army, being finally regarded as commander-in-chief. Eventually the office, as such, was abolished. It later evolved into a royal court of law whose jurisdiction covered military persons and matters and, in addition, extended to crimes of violence committed outside the jurisdiction of towns.

The term "constable" did not appear in England until after the Norman Conquest, though a somewhat similar office under a different title did exist. After the Conquest, a constable first appeared as quartermaster general of the court and of the army. In feudal times the preservation of the king's peace was largely a function of the military, so there was an overlap between the responsibility of the constable and that of purely civilian officials.

The Statute of Westminster of 1285 organized a national militia by blending the military with the constitutionally appointed officials of the shires. This resulted in a high constable being appointed for every "hundred" and generally the village bailiff was appointed

H. S. Cooper, recently deceased, was Regional Director for the Ontario Department of Correctional Services. Prior to that he was Deputy Commissioner of the RCMP.

It is not within the scope of this chapter to give any detailed history of the Royal Canadian Mounted Police, as the North West Mounted Police came to be called. Many books have been written on this subject, some historical and some detailing personal experiences. The reader who is interested can find a great amount of material in a public library. Unfortunately this is not true of other Canadian police forces, on which there is relatively little published material. A useful reference in this regard is *Policing in Canada* by William and Nora Kelly (Toronto: Macmillan Co.).

petty constable. These remained the executive legal officers of the counties until Acts were passed in the first half of the nineteenth century reorganizing the county police. These, in effect, set up the forerunners of today's county police forces. Justices for some time retained their function as constables, until eventually, about the middle of the nineteenth century, paid county forces were established. From this brief history it will be seen that the appellation "constable" is an old and honourable one and is an office that has had a long association with the police function.

The Statute of Westminster of 1285 stated as its object "to abate the power of felons." Basically, it codified many parts of existing systems which appeared to have stood the test of time. It affirmed the principle of local responsibility for policing. The system of "watch and ward" was established. A watch of a certain size, depending on the size of the town, was organized under the constable. All the men of the town had to serve on a roster basis and punishment was provided for refusal to serve. Chiefly the watches were employed for night duty only. Day watches followed in later years. Members of the watch had the power to arrest during hours of darkness and any prisoners were turned over to the constable the next day. The Statute also revived the custom of "hue and cry." This meant that any fugitive was to be pursued by all citizens after the watch had raised the alarm. Citizens were required to maintain arms in their homes, according to their status.

This system continued, with minor modifications, for hundreds of years. With the advent of urbanism and of a more affluent middle class, a practice developed whereby those who could afford to do so hired others, at minimum rates, to substitute for them in the watch roster. Gradually more and more citizens began hiring others until the quality of the watch degenerated, and in many cases it became almost meaningless. By the mid-eighteenth century, crime was flourishing. It was this condition which eventually led to the establishment of paid, full-time police forces.

In 1785 a bill was introduced in the British Parliament that, if passed, would have provided for the formation of a police force for the whole of the London metropolitan area. The bill was strongly opposed, particularly by the City of London (which even today has its own force separate from the London Metropolitan Police). The bill was seen as a threat to the liberty of the individual and an unnecessary encroachment on personal freedom.

It is interesting to note, however, that Pitt's bill of 1785 had not been entirely lost. The bold plans that England rejected, Ireland was quick to seize. The abortive bill was enacted, substantially in its original form, by the Dublin Parliament in the following year, 1786, and thus laid the first slender foundations for the Royal Irish

Constabulary.[1] Nearly one hundred years later, in proposing the formation of the North West Mounted Police, Sir John A. Macdonald is reputed to have said he envisaged an organization on the lines of the Royal Irish Constabulary.

It was not, however, until some fifty years later that the Metropolitan Police Act, sponsored by Sir Robert Peel, then home secretary, was passed by the British Parliament in 1829. Thus was established what is generally considered to have been the first metropolitan police force in the English-speaking world. The principles laid down at that time are still valid today and were as follows:

> It should be understood at the outset, that the *object to be attained is the prevention of crime.
> To this great end every effort of the police is to be directed. The security of person and property and the preservation of a police establishment will thus be better effected than by the detection and punishment of the offender after he has succeeded in committing crime. . . .
> He [the constable] will be civil and obliging to all people of every rank and class.
> He must be particularly cautious not to interfere idly or unnecessarily in order to make a display of his authority; when required to act, he will do so with decision and boldness; on all occasions he may expect to receive the fullest support in the proper exercise of his authority. He must remember that there is no qualification so indispensable to a police-officer as a perfect command of temper, never suffering himself to be moved in the slightest degree by any language or threats that may be used; if he do his duty in a quiet and determined manner, such conduct will probably excite the well-disposed of the bystanders to assist him, if he requires them.
> In the novelty of the present establishment, particular care is to be taken that the constables of the police do not form false notions of their duties and powers.[2]

In the next few years further legislation established police forces in the counties and in other cities and towns.

Canada too had the watch system, justices and, in many places, high constables or county constables. Again, as in Britain, it was found that as population and urbanization increased, so did crime, and a voluntary, non-professional system was no longer viable.

The first police force in Canada probably was formed in Toronto. In 1834 the town of York became a city and the name was changed back from York to the earlier Toronto. At that time, a full-time high constable was appointed with authority to hire and appoint special constables as needed. In the following year, five full-time paid constables were added, plus a reserve of fourteen special constables. So it may be said that the present Metropolitan Toronto Police had its beginnings in 1834. It was not, however, until 1837 that a uniform was authorized.

*In a second draft of the instructions, Peel changed the wording to "principal object."

In the early years the police force was under the control of the municipal council. This was changed in 1859 by an Act of the Parliament of Upper Canada, which created boards of commissioners of police. These boards were to consist of the mayor, the recorder or county judge and the police magistrate. From that time onward the Toronto police have operated under the control of such a board. There have been changes in the make-up of the board, but the basic principle still applies.

A similar pattern was followed by other cities in Canada as the need became apparent. Montreal established a police force in 1843 and Quebec City a few years later. Though Newfoundland was not to become a part of Canada for nearly seventy-five years, it should be recorded that the Newfoundland Constabulary, with jurisdiction over the whole island, was formed in 1871, along the lines of the Royal Irish Constabulary. Halifax became a city in 1841 and a police force was established shortly thereafter. Other cities followed suit.

In 1867 Canada came into being as a nation after the passage by the British Parliament of the British North America Act. Most of the provinces entered into Confederation. Among its provisions, the BNA Act gave exclusive jurisdiction in certain areas to the federal government and in others to the provinces. It assigned the responsibility for the enactment of criminal law to the federal government. However, the responsibility for enforcement was placed on the provinces. There are federal laws that provide sanctions, such as the Customs Act, Immigration Act, and may therefore be classed as criminal law. The enforcement of such federal Acts was, and is, a federal responsibility. However, enforcement of the Criminal Code is primarily a provincial responsibility.

The provinces in turn have assigned certain authority and responsibilities to cities and towns, and among these is policing within their own jurisdictions. Thus we have in Canada what may be described as a three-tiered system of policing. City and town police forces are responsible for general law enforcement within the boundaries of their municipalities, the exception being certain federal statutes, such as those mentioned above.

Rural areas also required policing—areas outside the jurisdiction of towns, cities and in some cases townships. This was a provincial responsibility and led eventually to the formation of provincial police forces. The advent of the automobile added impetus to this requirement, and today traffic law enforcement on most provincial highways is a provincial police responsibility.

Quebec established a provincial force in 1870. Initially it had very limited responsibilities, but these were gradually enlarged to meet growing needs and the force expanded accordingly. Ontario followed a similar pattern but much later, the Ontario Provincial Police (OPP) being formed in 1909. New Brunswick formed its provincial police in 1927, Nova Scotia in 1928 and Prince Edward Island in 1930.

There remain those areas for which the federal government has responsibility, requiring a federal police force. The federal government had been involved in policing to a limited extent prior to Confederation. In 1868 the Dominion Police Force was formed and although given jurisdiction for the whole of Canada, in practice its functions were confined primarily to eastern Canada. This force carried out federal duties on an expanding scale until it was absorbed by the Royal Canadian Mounted Police in 1920. To the Dominion Police must go the credit for the formation, in the early 1900s, of a national fingerprint bureau.

Prior to Confederation, western Canada—Rupert's land—was a fiefdom of the Hudson's Bay Company. Such law enforcement as existed was provided by the company. In 1869 Rupert's Land was purchased from the Hudson's Bay Company for 300,000 pounds. In addition, the company received approximately six million acres of land and retained certain trading privileges. In 1870 the Province of Manitoba was created, but it was a much smaller province then than it is today. Before 1870, the Red River Settlement had a volunteer police organization, formed about 1848. It was more like a militia than a police force, and its chief function was the maintenance of local law and order. When the new province was formed, it set up a small provincial police force. As the population increased and the province grew, the force was enlarged accordingly. It remained in being until 1932, when the province contracted with the federal government to have the Royal Canadian Mounted Police assume the duties of its provincial police. The Manitoba Provincial Police were then absorbed by the RCMP.

In 1871 British Columbia joined Confederation. It already had its own small police force. This provincial force, which claims the distinction of being the oldest in Canada, remained in being as an efficient organization until its responsibilities were taken over by the RCMP in 1950.

The acquisition of Rupert's Land placed the responsibility for policing this vast area squarely on the federal government, since it was all federal property, with the exception of Manitoba. The provinces of Saskatchewan and Alberta were not created until many years later, and it was only very recently that the Yukon and the present Northwest Territories acquired a commission form of government.

It was not until May of 1873 that an Act was passed by Parliament creating a force to be known as the North West Mounted Police.

Recruiting commenced shortly thereafter, with a government-imposed limit of three hundred members, and by late in the year the first contingent had reached what is now Winnipeg. The following year the force made its famous march west and assumed the policing of the Northwest Territories.

In the Northwest Territories and Manitoba, municipal forces developed much as they had in eastern Canada. Winnipeg led the way with the establishment of a small force in 1874; Calgary followed about ten years later with one paid constable. Other than in the cities the North West Mounted Police carried out policing throughout the whole of the Northwest Territories. Their posts were gradually expanded and extended as the population grew and frontiers were pushed further and further back.

The North West Mounted Police became the Royal North West Mounted Police in 1904. In 1905 the provinces of Saskatchewan and Alberta were created. Rather than establish their own provincial police, these new provinces contracted with the federal government for the RNWMP to take on the duties of provincial police. Thus for the first time this force carried out the function of provincial police in two provinces, in addition to their duties as a federal force. As the provincial police, the force was, and still is, responsible to the provincial government for those matters under provincial jurisdiction and to the federal government for federal responsibilities.

By 1917 the strength of the RNWMP had dropped dangerously low, in fact nearly to its original authorized strength of 1873. The provinces of Saskatchewan and Alberta formed their own provincial police. The RNWMP were now solely a federal force with jurisdiction only in western Canada.

In 1920 the federal government extended the jurisdiction of the force to the whole of Canada and its name was changed to the Royal Canadian Mounted Police. This extension involved the taking over of the Dominion Police by the RCMP. By this absorption, responsibility for the National Fingerprint Bureau was assumed by the RCMP, and their headquarters were moved from Regina to Ottawa.

World War I threw a strain on all police forces as they lost members to the military service. Added to their regular functions were the security problems caused by the war. Canada entered the war in 1914, the United States in 1917. Consequently there was continual concern that enemy agents or sympathizers could use the United States as a point of entry to Canada.

The advent of the automobile and its increased popularity through the years has had a dramatic effect on our society. Prior to the motor car, most police patrols in urban areas were by foot, or by bicycle in the more outlying parts of the town or city. Our cities and towns were smaller and the policeman on the beat came to know, and be known by, most citizens on his beat. Since World War I the police have become motorized, so that now, except in the smallest towns and villages, there are very few police on foot patrol.

Increased urbanization and the needs for an ever more complex society have spawned a host of laws, bylaws and regulations, so that even the most law-abiding citizen can find himself afoul of the laws. These developments have greatly increased the difficulties of police work. The police have had to keep up to date with a host of new technological advances and train staff accordingly. They have also had to keep abreast of a society in which great social changes continue to occur and result in the assumption by the police of responsibilities only loosely related to law enforcement *per se.*

The growth of the Toronto Police, now the Metropolitan Toronto Police, is fairly typical.

1874—Chief constable requested permission to have the photographs of all criminals and suspected characters taken, as occasion may demand.

1881—Chief constable reported new telephones and transmitters had been put in all stations. However, telephones had been used prior to 1881.

1886—A mounted unit was organized.

1888—Telegraph and telephone systems for callboxes were installed.

1895—Bicycles were first used on regular patrol.

1906—Fingerprinting began to be used for identification purposes.

1912—First traffic branch was organized.

1913—First policewoman was employed. Motorized vehicles were first used for police and ambulance service.

1929—Teletype was installed.

1935—Radio was used in police vehicles; one-way until 1938, when two-way radio came into use.

1957—Police forces of the City of Toronto and twelve suburban municipalities were united to form the present Metropolitan Toronto Police.

1972—Installation of a Computer Assisted Despatch (CAD) radio communication system commenced. This system became operational in 1975.[3]

As of January 1, 1977, the Metropolitan Toronto Police had a strength of 5,293 police personnel and 1,312 civilian personnel, for a total strength of 6,605. They operated 1,028 vehicles of various kinds, the greatest number being patrol cars. The growth of other police forces has been as dramatic in relation to the size of the area they police and the population growth. The increase in the number of civilian personnel, in proportion to police personnel, has been great. The need for more sophisticated records and reports has greatly enlarged clerical staff. Experts in different areas, such as finance, telecommunications, etc., have had to be added to keep pace with social and technological change.

Women first became actively involved in police work—as distinct from purely clerical work—in the early 1900s. There has been a steady growth in their participation since that time. Today all larger forces have female members performing the same duties as their male colleagues.

Many changes also affected the federal police force, the RCMP. In 1928 that force became once again the provincial police in Saskatchewan and absorbed the Saskatchewan Provincial Police. The RCMP Act provides that the federal government may enter into a contract with any province for the RCMP to perform provincial police duties in that province. It also provides that a similar arrangement may be made with a municipality for municipal policing but only with the concurrence of the lieutenant-governor in council of the province concerned.

In 1932 the federal government entered into similar agreements with the provinces of Nova Scotia, New Brunswick, Prince Edward Island, Alberta and Manitoba, and the RCMP absorbed the provincial police forces of those provinces. In the same year the federal government ordered the RCMP to take over the functions of the Preventive Service of the Department of National Revenue. The RCMP Act provides.

> *Section 17(3)* "Every officer, and every person appointed by the Commissioner under this Act to be a peace officer, is a peace officer in every part of Canada and has all the powers, authority, protection and privileges that a peace officer has by law."

> *Section 17(4)* "Every officer, and every member appointed by the Commissioner to be a peace officer, has, with respect to the revenue laws of Canada, all the rights, privileges and immunities of a customs and excise officer, including authority to make seizures of goods for infraction of revenue laws and to lay informations in proceedings brought for recovery of penalties therefor."

Members of the RCMP thus have the powers of a peace officer and those of a customs and excise officer for the whole of Canada. They are the only police force in our country with such authority. Defining "the powers, authority, protection and privileges" of a peace officer is a large subject that cannot be covered here. The Criminal Code of Canada outlines many of these rights. Certain statutes, both federal and provincial, contain specific provisions relating to those statutes.

In addition there is quite a body of case law bearing on this subject. Reference has already been made to the book *Policing in Canada*, where this subject is discussed at some length.

Newfoundland entered into confederation with Canada in 1949. In 1935 the colony had established a force known as the Newfoundland Rangers, which served in the same capacity as a provincial police force for Newfoundland and Labrador. Mention has been made earlier of the Newfoundland Constabulary, which policed St. John's and some of the larger municipalities. In 1950 the new province of Newfoundland entered into an agreement for the RCMP to do its provincial policing. The Newfoundland Rangers and some of the Constabulary were absorbed. The latter force still polices the city of St. John's.

In the same year British Columbia entered into a similar agreement and the British Columbia Provincial Police were absorbed by the RCMP. Thus by that year all but two provinces of Canada, Ontario and Quebec, had as their provincial police the RCMP. This situation continues to the present, as does the RCMP's policing role in the Yukon and the Northwest Territories.

The RCMP had also begun, in the 1930s, to police under contract some municipalities. This role has expanded over the years and the force now polices over 150 municipalities across Canada in those provinces in which they also act as the provincial police.

The Ontario Police Act also provides that under certain conditions the Ontario Provincial Police may police municipalities, and that force acts as municipal police in several towns in the province. In Quebec, there is no provision for its provincial police to enter into contract for the policing of municipalities. However, it may be directed by the attorney-general, where he considers it in the public interest, to take over for a limited time the direction of policing in any municipality.

Canada has a large number of police forces that are responsible to various authorities at different levels of government. This is generally the case also in other countries in the English-speaking world. There are, however, many countries where all policing is done by a federally controlled force or forces.

Federally the RCMP are responsible to the solicitor-general of Canada. In the provinces, the provincial police—including the RCMP where they act in that capacity—and the municipal police are ultimately responsible to the attorney-general (most provinces), the provincial minister of justice or solicitor-general. Like the growth of police forces, the machinery of control has grown and developed with experience and need.

Most municipal police forces in Canada, and certainly the larger ones, are directly responsible, under their chief constable or chief of police, to a police board or commission. The police board system of Ontario is fairly typical, and the Ontario Police Act (R.S.O. 1970, C. 351 Section 8) provides as follows:

(1) Notwithstanding any special Act, every municipality that provides and maintains a police force and that has a population of more than 15,000 according to the last municipal census shall have a board, and,
(a) any county or town having a population of 15,000 or less according to the last revised assessment roll;
(b) any village or township having a population of more than 5,000 and not more than 15,000 according to the last revised assessment roll; and
(c) with the consent of the minister [of justice], any village or township having a population of 5,000 or less according to the last assessment roll,
that provides and maintains a police force may, by by-law, constitute a board.

(2) The board, except as provided in subsection 3, shall consist of,
(a) the head of the council;
(b) a judge of any county or district court designated by the lieutenant-governor in council; and
(c) such person as the lieutenant-governor in council may designate.

It is recommended that readers should become familiar with the Act governing the police in their provinces. Provincial and federal statutes are available in most public libraries.

A more recent development has been the establishment in several provinces of provincial police commissions. Ontario was the first province, in 1962, to establish such a commission As other provinces followed they assigned functions similar to those already set out in Ontario. Section 41 of the Ontario Police Act sets these out as follows:

(1) It is the function of the commission,
(a) to maintain a system of statistical records and research studies of criminal occurrences and matters related thereto for the purpose of aiding the police forces in Ontario;
(b) to consult with and advise boards of commissioners of police, police committees of municipal councils and other police authorities and chiefs of police on all matters relating to police and policing;
(c) to provide to boards of commissioners of police, police committees of municipal councils and other police authorities and chiefs of police information and advice respecting the management and operation of police forces, techniques in handling special problems and other information calculated to assist;
(d) through its members and advisers, to conduct a system of visits to the police forces in Ontario;
(e) to require municipalities to provide such lock-ups as the commission may determine;
(f) to assist in co-ordinating the work and efforts of the police forces in Ontario;

(g) to determine whether a police force is adequate and whether a municipality is discharging its responsibility for the maintenance of law and order;

(h) to inquire into any matter regarding the designation of a village or township under subsection 4 of section 2 and, after a hearing, to make recommendations therefor to the minister;

(i) to operate the Ontario Police College;

(j) subject to the approval of the minister, to establish and require the installation of an inter-communication system for the police forces in Ontario and to govern its operation and procedures;

(k) to conduct investigations in accordance with the provisions of this Act;

(l) to hear and dispose of appeals by members of police forces in accordance with this Act and the regulations; and

(m) to exercise the powers and perform the duties conferred and imposed upon it by this Act.

(2) Subject to the approval of the minister, the commission may, by order, regulate or prohibit the use of any equipment by a police force in Ontario or its members.

Other sections of the Act deal further with the authority of the commission in more specific terms particularly relating to amalgamations, investigations, hearing of grievances, etc.

It will be seen that wide powers are conferred on the Ontario Police Commission. The general effect has been to bring about greater uniformity and higher standards, particularly in smaller municipal forces. Not all provinces with commissions have set up police training schools, but the trend is in this direction.

The RCMP, provincial police and larger municipal forces have maintained their own training establishments for many years. The scope and quality of training has steadily broadened and improved, as greater demands are made on police and more difficult decisions are required of them. Advances in technology have required training in many areas, and social change and diversity have necessitated more emphasis on sociology as part of police instruction.

Obviously, smaller forces usually do not have the manpower, the facilities or the money to provide the extensive training a recruit should have. Nor is recruitment training sufficient; there must be ongoing refresher and upgrading courses. Changes in the law, particularly the Criminal Code, require immediate instruction so that the police will understand the application of such changes. The provincial training schools fill a very real and very important need.

The federal government, through the RCMP, has also assisted. Many advanced and specialized courses are now available at the Canadian Police College at Rockcliffe, Ontario. These are open to all police forces and their cost is minimal, as tuition and accommodation are provided without charge. While, obviously, all police cannot be accommodated, those who do attend pass on to their colleagues the knowledge they have gained.

To this point mention has been made only of federal, provincial and municipal police. There are many other organizations of a police or quasi-police nature. Some have been in existence a long time, and others have recently developed. The jurisdiction of these forces varies according to the legislation for which they are responsible. Under federal law customs and excise officers possess certain police powers, as do immigration officers, postal inspectors, income tax investigators and others. Under provincial law game wardens and liquor licensing inspectors are invested with police powers relating to their functions. There are many other agencies, both provincial and municipal, that possess limited enforcement powers in relation to the Acts for which they are responsible, and the number continues to grow. One has only to think of licensing regulations, public health, building codes, etc., to appreciate how such agencies have increased in number. In addition, many police forces have auxiliary police and/or reserve members who, when summoned for duty, possess police powers. Police cadets are also considered to be members of the force to which they belong. Many forces also use special constables who have police powers.

Quite a large number of private organizations or companies, particularly larger manufacturers, have their own police and security forces. Their jurisdiction and powers vary depending on their appointment. In many cases, some or all members may be appointed as constables or special constables under the appropriate provincial legislation.

The railways, particularly the two national railways, have employed police in some form almost since the days of their construction. In the early 1900s the Canadian National and Canadian Pacific railways reorganized their respective forces and since then have had recognized police forces as authorized under the Railway Act. Many other company police forces came into being because of the security requirements of World War II.

In addition to these private forces, there are a large number of private investigative agencies and protective or security services. They provide security and other services on a hire or contract basis. Protective and security services in particular serve an ever-widening clientele. They provide security services to all levels of government, and to an increasing number of business firms and factories. Their numbers have increased dramatically in the postwar years, and it is now estimated that employees of such agencies far outnumber members of regular police forces. Their powers vary according to the authority given them under provincial statutes.

Obviously in a country as vast as Canada law enforcement would be impossible without close co-operation between police forces. With improved travel and communications crime is no longer a local matter. Today there is continuous co-operation and exchange of information between all forces on a nationwide basis.

This co-operation has been helped by the federal government establishment, through the RCMP, of national services and centralized information banks contributed to by all police forces and available to all. Their cost is borne by the RCMP. In 1933 the single fingerprint collection was started. By 1935 a new law required the national registration of handguns and these records are maintained by the RCMP. The next year a modus operandi section was established, followed by the first crime detection laboratory in Regina in 1937. There are now six such laboratories operated by the RCMP across Canada. Ontario and Quebec have established similar facilities.

Also in 1937, the RCMP *Gazette* appeared, the photographic and crime index sections were set up at headquarters, and the aviation section was created. In 1957–58 the force established a national telex system, and other forces rapidly acquired similar equipment, enabling them to communicate with each other and directly with RCMP headquarters. A fraudulent cheque section was created at the same time. Three years later the RCMP established national crime intelligence units, concerned primarily with intelligence on organized crime. As these developed, information was contributed by and made available to other forces. Commercial fraud sections were established in 1966.

In 1972, after many years of planning and data collection, a large computer became operational which stores information about known criminals, motor vehicles, firearms and stolen property. All police forces can be linked by telecommunication directly to the computer and can secure available information almost instantly. By radioing his local centre, a policeman on car patrol can receive information in a matter of seconds. During this same period, automated storage of fingerprints was commenced. This greatly reduced search time.

Co-operation has been increased also by other means. In 1905 the Canadian Association of Chiefs of Police was formed. It has increased in strength and influence through the years and is now a dynamic organization. In subsequent years provincial associations of chiefs of police were formed, increasing contact between forces. Police associations also developed and today the majority of forces have such associations. They serve many of the functions of a union and have contributed to bettering working conditions and salaries, thereby making police work more attractive.

Traditionally there has been co-operation between Canadian and American police forces, particularly those near the border. Today many Canadian chiefs of police are members of the International Association of Chiefs of Police, a primarily American organization with a secretariat in Washington, D.C. In 1923 the International Criminal Police Organization—better known as Interpol—was formed. Today over one hundred countries are members of this organization. It has a secretariat in Paris, France, which serves as a clearing house and repository of information on international criminal matters. There is a common misconception concerning Interpol. It is not in itself an investigative agency. Each member country nominates one of its federal law enforcement agencies to be its representative to Interpol. That agency is the channel for supplying information and for making requests for information or aid. These representative agencies may deal directly with one another, while keeping Interpol advised of their activities. The RCMP are Canada's representative to Interpol.

As the national police force, the RCMP have been assigned primary responsibility for national security. This is a counter-intelligence function. Several foreign countries operate espionage systems in Canada and seek to acquire agents and information by recruiting Canadian citizens. As a counter-intelligence agency, the RCMP combats such subversion. Other forces in Canada supply relevant information to the RCMP.

With the tremendous increase in Canadian immigration the RCMP have established posts in many countries. Their function is to ensure that undesirables do not gain entrance to our country. Provincial and municipal forces also do security checks as required by the governments they serve.

The police have had to expand in several directions to deal with specific problem areas. Larger forces have special squads to work in the juvenile field, with so-called morals offences, with the drug problem, with terrorism, with racial problems, and in other areas. Gaining prominence are those squads that work in the field of community relations. They supply speakers to many community groups, particularly in the schools, train students in the school patrol system, provide displays and materials to help the public increase the security of their homes and businesses. The list is almost endless.

The police are a public body, continually in the public eye, and therefore an open target for attack. They are in a profession where the temptations and pressures are probably greater than in any other. Any large organization or profession will occasionally have those who do not measure up. That the number of police who violate the public trust is so small is a tribute to the sincerity and dedication of the overwhelming majority.

No record of the development of our police would be complete without a tribute to the families of the members of our forces. Particularly in earlier days, members of the RCMP and provincial forces often served in relatively isolated places and on one-man detachments. Families shared the isolation, the work—and the worry. Police work still offers dangers not present in other fields. An increasing incidence of violence and the use of firearms by criminals have added to the dangers. Perhaps the poet John Milton best expressed it when he wrote, "They also serve who only stand and wait."

In the introduction to his book, *A History of Police in England and Wales*, T. A. Critchley states:

> Total freedom is anarchy, total order tyranny. The police, who represent the collective interests of the community, are the agency which holds a balance somewhere between. Their standing is a rough index of society's own attitude towards the regulation of civilized living: regard for the police, which should not of course be uncritical, is regard for law and order. Patrick Colquhoun did not exaggerate when, writing at the end of the eighteenth century, at a time when the English were resisting the idea of paid professional police as being incompatible with liberty, he declared: "Everything that can heighten in any degree the respectability of the office of constable, adds to the security of the state, and the safety of the life and property of every individual."[4]

This was true when the first police forces were formed and is equally true today.

NOTES

1. T. A. Critchley. *A History of Police in England and Wales*. Montclair, N.J.: Patterson Smith Publishing Corp., 1972.
2. *Ibid.*
3. Metropolitan Toronto Police, *A Brief History*. Toronto: Metropolitan Toronto Police Information Services.
4. Critchley, *op. cit.*

FURTHER READINGS

Chambers, Captain Ernest J. *The Royal North West Mounted Police*. Originally published in 1906 by the Mortimer Press, Montreal. Facsimile edition published by Coles Publishing Company, Toronto, 1972.
Critchley, T.A. *A History of Police in England and Wales*, 2nd. ed. Published by special arrangement with Constable & Co., Ltd. Montclair, N.J.: Patterson Smith Publishing Corp., 1972.
Kelly, William and Nora Kelly. *Policing in Canada*. Toronto: Macmillan Co. of Canada.

Kelly, William and Nora Kelly. *The Royal Canadian Mounted Police—A Century of History*. Edmonton, Alberta: Hurtig Publishers.
Metropolitan Toronto Police. *A Brief History*. Metropolitan Toronto Police Information Services, Toronto.
The Police Act. Revised Statutes of Ontario.
The Royal Canadian Mounted Police Act. Revised Statutes of Canada.
Turner, John Peter. *The North West Mounted Police, 1873-1893*. Published by Edmond Cloutier, King's Printer and Controller of Stationery, 1950.

Chapter 4

Private Security in Canada: Some Questions and Answers
C. D. Shearing

This chapter considers a significant, and hitherto neglected, aspect of the order maintenance process: private security. Private security has grown enormously over the past two decades. It touches all of us quietly, yet pervasively. In office buildings, stores, universities, libraries, shopping centres, apartment buildings, and subdivisions, we frequently and regularly see private security persons and are in turn seen by them. Our contact with private security has increased so unobtrusively that it has become an accepted part of modern life. We tend, somewhat patronizingly, to treat private security as peripheral to our lives, yet it plays a critical role, and is an essential part of the social control process.

Every so often private security intrudes on our activities; for example, when we are stopped on leaving a library to have our bags searched, or are searched before entering the boarding lounge at airports, or are scrutinized on entering a residential complex. Occasionally, some action by a security person might alarm us—for instance, when we learn that security guards have fired on militant strikers. For the most part, however, private security remains in the background.

Not only are our contacts with private security barely noticed, but frequently we are unaware that contact has taken place. These "invisible" contacts sometimes have an even more profound effect on our lives. When we apply for credit or insurance, for example, we typically grant the company concerned permission to undertake a "background check" on us. This investigation is often completed without our having any concrete evidence of what was done or what conclusion was reached.

There has always been the equivalent of what we call today private security. What is significant is the recent enormous increase in private security. Pleece (1972), for example, has estimated a growth

Dr. Shearing is a Senior Research Associate and Graduate Secretary at the Centre of Criminology, University of Toronto. Previously, he was a member of the Ontario Working Group on Police Training established by the Solicitor General of Ontario in 1974.

rate for contract security in England of 20 percent per annum. Similarly, Kakalik and Wildhorn (1972) have noted a growth rate for private security generally in the United States of 10 to 15 percent per annum. Both argue that private security forces are larger, or will soon be larger, than public police forces.

The growth of private security is the consequence of a fundamental reorganization of social control. The most visible, and in numerical terms the largest, change in these arrangements has occurred with respect to the patrol function. The "new police" in England, formed in 1829, were established as a patrol force. Since then the public police have developed other components, most notably a detective function. They have, however, always remained primarily a patrol force, although they have changed, over the last half century, from a force of foot patrolmen to a motorized force that relies on citizens' telephone calls to inform them of problems (Reiss, 1971; Shearing, 1974).

This situation has led a police sergeant in England's Northumbria Police to comment that "we are neglecting the most ingenious and efficient piece of equipment the police force has ever known: the foot patrol beat officer" (cited in Lewis, 1976: 208). While the police may be neglecting this "piece of equipment," it has not been neglected by others. The foot patrolman remains an essential part of our order maintenance system, however he is no longer a policeman, but rather a private security guard.

Like his predecessor, the police foot patrolman, the private security guard patrols to protect property and persons and to ensure that public order is maintained. In addition to those similarities, however, there are important differences. For example, the security guard usually is *not* a peace officer, and so does not have the rights, powers and duties of a policeman. Similarly, unlike policemen who typically patrol public property, the security guard usually patrols private property, although this may be property to which members of the public have easy and routine access (as is the case, for instance, in a commercial shopping centre).

The existence of private security raises questions about its consequences for our quality of life. What, for instance, is the significance of the fact that we are now policed, and hence supervised, more and more by private security forces that are often employed by private individuals and institutions, rather than by governments?

Before such questions can be addressed, it is essential that we develop an understanding of private security. For the last several years, the Centre of Criminology at the University of Toronto has been attempting to establish a factual and conceptual framework for the definition and understanding of private security. In the remainder of this chapter, we will draw on this research to answer questions about private security in Canada.

What Is Private Security?

We begin with a question of definition. In doing so we must attempt to explicate the principles that underlie common usage—no easy task.

The definition of private security has been considered by several authors (see, for example, Becker, 1974; Kakalik and Wildhorn, 1972; Freedman and Stenning, 1977). All, however, are unsuccessful in providing a definition that distinguishes private security from other security forces, as well as from private citizens. A useful starting point is Freedman and Stenning's definition of the concept "security." In defining security, they cite a senior police official in Australia who wrote:

> Security means much more than the locking of doors and windows, the conveyance of money and the collection and delivery of valuable property. These days security is big business and I am referring not only to the patrol services which are a common part of the scene in big cities, but also to such services and devices as document shredders, safes, alarms, armoured transport, communication equipment, bullet-proof glass, courier services, identification systems, private investigations into industrial espionage, and armed guards. (1977: 9)

In commenting on this statement, they add the following security functions:

> . . . credit reporting agencies, electronic surveillance, polygraphs and other forms of "lie-detector," fire alarms, equipment for opening suspected letter bombs, guard dogs, and even strictly financial services such as credit cards and traveller's cheques, with their advertising slogans on the lines of "You never know when you might be robbed." (1977: 9)

The difficulty with this "definition" is that it is a list of security functions, not a definition of security. In order to transform this list of functions into a definition, we must look to what it is that these activities have in common. What appears to unite these activities is that they all involve the *protection* of information, property, or persons. This conclusion is consistent with the usual dictionary definitions of security. For instance, *The Little Oxford Dictionary* (1969) defines the adjective "secure" as: "untroubled by danger or fear; impregnable, safe. . . ." In short, something is secure when it is protected from danger.

With a definition of security established, our next task is to differentiate between different categories of persons who perform security functions. Perhaps the first distinction to be made in this regard is between persons whose jobs centre around security functions and persons who perform security functions either outside of an occupational context or incidental to some other occupational focus. This allows us to distinguish private security persons from private citizens who routinely perform security functions (for example, locking doors), and other occupations that involve security functions, but are not security occupations *per se* (e.g., a bank manager who checks the vault door before leaving work).

However, even the category "security occupation" includes more than private security. There are at least two major security occupations that must be segregated if we are to identify private security; namely, the military and the public police. Further, given the commonsense definition of private security and the definition found implicitly in legislation that refers to private security, it appears that public officials other than police with peace officer status, such as prison guards, mayors, game wardens, customs officers (Freedman and Stenning, 1977: 18) should also be segregated within the category of security occupations if private security is to be identified as a separate sub-category.

On the basis of this line of reasoning, private security persons may be defined as *persons employed in security occupations other than the military and the public police, and other public officials with peace officer status*. This definition may, at first glance, appear troublesome because it identifies private security indirectly as a residue category. That is, it tells us what private security is not, not what it is. However, rather than being a problem, this feature is an asset as it is consistent with how private security is defined in practice. Private security is, to most people, a security occupation other than the public police and the military.

The definition also suggests another feature of the commonsense definition of private security. In practice the line separating private security from other security forces is somewhat fuzzy. It is fuzzy in two ways. First, it is not always clear precisely which persons are to be included in other security occupations. Should traffic wardens, for example, be included in the category public police, as Freedman and Stenning (1977: 18) suggest, even though their peace officer status is strictly limited? Secondly, besides the police and the military, just what other occupations should be excluded from the category private security appears to be as much a matter of convention as principle. For instance, game wardens could, it seems, be as easily treated as private security. Similarly, the Canadian National Railway police, the Canadian Pacific Railway police, and the harbour police, although not accorded full peace officer status, do have a limited peace officer status that places them, as Freedman and Stenning note, "on the borderline between public police and private security" (1977: 37).

What Types of Private Security Are There?

Private security is usually classified in terms of four criteria: first, the relationship between the security force and its clients; second, whether it is licensed or unlicensed; third, whether the work is guarding or investigation, and finally, whether the security persons provide security functions directly, or indirectly as operators of security equipment.

Contract Versus In-House Security

The two most frequently used categories of security are contract and in-house. Contract security refers to "agencies and agents who are in the business of providing ... [security] services to others [clients] for hire or reward. 'Contract' agencies and agents may thus be distinguished from in-house ... [security] services, which provide services exclusively for one company [institution or individual] which employs them on a more or less permanent basis" (Freedman and Stenning, 1977: 46).

Licensed Versus Unlicensed Private Security

In Canada, not all private security is regulated by licensing statutes. Although the scope of licensing legislation varies somewhat from province to province and within provinces, in all provinces with licensing statutes most contract security is licensed, while in-house security is not. Throughout Canada, there is one important sub-category of contract security which is not required to be licenced under legislation regulating private security; namely, credit reporting. However, in British Columbia, Manitoba, Nova Scotia, Ontario and Saskatchewan, "under the consumer protection legislation ... they are required to hold licenses in order to operate legally" (Freedman and Stenning, 1977: 48).

Security Guards and Investigators

It is customary within the security field to distinguish between security persons in terms of whether they provide a guarding or an investigative service. In Canada, this distinction has gained weight by being incorporated into licensing legislation. This has tended to make the distinction more important for contract security. The definition of a security guard common to most provincial statutes is a person who "acts as a guard or watchman, or guards or patrols, or provides other security services for the purposes of protecting persons or property" (Freedman and Stenning, 1977: 46).

While there is less agreement in provincial legislation about the definition of private investigators, it is possible, as Freedman and

Stenning demonstrate, to develop a "synthesized definition." Canadian licensing legislation defines a private investigator as a person who:

(a) searches for and furnishes information regarding,
  (1) the character or actions of persons,
      and
  (2) the nature of the business or occupation of persons (not in Quebec)
(b) searches for offenders against the law (not in Alberta or British Columbia)
(c) searches for missing persons or property (not in Quebec or British Columbia) (1977: 47)

Security Equipment

In all fields of human activity, the development of technology frequently means that activities once performed by people can be, and often are, taken over by machines. There is nothing new about this. The nineteenth and twentieth centuries, however, have seen enormous developments in technology, with profound social consequences. Developments in electronic technology, particularly, have had a profound effect on security. Prior to the developments that electronic technology has made possible, mechanical methods of protection had changed little since time immemorial. While we have, for instance, developed, and continue to develop, new and more efficient locks, there is nothing new about locking devices. Electronic technology has, however, radically changed the nature of security equipment. Freedman and Stenning note that "it is indeed arguable that the human element is, or is becoming, a secondary consideration in many areas of private security" (1977: 209).

The advance of electronic technology in the security field has led to a growing distinction between security persons who man security equipment such as alarm respondents and persons who act relatively independently of such equipment.

What Do Private Security Persons Do?

Public and "Private" Peaces

In defining private security, we have already done much to delineate the activities of private security persons. They protect information, persons and property. In doing so, they, like the public police, act to preserve the peace. This is not surprising, as the concept of the peace arises out of a concern with persons and their belongings. As Keeton has recently indicated, the ancient Anglo-Saxon concept of "frith," from which our concept of "the peace" arises, refers to "the right of inviolability which attaches to persons, places and communities" (1975: 3).

This similarity of function between private security and the public police has been noted by commentators in Britain (see, for example, Wiles and McClintock, 1972), in the United States (see, for example, Post, 1971) and in Canada (Jeffries, 1977), and is responsible for the preference some authors have for the term "private policing" in referring to private security.

Private security forces, however, do more than preserve the public peace. Unlike the public police, who are not "legally charged with enforcing privately established rules and regulations" (Kakalik and Wildhorn, 1972: 57), enforcing such rules forms an integral part of many private security persons' responsibilities. Thus, the responsibilities of private security typically extend beyond those of the public police and include, for want of a better term, what might be called the preservation of "private peaces."

Security Activities

We turn now to a more detailed analysis of the functions private security persons perform. At present, the only published research on the activities of private security in Canada is a study of in-house security in Ontario by Jeffries (1977). While this research is limited to Ontario and in-house security, and by the elementary level of analysis used, it provides a useful initial basis for assessing the range of functions performed by private security, as Jeffries' sample covers a wide spectrum of users of security services. Jeffries' findings are based on an analysis of twenty-one in-house security organizations working within commercial, manufacturing, mining and personal service organizations. While there will undoubtedly be some differences in the activities performed by contract security and by private security in other parts of Canada, similar categories of users are likely to place similar demands on private security no matter where they work or how they are organized. In interpreting Jeffries' findings, however, it must be noted that a significant gap in her sample is the absence of government private security organizations. With this limitation in mind, we proceed to examine her findings.

Jeffries described the functions performed by persons in various security positions within in-house security organizations. If her findings are classified in terms of whether the activities performed are primarily investigative or guard functions, the following analysis results (1977: 15).

These findings support our general conclusions about the relationship between the public police and private security work. The private security persons studied by Jeffries, like the police, investigated crimes, maintained order, and responded to emergency and crisis situations. In addition they were, unlike the police, responsible for enforcing private regulations, for example, access to certain areas.

Investigative Functions

Position	Function
Investigator	Investigates specific cases of fraud, theft or other abuse.
Floor detective	Detects and apprehends shoplifters in accordance with company policy.
Retail honesty shopper	Conducts "integrity" checks on cashiers.
Floor patrolperson	Patrols company property at irregular and unknown intervals.
	Reacts to emergency situations encountered during the course of rounds.

Guard Functions

Position	Function
Stationary guard	Stationed at "control point" on company property.
	Controls access to and egress from particular areas.
	Responds to emergency situations as required.
Punchclock patrolperson	Performs routine patrols according to a punchclock program.
Nightwatchman	Responsible for physical security during "off" hours.

Jeffries' findings serve, in addition, to point to a further important difference between the police and private security. While private security is concerned with the enforcement of both laws and private regulations, it generally restricts its activities to the property of its clients. Private security has routine and regular access to private property, whereas the public police generally only enter private property when specifically invited to do so. This means that private security is, with respect to the areas for which it is responsible, generally free from a major restriction imposed on the public police, namely their limited access to private places. This difference is frequently referred to by private security persons to support the argument that they are in a much better position to prevent crimes than the public police, who are generally limited to responding to crimes after they have occurred.

This discussion of the activities of private security raises the question of whose interests it serves, that is, whom do private security employees work for? The public police, in theory, work as agents of the people, while private security persons clearly act as agents of individuals or organizations. Although private security persons do not thereby relinquish their responsibilities as citizens, they take their instructions, as security persons, from their employers, whose interests they are employed to protect. Thus, when we are policed by the public police we are, in theory being policed in our own interest. When we are policed by private security, any community of interest is both in theory and in practice an incidental feature of the relationship; we are being policed, within the protection offered by law, in the interests of the security person's employer.[1]

What Are the Historical Origins of Private Security?

In understanding the relationship between the public police and private security with respect to their responsibilities, it is useful to consider briefly the historical roots of private security and the public police.

The concept of "the peace," which is central to our notion of security, has its origins, we have argued, in the ancient Anglo-Saxon concept of "frith." This concept, we saw, referred to peace in a very local sense, focussing as it did on the inviolability of persons, places and communities. The modern concept of the public peace represents an extension and modification of this early idea.

The first step in this development was the identification of the king's peace as a peace of a special order. The king's "frith" or "grith," as it was called, applied not only to his person but extended to his household. Gradually its boundaries grew until it came to encompass the entire kingdom. The king's peace, in Maitland's (1913: 108) words "devours all other peaces." It becomes the public peace and the sovereign becomes responsible for securing not only the peace of his household, but the peace of the kingdom.

This extension of the king's peace has tended to obscure the original concept of "frith" so that now it strikes us as strange to talk of private peaces. Yet this concept is embedded in other more familiar notions; for example, the distinction between civil and criminal law and between private and public wrongs. The ancient concept "frith" provides a historical basis for the scope of the peace preserved by private security, its loyalty to specific employers, and the narrow geographic focus of its responsibilities.

Originally, community officials responsible for preserving the "frith" derived their authority directly from the local community or kinship group, on whose behalf they acted (Critchley, 1967). With the emergence of the concept of the public peace, these community officials found themselves in a difficult and ambiguous position, as they were at once responsible to two authorities, the sovereign and their local community. This tension has, over the centuries, been systematically reduced so that today the police, while often organized on a local basis, are limited in their responsibilities to preserving the public peace and derive their authority as peace officers directly from the sovereign authority (Critchley, 1967).

The tension of dual authorities, however, remains for the private security person, whose position is similar in many respects to that of the ancient hundredsman responsible for maintaining the "frith" of a community or kinship group, but with obligations to the king. The private security person, as a citizen, has responsibilities to the sovereign authority; yet as a private security person *qua* private security person, his responsibilities are to his employer. Unlike the hundredsman, however, he does not often hold public office, except when he is appointed a special constable. His loyalty is primarily to his employer.

What Are the Legal Powers, Rights and Duties of Private Security Persons?

As we have implied in our discussion of the historical origins of private security persons, they usually only have the powers, rights, and duties of private citizens or the powers delegated to them by their employer, who in a great many cases, is "the owner or a person in lawful possession of property" (Canadian Criminal Code, s. 449(2)).

Our law gives certain powers, duties and rights to private citizens and property owners. As agents of property owners and private citizens, private security persons assume these powers, duties and rights. If we are to understand the legal status of private security persons, we must therefore understand the position of private citizens and owners of property. With respect to the preservation of the public peace, Justice Morand (1976) has recently argued that private citizens have a common law obligation to preserve the public peace. Freedman and Stenning (1977: 259-60), in contrast, have argued that the position of private citizens in Canada is not at all clear. Canadian law, they point out, speaks to citizens with respect to their involvement in preserving the public peace with considerable ambivalence. They conclude that while the public have a very clear *right* to preserve the public peace, it's doubtful whether they also have a *duty* to do so.

In exercising this right to preserve the public peace, Canadian law grants citizens certain legal powers with respect to such actions as the use of force, search, seizure and arrest. It is not possible here to consider the limits of these powers in detail.[2] Instead we will, by way of illustration, refer to the powers citizens are accorded with respect to one of these legal acts, namely, arrest.

The Canadian Criminal Code provides the most general source of authority for citizen powers of arrest. The Code, as we have indicated, distinguishes between private citizens on the one hand, and property owners and persons in lawful possession of property and their agents on the other. For both classes of citizens the Code limits citizen powers of arrest to arrest without warrant. Within this general limitation, the powers of arrest of private citizens are defined in Section 449 as follows:

(1) Anyone may arrest without warrant:
(a) a person whom he finds committing an indictable offence, or,
(b) a person who, on reasonable and probable grounds, he believes
  (i) has committed a criminal offence, and
  (ii) is escaping from and freshly pursued by persons who have lawful authority to arrest that person.

As this section makes clear, under normal circumstances a citizen may arrest persons only for indictable offences; that is, for more serious offences such as rape, arson, robbery, breaking and entering and so on. Further, he may, under normal circumstances, only arrest for these offences if he *finds* the person committing the offence.[3] This means that a citizen normally cannot arrest a person simply because he believes, or indeed "knows," that the person has committed an indictable offence.

The Criminal Code provides somewhat broader arrest powers for private citizens when they are engaged in assisting someone with lawful authority to arrest, provided this person is "freshly pursuing" the person to be arrested. Under these circumstances, the citizen may arrest for criminal, and not merely indictable, offences. Understandably under these circumstances, the Code does not require that the person to be arrested by the assisting citizen be seen committing the offence, but simply that the citizen in question have "reasonable and probable grounds" for believing that the person he is assisting has lawful authority to arrest.

These citizen powers of arrest become more extensive when a citizen is an owner of property, a person in lawful possession of property, or the agent of such a person.[4] Under these circumstances a person may arrest anyone whom he "finds committing" a criminal offence (as opposed to an indictable offence), provided the offence is committed "on or in relation to" the property in question. This provision provides property owners, those in lawful possession of property, and their agents with arrest powers more extensive than those of other citizens by extending the scope of their arrest powers beyond the more serious indictable offences to all criminal offences even when there is no suggestion of "fresh pursuit."

This extension of arrest powers reflects the centrality of the institution of private property to our society and the fact that our law establishes rights of ownership and provides owners and those in lawful possession of property with state-backed coercive means of securing and protecting these rights (Chambliss and Seidman, 1971; Freedman and Stenning, 1977).

Under the provisions just considered, it is clear that the legal powers of most security persons to arrest are considerably less than those of the public police who, for indictable offences, are generally not restricted by the "finds committing" stipulation, but may arrest provided they have reasonable and probable grounds for believing a criminal act has been or is about to be committed (Canadian Criminal Code, s. 480(1)). In practice, however, the effect of this difference is not nearly as great as one might suspect. Private security persons acting as agents of property owners or those in lawful possession of property, frequently, and in contrast to the public police, have routine access to private places where crimes against property are likely to be committed. This means that they are more likely than the public police to find someone committing a criminal offence and therefore are less likely than the public police to need to be able to arrest on suspicion. Significantly, in those areas where a private security person does not find a person committing a criminal offence, but finds the person on the property he is protecting, he may usually still arrest if he wishes to detain the person under the provisions of the provincial Trespass Acts, which, as Freedman and Stenning have pointed out, provide "grounds for arrest even where no criminal offence has been committed" (1977: 110). Thus, in cases where a person is suspected of having committed a criminal act, but is not found committing the act, private security persons have little difficulty in legally detaining the person to allow for further investigation, if they wish to do so. Significantly, in those cases where there is no urgency to detain, private security persons may *in practice* avail themselves of the more extensive arrest powers simply by calling the police and persuading them that there are reasonable and probable grounds for suspecting that an indictable offence has been committed.

In the light of these considerations, it is evident that where property is being protected, private security persons *in practice* are in much the same position as policemen in their access to arrest as a means of dealing with the problems they encounter.

Not only do private security persons in practice have much the same access to powers of arrest as the public police, but some private security persons in certain circumstances have legal powers identical to those of public police because they have been appointed as peace officers via special constable appointments. When private security persons are appointed special constables, they become, by virtue of the peace officer status that these appointments confer, quasi-police-men.[5] In those cases where a private security person is appointed as a special constable with his peace officer status limited only by a geographic constraint (for example, campus "police"), he has with reference to this area the same legal powers as a regular policeman. His special access to private property, however, means that he is not constrained to the same extent as policemen are, within his area of jurisdiction, by our institutions of privacy (Stinchcombe, 1963).

Where private security persons are appointed as special constables, the conflict of wearing two caps, referred to above, becomes most acute. Under these circumstances, their situation corresponds very closely to that of the Anglo-Saxon hundredsman. They are, on the one hand, officers of the Crown who take their authority and direction directly from the law. On the other hand, however, as employees who act as agents of their employers, they derive their authority from their employers. Theoretically, this dual authority should serve to reduce the control of employers over security persons who become by virtue of their peace officer status independent Crown officials. In practice, however, this is unlikely to be the case as it is their employer whom they must satisfy if they are to keep their jobs.[6]

In addition to these considerations, there is a further aspect of the private security person's practical circumstances that must be considered if the relative insignificance of the differential in legal powers between the police and private security is to be fully appreciated. This is the issue of consent.

In establishing limits as to what people can do to each other, our law, in most instances, acts to protect persons when they are being imposed upon against their will. For the most part our laws (with the exception of certain primarily moral offences) are relatively unconcerned with what people do to each other provided they consent to what is being done. This legal principle is of great importance for the relationship between security forces and those they supervise. With reference to the legal restrictions we have been considering, if "the citizen can be shown to have consented to such interferences (e.g., by voluntarily submitting to a detention or search) . . . the whole picture changes. The police or private security official no longer has to rely on the various powers conferred upon him by the Criminal Code and other statutes; for consent of the person being searched, detained, interrogated, etc., is sufficient to render the interference legally justified in almost every case" (Freedman and Stenning, 1977: 68). Consequently, "the private security official who carefully sets about obtaining valid consent from the persons with whom he interacts, need worry very little about the various laws which have been enacted, or formulated by the courts, to protect such persons from undue interference or restraint" (Freedman and Stenning, 1977: 76).

For most security personnel, consent is not difficult to obtain. Indeed, very often the consent is implied by virtue of the person's presence in the situation in question. For example, a condition of employment may be that the employee be willing to submit to a search on leaving the job site. Similarly, an airline can make consent to a search a requirement of boarding one of its aircraft. Whatever the reason, it is clear that private security persons are often able to obtain consent for what they wish to do with relative ease. This fact further erodes the practical impact of the differences in legal powers between the public police and private security. Indeed, it could be argued that the private security person probably finds himself in a "better" position than most policemen, as he is more likely to be able to persuade people to consent to his interference.

In summary, it appears that in practice, private security persons are not only frequently able to exercise control over a greater part of our lives than do the public police because their responsibilities extend beyond the public peace to "private peaces," but in addition their *de facto* ability to interfere with our liberty may be as great, and perhaps even greater, than that of the public police.

How Is Private Security Regulated in Canada?

The question of the regulation of private security has been carefully analyzed by Stenning and Cornish (1975). The broad outlines of the regulation of private security in Canada have more recently been summarized by Freedman and Stenning (1977), and it is to their report that we once again turn.

They indicate that the legal significance of licensing is that persons and organizations that require security licences may not perform security services without first obtaining a licence. Significantly, "apart from conferring the right to do business legally ... such licences do not directly confer any other legal status or powers on licencees," although, "the fact that someone has been officially licensed to perform certain functions ... may ... provide them indirectly with a stronger defence against criminal or civil liability

(e.g., 'lawful excuse') under certain statutory provisions" (1977: 47).
In Canada, not all private security needs to be licensed. We will, in the remainder of this section, identify several categories of manned security and indicate which persons and organizations within each category require licences.

Contract Security Guard Agencies and Agents

Freedman and Stenning write that "Alberta, British Columbia, Manitoba, Ontario, Quebec, New Brunswick and Nova Scotia all have legislation in force which requires contract security guard agencies and agents to be officially licensed in order to do business legally" (1977: 45-46). Since then, similar legislation has come into force in Newfoundland and is being drafted in Prince Edward Island. As the passage from Freedman and Stenning (1977) implies, Saskatchewan excludes contract security guards from its legislation. While it is the only province to exclude security guards, all provincial legislation specifically excludes some categories of contract security. In identifying those persons and organizations excluded, Freedman and Stenning write:

> Into this category, we may place designers, manufacturers, distributors, installers, and service personnel for all manner of security "hardware" items, including locks, safes, alarms, hazard control systems, bullet-proof and fire-resistant panels and clothes, trained dogs, weaponry of various kinds other than "restricted weapons," access control systems, stock control systems, and surveillance and monitoring equipment. Also included in this category are commercial lie detector operators (polygraphists, psychological stress evaluator operators), voice analysts (spectrograph operators) and other forensic scientists (e.g. fingerprint or handwriting analysts, ballistic experts, etc.), industrial and security psychologists, and other "security consultants" or management consultants who, although primarily skilled in security matters, do not provide the kind of security services which would require them to be licensed under the various Provincial licensing statutes. Some courier services may also operate without being licensed, and alarm monitoring and response personnel (not necessarily the same as installation and service personnel) will also generally fall into the category of unlicensed contract security personnel (1977: 50-51).

Elsewhere, Freedman and Stenning note that in addition other groups are also exempted from licensing legislation; these include railway police and the Canadian Corps of Commissionaires.

Contract Private Investigative Agencies and Agents

"All provinces except Newfoundland and Prince Edward Island ... require contract private investigation agencies and private investigators to be licensed in order to operate legally" (Freedman and

Stenning, 1977: 47). Since 1977, similar legislation has come into effect in Newfoundland and is being drafted in Prince Edward Island. In all provinces where legislation exists, however, various categories of security persons are, once again, specifically excluded from the licensing statutes. In addition to the obvious exemption of the public police, the statutes exempt "railway police, barristers and solicitors and their employees, credit rating and employment suitability investigators, insurance investigators and adjusters, certain government employees, and persons licensed in other jurisdictions and on temporary assignment in the province concerned" (Freedman and Stenning, 1977: 48).

Contract Credit Reporting Agencies and Agents

Although credit reporting agencies and their agents are exempted from licensing statutes dealing with contract security guards and investigators, they are, in some provinces, required to be licensed under the provisions of other statutes. Five provinces (British Columbia, Manitoba, Nova Scotia, Ontario and Saskatchewan) require these persons and organizations to be licensed under consumer protection legislation. These statutes "restrict the collection and dissemination of information to that required for credit, tenancy, employment or insurance purposes. They also limit the kinds of information which may be collected, and generally require either that the subject of an investigation should consent to it, or at least that he or she should be notified that such an investigation is taking, or has taken place. Access by the subject to such information as is collected is also provided for" (Freedman and Stenning, 1977: 48-9).

Dealers in Restricted Weapons

The position with respect to dealers in restricted weapons is stated by Freedman and Stenning as follows:

> Persons who carry on the business of selling at retail, repairing or taking into pawn weapons which are defined as "restricted weapons" under s.82 of the Criminal Code are required by s.96(2) of the Code to be holders of a permit for that purpose issued by the Commissioner of the RCMP, a Provincial Attorney General, or a person expressly authorized by either of them (s.97(1) and (4)). Section 96(1) of the Code also imposes upon these persons a duty to maintain certain records relating to transactions involving restricted weapons, to produce such records for inspection at the request of a peace officer, and to mail a copy of them to the Commissioner of the RCMP if he requests one in writing. Persons who manufacture, buy or sell at wholesale, or import restricted weapons are also subject to these record-keeping obligations, but are not required to have a permit as such in order legally to carry on business (1977: 49-50).

In-House Security Personnel

In-house security is at present not required to be licensed in Canada even though in-house security persons perform functions similar to those of contract security, and even though, from the perspective of the persons being supervised and controlled, the in-house/contract distinction may be inconsequential.

The difference in the treatment of contract and in-house security by legislators appears to suggest that they are much less concerned about protecting the public from the activities of private security than they are with protecting employers of contract security forces, who cannot, supposedly, adequately protect themselves because they do not control the process whereby security persons are selected. This suggestion was made in 1973 by Michael Warren, then Deputy Solicitor General for the Province of Ontario, in a speech to a workshop on private policing and security in Canada. He noted that in the position favouring the exclusion of in-house security from licensing, "it is argued that the 'in-house' employer's self-interests cause him to exercise care in selecting trustworthy and competent employees and in supervising their work" (1973: 56). In his remarks, Mr. Warren questioned the validity of this philosophy. He suggested that this distinction between in-house and contract security might be unjustified and that perhaps licensing legislation should be concerned primarily with citizens affected by private security. Mr. Warren stated his argument as follows:

> There can be no doubt that in the performance of his job, the "in-house" security guard or investigator is often faced with situations which have the potential for interference with the individual's privacy and freedom.
> The performance of arrest, searches, and interrogations by "in-house" personnel highlights the problem. . . .
> Wildhorn and Kakalik, in their report *Private Police in the United States*, suggest that "contract" employers have self-interest similar to "in-house" employers in the selection and supervision of personnel, and that on all counts the reasons for regulating the "contract" security and investigative personnel apply to "in-house" agencies and personnel.
> Clearly, there is room for questioning the exclusion of the "in-house" personnel from our legislation (1973: 56–57).

In light of these arguments, it will be interesting to see whether in-house security will be included in the new licensing legislation being prepared in British Columbia and Ontario.

Who Are Private Security Persons?

Now that we have considered the legal status and regulation of private security persons, the question that arises is, who are the people who occupy this status?

Private Security Executives

At present there is relatively little information available in Canada with respect to private security executives. Some information on this subject was collected by Fern Jeffries (1977) during 1974 and 1975 in her study of in-house security.

Jeffries' sample included twenty-four persons whom she classified as security managers. This group was overwhelmingly male and had a mean age of forty-three years. Almost all the security managers had had some high school education. In addition, half the managers had attended university. About one third of them had attended a community college.

In examining security managers' backgrounds, Jeffries found that one third of the managers with previous employment experience had worked as public policemen. With respect to salary, in-house security managers earned significantly more than their employees, with 45 percent of them earning more than $20,000 per year. Only 5 percent of security supervisors earned more than $18,000 per year.

Security Guards

With respect to security guards and private investigators, we are able to provide a national profile. To do so we rely on the report by Farnell and Shearing (1977). Before proceeding to examine their results, however, attention must be drawn to their proviso that they encountered considerable difficulty in satisfactorily extracting data on private security persons from the available census data, and that their analysis depends on the adequacy of the assumptions underlying the methods they used.

Security guards in Canada in 1971 appeared to be very similar to security guards in the United States. Like Kakalik and Wildhorn (1972, Vol. 1: 30), Farnell and Shearing report that security guards tend on average to be aging males who are both poorly paid and poorly educated. They note that in Canada, only 7 percent of the security guards were women; that 41 percent were fifty-five years of age or older; and that security guards tended to earn less than the national average wage of $5,133, with an average annual salary of $4,707. Given this salary level, it is significant to note that security guards tended to work long hours with 14 percent working more than fifty hours per week, and 78 percent working more than forty hours per week. With respect to education, Farnell and Shearing note that as many as 46 percent of security guards have less than grade nine education.

Casual observation suggests that this profile of security guards appears to apply as much today as it did in 1971. There is, however, one obvious exception that applies to many of the larger centres in

Canada. Farnell and Shearing report that in 1971 over 80 percent of security guards were born in Canada. Since then, especially in large cities, there appears to have been an influx of immigrants into security guard positions both within the contract and in-house sectors.

Private Investigators

Private investigators, in contrast to security guards, tend on an average to be younger, better educated, and better paid. In addition, there were relatively more women working as private investigators than as security guards, although the number remained small (16 percent). Seventeen percent were over fifty-five years old, they earned an average annual salary of $6,520, and were as a group better educated than security guards. Only 18 percent of the private investigators had not attended school beyond grade eight.

As with security guards, the 1971 census data indicated that private investigators work relatively long hours with 81 percent working forty hours a week or more. The vast majority (84 percent) of private investigators were born in Canada. In contrast to security guards, it appears that relatively few immigrants have moved into private investigative positions.

How Much Private Security Is There?

In this section we complete our description of private security in Canada by discussing its size, growth and cost.

On the basis of their analysis of the census data, Farnell and Shearing (1977) estimate that there were 50,200 persons employed in security occupations, including government security employees in correctional institutions, etc., in Canada in 1971. The distribution of these persons by type of force and by province is presented in the following table (Farnell and Shearing, 1977: 36).

The distribution of these persons across the "industrial divisions" used by Statistics Canada is given in the following diagram (Farnell and Shearing, 1977:97).

When correctional guards and the like are excluded from these figures (they are not usually considered to be private security), Farnell and Shearing estimate the total number of persons working in private security occupations in 1971 to be 36,525. This compares with a public police strength reported by Statistics Canada for 1971 of 39,724.[7]

The number of persons employed in private security appeared to grow rapidly during the 1960s. Farnell and Shearing note, however, that census data, because of changes in format, make it impossible

TABLE 4 - 1
Distribution of Private Security Personnel, 1971 by Province and Type of Force*

Province	Contract Security Total	Contract Security % of Total	In-House Security Private Total	In-House Security Private % of Total	In-House Security Government Total	In-House Security Government % of Total	Private Security Total	Private Security % of Total
Newfoundland	100	.9	760	3.0	200	1.4	1,060	2.1
Prince Edward Island	60	.6	45	.2	40	.2	145	.2
Nova Scotia	570	5.0	880	3.4	460	3.4	1,910	4.0
New Brunswick	435	4.0	845	3.3	410	3.0	1,690	3.3
Quebec	3,295	28.5	9,170	36.4	4,250	31.5	16,715	33.2
Ontario	4,780	41.4	8,325	33.0	4,785	35.4	17,890	36.0
Manitoba	510	4.4	750	3.0	520	4.0	1,780	3.5
Saskatchewan	255	2.2	600	2.3	400	3.0	1,255	2.5
Alberta	675	5.8	1,285	5.1	865	6.4	2,825	6.0
British Columbia	850	7.3	2,475	10.0	1,435	10.6	4,760	9.4
Yukon, Northwest Territories	10	.08	45	.2	115	.8	170	.3
TOTAL	11,540	100	25,180	100	13,480	100	50,200	100

Source: Data Dissemination Service, Statistics Canada.

*Since Statistics Canada's data are subject to a random rounding procedure, totals do not necessarily equal the sum of rounded figures in distributions.

to estimate with any degree of accuracy the growth of private security. They do argue, nevertheless, that some estimates suggest the growth of contract security may have been as high as 700 percent during the period 1961 to 1971. If in-house security has grown at only a fraction of this rate, it could be that today in Canada private security persons may well exceed by a significant margin the number of public policemen.

While private security persons (broadly defined to include government security forces) outnumbered the public police in 1971, the expenditure for private security during that year was much less than the expenditure for the public police. It cost Canadians $646.9 million in 1971 to provide public police services. The cost of private security payrolls for the same period is estimated by Farnell and Shearing at $254.9 million. While they note that this estimate probably underestimates payroll expenditure, and although it cannot be directly compared with the public police figure (which is not limited to payroll expenditures), it is clear that the total, as well as the per-man, cost of private security was considerably less than the cost of the public police.

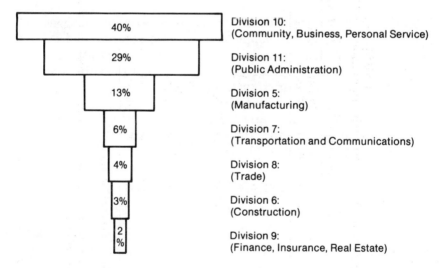

Figure 4 - 1
Percentage distribution of private security personnel
by industrial division.

Conclusion: The Quiet Revolution

There appears to be little doubt that private security is here to stay and that it will form an increasingly important part of the total social control apparatus. What does this mean? What will the impact of private security be on the quality of life in Canadian society? The immediate reaction to these questions might well be that it appears to have had very little impact. There is, as we indicated at the outset, some truth to this. Private security has developed quietly. The increased presence of private security has hardly been noticed. However, these quiet changes appear on inspection to have revolutionary implications. With the development of private security there has been a shift in the locus of social control from the public to the private sector, from governments to corporations, local groups to individuals. This raises critical questions that we are only beginning to appreciate. Does such a move represent, as Freedman and Stenning (1977: 53) suggest, disenchantment with the public police? Does this mean an increasing influence of private local interests over the "public interest" in social control? Is this a good or a bad thing? Is the "privatization" of policing part of a general movement being felt in other areas of public service, such as education and mail service? If so, what does this mean for the role of central government? In Canada, are the political pressures connected with the constitution and the autonomy of the provinces related to the erosion of the role of governments in the social control processes we have suggested? What effect has the development of private security had on the power of corporations, especially multinational corporations, vis à vis the individual and the state? Has it, as Friedenberg (1975) suggests, enhanced their stature and power?

These are the questions that the facts about private security raise. It is to these issues that research is now being directed, as the research program at the Centre of Criminology, University of Toronto, is extended beyond its initial fact-finding stage.

NOTES

1. Where private security work for governments, their position vis à vis the interests they serve is similar to that of the public police.
2. See Freedman and Stenning (1977) for a more comprehensive discussion.
3. The Canadian courts have interpreted the phrase "finds committing" to mean "finds apparently committing." As a result, a person will not be convicted for having made an unlawful arrest even if it is subsequently proved that the arrested person was not actually committing the offense in question, provided he can successfully argue that the arrested person was apparently committing the offence. See Freedman and Stenning (1977: 79–82) for a discussion of this distinction.

4. The relevant section of the Criminal Code is s.449(2). It provides that:

(2) Anyone who is
   (a) the owner or a person in lawful possession of property
   or
   (b) a person authorized by the owner or by a person in lawful possession of property,
   may arrest without warrant a person whom he finds committing a criminal offence on or in relation to that property.

5. This is a quasi-police status as these appointments seldom accord the persons so appointed full peace officer status, but limit their powers to specific areas, and/or for specific time periods, and/or for specific purposes. For example, a private security person might be appointed as a special constable to enforce a parking by-law in and around an exhibition site for the duration of the exhibition.
6. For an extensive examination of special constable appointments and their use in Canada, see Stenning and Cornish (1975: 196-212).
7. This total excludes "data for the R.C.M.P. Headquarters, Divisional Headquarters and Training divisions located at Ottawa, Ontario. [It also excludes] data for the several R.C.M.P. Headquarters [in Ontario] and the eastern training centre at Ottawa." (Statistics Canada, Police Administration Statistics, cat. no. 85-204, p. 29), cited by Farnell and Shearing (1977: 238).

FURTHER READINGS

Becker, Theodore M. "The Place of Private Police in Society: An Area of Research for the Social Sciences." *Social Problems*, Vol. 21, No. 3, January, 1974.

Chambliss, W. J. and R. B. Seidman. *Sociology of Law: A Research Bibliography.* Berkeley, Calif.: Glendessary Press, 1970.

Critchley, T. A. *A History of Police in England and Wales, 900-1966.* London: Constable, 1967.

Draper, Hilary. *Private Police.* Harmondsworth, England: Penguin Books, 1978.

Farnell, Margaret B. and C. D. Shearing. *Private Security: An Examination of Canadian Statistics, 1961-1971.* Toronto: Centre of Criminology, University of Toronto, 1977.

Freedman, David J. and Philip C. Stenning. *Private Security, Police and the Law in Canada.* Toronto: Centre of Criminology, University of Toronto, 1977.

Friedenberg, E. Z. *The Disposal of Liberty and Other Industrial Wastes.* New York: Doubleday, 1975.

Jeffries, Fern. *Private Policing: An Examination of In-House Security Operations, 1977.* Toronto: Centre of Criminology, University of Toronto, 1977.

Jeffries, Fern (ed.) *Private Policing and Security in Canada: A Workshop, 1973. Report of the Proceedings.* Toronto: Centre of Criminology, University of Toronto, 1974.

Kakalik, J. S. and S. Wildhorn. *Private Police in the United States, Vol. IV: The Law and Private Police.* Santa Monica, Calif.: Rand Corporation, 1972.

Kakalik, J. S. and S. Wildhorn. *The Private Police: Security and Danger.* New York: Crone Russak, 1977.

Keeton, G. W. *Keeping the Peace.* Chichester: Barry Rose, 1975.

Lewis, Roy. *A Force for the Future: The Role of the Police in the Next Ten Years.* London: Temple Smith, 1976.

Maitland, F. *The Constitutional History of England.* Cambridge: University Press, 1913.

Morand, D. R. *The Royal Commission into Metropolitan Toronto Police Practices.* Toronto: The Commission, 1976.

Pleece, Sydney. "The Nature and Potential of the Security Industry." *Police Journal.* Vol. XLIV, No. 1 (January-March), p. 41, 1972.

Post, R. S. "Relations with Private Police Services." *The Police Chief.* (March), p. 54–56, 1971.

Reiss, Albert J. Jr. *The Police and the Public.* New Haven, Conn., and London: University Press, 1971.

Shearing, Clifford D. "Dial-A-Cop: A Study of Police Mobilization." *Crime Prevention and Social Defense,* ed. R. L. Akers and E. Sagarin. New York: Praeger, 1974.

Stenning, Philip C. and M. F. Cornish. *The Legal Regulation and Control of Private Policing and Security in Canada: A Working Paper.* Toronto: Centre of Criminology, University of Toronto, 1975.

Stenning, Philip C. and Clifford D. Shearing. *Search and Seizure: Power of Private Security Personnel.* (A Study Paper prepared for the Law Reform Commission of Canada). Ottawa: Ministry of Supply and Services, 1979.

Stenning, P. C. and C. D. Shearing. "Private Security and Private Justice: Doing Justice to Justice," *British Journal of Law and Society,* forthcoming.

Stinchcombe, A. L. "Institutions of Privacy in the Determination of Police Administrative Practice." *American Journal of Sociology,* Vol. 69 (September), p. 150, 1963.

Wiles, Paul and F. H. McClintock, (eds). "The Security Industry in the United Kingdom; Papers Presented to the Cropwood Round-Table Conference, July 1971." Cambridge: Institute of Criminology, 1972.

Chapter 5

The Role of Police in Society
J. A. Blake

Obviously, any chapter entitled "Role of Police in Society" should give one a clear definition of what the police role is. But is there such a clear, precise, or definitive role for police in Canadian society?

We have role definitions for police by police. Some definitions go further and become tenets, generally accepted and acted upon by most police, while others are merely policy, leaving the individual policeman to interpret for himself exactly what he should be doing. In addition, there are role definitions of the police formulated by the public and the public's expectations, which may be quite different from those defined by the police. We must start by looking at what has traditionally been the role of the police in Canada. From this we can examine this role a bit more carefully.

Most police manuals state that the primary functions of the police are: (1) to prevent crime; (2) to detect crime and apprehend offenders; (3) to maintain order in the community; and (4) to protect life and property. The *Concise Oxford Dictionary, Fifth Edition*, says that a role is "an actor's part; one's function; what one is appointed to or is expected of or has undertaken to do." The same dictionary defines function as "an activity proper to anything; mode of action by which it fills its purpose; office holder's duty, employment, profession, calling; religious or other public ceremony or occasion, social meeting of formal or important band."

Historically the role of the police has been to enforce the law, especially the criminal law. But this role is changing and changing drastically. In this chapter, I will examine not only the police role but police role conflicts; in other words, the ambiguities of the police role (none of which are mutually exclusive) as they are seen by the police and by the public. These ambiguities concern public expectations of law enforcement, order maintenance, service functions, public demands and police responses to these demands, and the contradictory skills and interpersonal relationships required by the role. It is ironic that most people fear crime yet many also mistrust the police. Why?

In certain contexts, the police officer is seen as the enemy, the

J. A. Blake is an instructor and Program Head of the Law Enforcement Program, Grant MacEwan Community College, Edmonton.

representative of an unjust society. Traditionally, police have been thought of as protectors of the rich and defenders of the status quo. In defending property they often appear to be protecting the vested interests of certain groups. Due to the nature of their role at such occurrences as unruly picket lines, it may appear that the police are not impartial.

I would contend that the police of this country are not adequately prepared to fill their role in society. I am not talking about their strictly functional skills: marksmanship, unarmed combat, high-speed chases, and so forth. I am talking about their psychosocial skills as agents of social control. Society has changed, but the police have not changed with it. Their training is not geared to meet the needs of today's society. Quite simply, policemen are not being trained to deal with people. Available literature on time studies of a police officer's activities indicate that between 75 and 80 percent of his time is spent in community activities not directly related to the investigation of crime or the apprehension of criminals. These activities include non-enforcement functions such as intervention in family quarrels, work with juveniles, rescue and paramedical emergency work and crime prevention functions. However, in the training program, this ratio is reversed, and the majority of a recruit's time is spent learning enforcement functions, with very little training provided for the major portion of his job—community service and order maintenance functions. Most policemen are offended if they are referred to as social workers, yet they *are* Canada's most visible, front-line social workers.

Enforcing the law is an unambiguous and clear-cut function relative to other responsibilities with which the police are entrusted. Maintaining order, on the other hand, is much more difficult because it involves so many undefined conditions, so many discretionary decisions the policeman must make. Yet which is the most important function: enforcing the law or maintaining order? The question could be posed another way: Which function involves more of the policeman's time?

Once a policeman, in his role as a social control agent, enters the life of the ordinary citizen, he affects that citizen's attitude toward the police either negatively or positively. One source of frustration for the policeman is the confusion between what he *does* and what he *thinks* he should be doing. A policeman is in a real dilemma: he is expected to be close to the community yet not too close. If he does his job according to the book, he will likely be overly strict and arouse public antagonism; if he stays too aloof, he will likely be ineffective as a policeman. Either way, he will receive no public support and no co-operation.

In the past, the police have been considered skilled tradesmen who could learn their role, and how to fulfill it, on the job. Today, their training still gears them to catch offenders, when in fact their job is social control. Because they are untrained and uncomfortable in this role, they often project an attitude of condescension rather than service to the public.

Historically the role of the police has often been compared with that of the military, but the tasks of the soldier are more clearly defined. It is comparatively easy to determine whether or not a soldier is doing his job. It is much more difficult to measure the performance of a policeman outside the activities of investigation and arrest of criminals. What about the police who are doing public relations? What about the police who are performing law and order maintenance? What about the police who are doing public service? These activities cannot be measured and totalled at the end of the month.

So what are the effects of these frustrations arising out of the police role and role conflict? One result is that the police may direct their anger at the community because they are upset with the system. But these frustrations can also manifest themselves in much more subtle and serious ways.

For the sake of explanation, let us follow an arrest and the resulting consequences for one young, inexperienced police constable. Let us imagine he comes across a person committing a crime such as breaking and entering. He calls for assistance, but in the meantime he is there alone. During this period the officer undergoes many emotions. If there is resistance to arrest by the suspect, who has no discernible weapons, the policeman has first of all to overcome a natural fear of physical combat. He may be smaller than the offender but he must bear in mind that he can only use force equal to that which he encounters. During the course of the arrest, the suspect's coat is torn. Having succeeded in apprehending an offender, the policeman feels proud that he has served the public and lived up to his own role expectations. He returns to the station to write out his report. Meanwhile, in the jailhouse, the prisoner may draw attention to his torn coat or scrapes received during the arrest. The patrolman becomes aware that he stands a chance of being accused of police brutality.

For his appearance before a judge, the suspect will be defended by a lawyer, either his personal attorney or one supplied by legal aid if he cannot afford to pay the costs himself. Now if the accused has, in fact, made a confession to the police, or has been caught red-handed, the lawyer has little option but to try to discredit the testimony of the police constable. This is the basis of our "adversary system" of justice, with the lawyer and his client on one side, and the police and prosecution on the other. The lawyer's job is to win for his client; therefore he must try to discredit any evidence that the policeman gives. He must attempt to convince the judge that the policeman was mistaken and that what he thought he saw happen is incorrect—or he may even imply that the policeman is a liar.

After all of these events, the impressionable and inexperienced policeman may well ask, "Who is on trial here anyway?" After succeeding in carrying out a good night's work, overcoming his own fear of physical combat, and sustaining the protection of the public by his arrest of a criminal—all of which he thought coincided with his role as a law enforcement officer—he finds himself in conflict with and demoralized by an aspect of his role for which he has received little preparation.

The most serious charge is the one of police brutality. Often the public is unaware of how this charge can affect a police officer. The police have the responsibility of arresting offenders but are limited in the amount of force they can use. The policeman, in his conviction that he is doing right and is protecting the public, confronts the suspect, terror in his stomach, and makes the arrest. Frequently a scuffle ensues and sometimes it can get violent. It is very understandable that a person can get injured or have his property damaged. All of a sudden the officer is accused of police brutality. To him this seems unjust. Should he just say, "You're bigger than I am, so let's forget it?" The policeman may feel that he had maintained his composure in a difficult situation, yet he may end up in a court defending his actions.

Notwithstanding all the aforementioned happenings, my contention is simple. Unless a policeman understands that the fear which he experiences in making an arrest is natural, that the physical confrontation between himself and the suspect may be unavoidable, that he may even lose and the suspect may get away, that these are all conditions of his job and beyond his control, then he will always be frustrated with his role in society.

It is also necessary for the police to understand the purpose behind the checks and balances essential to our legal system. If an officer does not understand the reasons for these, he may begin to take his experiences too personally; his attitude toward society will become somewhat paranoid. Unfortunately, from his peers or experience, he may learn one salient motto: "Get them before they get me." The result is that the police develop a defensive isolationism. They feel they must protect each other verbally, physically and socially. They become a closed society, with its own values—and the public is the enemy. Right and wrong become like black and white and those who break the law (regardless of the seriousness of the offence) are "bad" and hence must be apprehended. The ability to distinguish between a minor lawbreaker and someone who is a serious, dedicated criminal becomes clouded. The young recruit who absorbs these values is on the road to becoming a cynical, cold, relentless, stereotypical cop.

This cynicism may turn into hostility and manifest itself in a number of ways. Suicide, alcoholism, domestic strife, separation and divorce, psychological problems, and a high rate of attrition in police forces are the result. Unfortunately attrition occurs chiefly among the high achievers, the humanistic idealists, who come to the realization that they can serve their fellow man in some more beneficial way. Those who want and need to control others stay on and perpetuate the unfavourable reputation of the police in society. I do not suggest that this behaviour pattern is the norm, but it is becoming much too prevalent.

We must remember that the policeman lives in an artificial world, that he sees a distorted picture of life, that in most cases, the people he deals with daily, particularly the criminal element or those in the crime-ridden areas of the city, are only part of society. Yet it is difficult for some police to understand or recognize that his perspective may be limited.

So how should we prepare policemen for their role in society, particularly as it applies to "people problems"? First, let us examine what happens now when a young person desires to be a police officer. When he reaches the admissible age, passes the required tests and enters the police academy, he is trained in psychomotor skills: how to carry out unarmed combat, how to swim and box, and similar activities. He is taught the Criminal Code, how to investigate minor offences, various provincial statutes, the Highway Traffic Act, the Liquor Control Act, and city ordinances. If he is a member of the RCMP, his training is more comprehensive. Immediately after his training, he is out on the street. It does not take him very long to discover that the public does not see him as a knight in shining armour; instead he is disliked by a significant portion of the population, and even hated by some. Nowhere in his education was he prepared to accept this. His police training has taught him skills and police procedures, but there has been little human relations education, or in such subjects as sociology, criminology and psychology, to aid in his understanding of himself and society's attitudes toward him.

There are a great number of explanations for this shortcoming. One is that the public have a lack of knowledge concerning the role of the police. Secondly, the public have expectations the police cannot fulfill. Thirdly, the police lack understanding of their own responsibilities and just how far they can go.

Not only is the recruit unprepared for the street, he has little practical understanding of the criminal justice system of which he is an integral part. For example, he may understand that both he and the judge agree that stealing is a crime and must be punished. However, is he capable of understanding other points of view? Will he accept the teacher who believes that stealing is a learned behaviour? Or the psychologist who says the thief is just acting out hostilities? Or the social worker who could tell that juvenile delinquency derives from a lack of love in the offender's home life? Yet all these people are also members of the criminal justice system and their viewpoints can influence the outcome of a trial.

So, what happens to the recruits we train in the enforcement role and whom we then expect to become practitioners in applied psychology and sociology? Some do very well. Others fail miserably; and their failure is not their fault. It is ours. If you train a man to operate a machine and he ends up sweeping floors, he is going to be frustrated and resentful. And he certainly is not going to do a very good job. If, however, in the beginning, you had explained to the man his job was not only to operate the machine, but to sweep floors as well, presumably you will have a satisfied employee or no employee at all. Instead of deriving satisfaction from their job as agents of social control, the police feel frustrated because they believe themselves to be doing a job that, although rightfully theirs, they receive little training and even less credit or support for.

The police work under tremendous and growing stress, a stress of which they are not even aware. This stress comes from their lack of understanding of the criminal justice system within which they work. Many policemen, because they were never trained to understand the system properly in the first place, grow to maturity in the police role viewing it as an encumbrance.

So how do we correct these faults? First by understanding that never before in our history have people learned more, gone to school for longer periods, travelled more, read more, and understood more. As a result, they do not want policemen, under their present training regime, to be just skilled tradesmen dealing with social problems. In fact, some people know more about the solutions to the problems than the police do. In this day and age, people will not accept being told what to do, or having their lives controlled or directed by the police, or anyone else in authority. The police must learn new skills in solving people problems.

If one concedes that "right" decisions are based mainly on knowledge, that knowledge comes (at least in part) from education, then education will enable the professional policeman to adapt to the situation of the moment. The most relevant education is one that allows the recruit to respond appropriately to the greatest number of variables or unpredictable situations. However, for the young recruit who has never been out on the street, or in the courts, and cannot judge the real need for any of the training or education he is exposed to, his view of relevance will come from the attitude and actions of his superiors towards such training and education. Behavioural science training, or any higher academic training, will become more relevant to the recruits only when it becomes recognized by the senior officers that it is an essential part of police preparation.

Surprising as it may seem, 90 percent of the population live out their lives with little or no contact with the police insofar as breaking the law is concerned. A simple truth is that this silent majority of the public like the police. So perhaps the job is to teach the police to like the public. They have to realize that the 10 percent of the population with which they most frequently deal do not represent the whole, and that their attitude to the whole should not be based on that 10 percent.

If, in fact, 90 percent of the population do not need to be treated as criminals and if in fact the largest portion of the police role is to act as agents of social control or solvers of "people problems," then it seems that we are committing a great travesty of justice: a travesty of justice both to the police and to the citizens of Canada in not preparing our police for what has been demonstrated to be their most important function. A better equipped police force will come only through education—not through training. Training is skill learning, whereas education is concerned not only with how, but also with why. The task will not be easy, as opposition will start with some constables themselves, their non-commissioned officers, and even a few officers, who perceive their role in only one way—as law enforcement agents. True, they must be prepared to meet force with force, but that is not their only role. It is time that the senior officers of police departments and the public insist that police be given the opportunity to learn psychology, sociology and other behavioural-related subjects.

Unless there is a recognition of the police social control role, unless we stop concentrating on bigger and better weaponry, machines, technology and so on, unless we educate policemen concerning the criminal justice system, I do not see a bright future for the police or the public of this country.

The police of the future must no longer be allowed to follow along para-professional lines as they have done in the past, with antiquated procedures and authoritarian methods of management. The quest for professionalism will demand senior policemen who have managerial skills rather than those who have simply been promoted by virtue of seniority. The realization that the skills necessary for police management are not necessarily the same as those possessed by a good law enforcer will lead to different assessment criteria for promotion.

Once we adequately prepare the policeman to fulfill his complete role in society, then and only then will he receive the quiet peace, the inner satisfaction that comes from serving his fellow man. For after all, is that not what police work is all about?

Chapter 6

The Police and the Judiciary

Ian V. Dubienski

To appreciate the correlation of the judiciary and the police, one must have an understanding of the relative position each holds in the criminal justice system. To achieve this the student must be clearly apprised of the jurisdiction of each in the relationship of one to the other.

The administration of justice in Canada with reference to the criminal law has its jurisdictions and legislative powers established by the British North America Act (1867), which created the Dominion of Canada.

To better understand the Act, examination should be made of various sections that have a bearing on our subject.

Section 91, sub-section 27 of the BNA Act enacts: "... the exclusive Legislative Authority of the Parliament of Canada extends to all Matters coming within the Classes of Subjects next hereinafter enumerated; that is to say . . . the Criminal Law except the Constitution of Courts of Criminal Jurisdiction but including the Procedure in Criminal Matters." This establishes the fact that only the federal government can legislate the criminal law or laws that have criminal sanctions in the federal area of competence.

Section 92, sub-section 14 of the BNA Act enacts: "The Administration of Justice in the Province, including the Constitution, Maintenance, and Organization of Provincial Courts, both of Civil and of Criminal Jurisdiction, and including Procedure in Civil Matters in those Courts." By this enactment the physical establishment of the courts and the court offices and the day-to-day administration are the responsibility of the provincial governments.

It is enacted under the BNA Act, Section 96: "The Governor General shall appoint the Judges of the Superior, District, and County Courts in each Province except those of the Courts of Probate in Nova Scotia and New Brunswick."

Further it is enacted by Section 92, (referred to above) sub-section 15, "The Imposition of Punishment by Fine, Penalty, or Imprisonment for enforcing any Law of the Province made in relation to any

Judge Dubienski is a Senior Judge of the Provincial Judges Criminal Court, Manitoba. Previously, he was a full-time magistrate to the Winnipeg City Magistrate's Court.

Matter coming within any of the Classes of Subjects enumerated in this Section." This empowers the provinces to pass laws in provincial jurisdiction such as Highway Traffic and Liquor Acts with penalties for non-compliance thereof. Such penalties are known as "quasi-criminal" offences and are called "petty" or "minor" regulatory offences.

Because of the provincial jurisdiction under Section 92, sub-section 14 of the BNA Act, the provinces have the exclusive power to appoint provincial judges, magistrates, justices of the peace and in the province of Quebec, judges of the session of the peace and provincial judges.

The Judicial System

At the time of the enactment of the BNA Act, levels of courts with criminal jurisdiction were established, and as each province became a member of the Dominion of Canada similar provision was made.

The jurisdiction of the various courts designates their authority and the powers they are able to exercise in the criminal law. The Criminal Code also indicates the appropriate court to which a matter shall go by reason of its classification as an offence and elective procedures. This is discussed elsewhere.

Magistrate's Court

It is proposed to discuss the various courts of criminal jurisdiction by commencing with the court that is the usual court of entry into the criminal justice system, that is the "magistrate's court" as defined by the Code but variously designated on a provincial basis, as is pointed out later.

The jurisdiction for criminal matters is given to this court by definition under Section 2 of the Criminal Code (the definition section) under the heading "Court of Criminal Jurisdiction." It is variously defined as:

(a) a court of general or quarter sessions of the peace, when presided over by a superior court judge, or a county or district court judge, or in the cities of Montreal and Quebec, by municipal judge of the city, as the case may be, or a judge of the sessions of the peace; and

(b) a magistrate or judge acting under Part XVI.

A magistrate is defined in the Criminal Code as "a magistrate means a police magistrate, a stipendiary magistrate, a district magistrate, a provincial magistrate, a judge of the sessions of the peace, a recorder, or any person having the power and authority of two or more justices of the peace, and includes:

(a) with respect to the Provinces of Ontario, Quebec, New Brunswick and British Columbia, a judge of the provincial court;

(a.1) with respect to the Provinces of Alberta, Manitoba and Prince Edward Island, a provincial judge;

(a.2) with respect to the Province of Nova Scotia, a judge of the Provincial Magistrate's court;

(b) with respect to the Province of Saskatchewan, a judge of the Magistrate's Court; and

(c) with respect to the Yukon Territory and the Northwest Territories, a judge of the Supreme Court, and the lawful deputy of each of them."

The judges of these courts defined as magistrates, usually legally qualified, are appointed to hold office by most provinces during good behaviour to retirement age. Those of the Yukon and Northwest Territories are appointed by the federal government.

The judges of the Magistrate or Provincial Court have jurisdiction over what are known as indictable and summary conviction offences as well as the quasi-criminal matters.

The County or District Court

The County or District Court criminal jurisdiction is established most often when the accused elects to be tried with judge without a jury. The jurisdiction of this court is established under Part XVI of the Code with the elective procedures for trial. In a few provinces this court may hear some offences with a jury.

In some provinces the court has jurisdiction in criminal appeal matters. These are appeals from the Magistrate's Court.

The Superior Court

The highest provincial trial court of criminal jurisdiction is known as the Superior Court of Criminal Jurisdiction, defined in the Criminal Code as being:

(a) In the Province of Ontario, the Supreme Court;

(b) In the Province of Quebec, Superior Court;

(c) In the Provinces of Nova Scotia, Prince Edward Island, and Newfoundland respectively, the Supreme Court;

(d) In the Province of British Columbia, the Supreme Court or the Court of Appeal;

(e) In the Provinces of Manitoba, Saskatchewan, Alberta and New Brunswick respectively, the Court of Appeal or the Court of Queen's Bench;
(f) In the Yukon Territory, the Supreme Court and,
(g) In the Northwest Territories, the Supreme Court.

The judges of these courts are appointed by the federal government (during good behaviour) to retirement age and have exclusive jurisdiction for what are known as capital offences. The offences over which they have jurisdiction are described in Section 427 of the Criminal Code as follows:

(a) Offence under any of the following sections namely, (i) Section 47—treason. (ii) Section 49—action against her Majesty. (iii) Section 51—intimidating Parliament. (iv) Section 53—mutiny. (v) Section 62—sedition. (vi) Section 75—piracy. (vii) Section 76—acts of piracy. (viii) Section 218—first- or second-degree murder.
(b) Accessory after the fact—treason or murder.
(c) Bribery by the holder of a judicial office.
(d) Offence of attempting to commit any of the offences in said Paragraph a(i) to (vii) or the offence of conspiring to commit any of the offences mentioned in Paragraph (a).

Such matters are tried in the Superior Court with judge and jury after committal for trial by the magistrate. It is the responsibility of the judge to make decisions of law such as evidence and to sentence the accused. The jury is charged with the responsibility of deciding the guilt or innocence of the accused, based on the facts.

The Court of Appeal
The appellate provisions are mainly dependent upon whether or not the matter was an *ab initio* indictable or a summary conviction offence.

If indictable, the appeal is to the Provincial Court of Appeal for appeal from a conviction by accused, acquittal by Crown, or assessment of sentence. The court in some jurisdictions is in reality a division of the Provincial Superior Court, being either a panel of judges or the Court *en banc* or a separate Court of Appeals. The courts are established, maintained and administered by the provinces. The judges are appointed and paid by the federal government. An appeal of conviction of an indictable matter may be generally taken to the Court of Appeal if (a) a sentence for murder there is automatic right of appeal on conviction, (b) on questions of law as of right but (c) on question of fact or mixed law and fact or other grounds—

with leave of the court. Appeal for sentence is allowed only on leave.

Upon hearing the appeal, the Court of Appeal may dismiss or allow an appeal and order a new trial or direct an acquittal. It may vary a sentence in any way it deems appropriate. Appeals from this forum are made to the Supreme Court of Canada.

If the offence is a summary conviction, the appeal may be in two forms: (a) by re-trial by judge alone—being in most provinces in the District or County Court, this procedure allows for the old evidence plus new evidence to be put forward; (b) the judge who heard the matter to submit to the Court of Appeal questions of law as he found them for its ruling as to whether he was correct or not in his interpretation. Upon decision, that matter is returned to the judge for his disposal. There can be no stated case on facts or mixed law and facts.

There are other controls that Superior Courts can assert over Summary Conviction Courts. They are known as extra-ordinary remedies. They are usually an order of the Appeal Court to the lower court to perform or not perform some act.

The Supreme Court of Canada

The final court of appeal of the nation is the Supreme Court of Canada, consisting of nine judges, sitting in Ottawa. Only those cases that involve a question of public interest or an important point of law that must have a final decision generally reach this court. There are some cases that go to the Supreme Court as a matter of right in the area of criminal law, and the main example of that is a person convicted and sentenced on a charge of murder whose appeal has been dismissed by the Court of Appeal. In other cases, appeals are within the discretion of the court itself and are decided on motions known as "applications for leave to appeal."

Juvenile Court

The Juvenile Court is a court established under the provisions of the Juvenile Delinquency Act, a federal Act passed for the purposes of dealing with young offenders.

This court is established, maintained and administered in much the same way as the Magistrate's Court and obtains its jurisdiction from the similar enactment of the British North America Act.

The jurisdiction of this court is established by the age of the offender and it varies throughout Canada from those under the age of sixteen to those under the age of eighteen.

It is important to understand the philosophy of the Juvenile Court, in that it is based on the fact that a child is to be treated as "a misdirected and misguided child and one needing aid, encouragement, help and assistance." The care, custody and discipline in the court or as a result of a court order must approximate those of parents. The child is not to be treated as a criminal. He is not charged with the offence, be it under the Criminal Code, provincial statute or bylaw, but with a delinquency of having committed such an infraction. Therefore, he obtains not a criminal record but a record of a delinquency.

Most of these courts now have two sections. The first is the Juvenile Section, which deals directly with the administration of the Juvenile Delinquents Act; the second is the Family Court, which deals with family matters having to do with marriage conflict, maintenance and custody of children. In the province of Quebec, these courts are called Social Welfare Courts.

Once a charge of delinquency has been heard against an offender, he can be dealt with informally or sent to a holding facility. In many jurisdictions the accused can be dealt with by an informal disposition by the probation officers without appearing before the court.

It should be pointed out that for some time there has been criticism and discussion concerning the Juvenile Delinquents Act and there have been several attempts at amendment and a change of philosophy.

The federal Department of the Solicitor General currently is proposing a new "Young Offenders Act" that is built on somewhat different principles than those of the Juvenile Delinquency Act. Brief reference is made to this Act at this time to show the difference in its approach.

The new Act stipulates that young persons who commit offences should bear responsibility for their contraventions. While young persons should not in all instances be held accountable in the same manner and suffer the same consequences for their behaviour as adults, society must nonetheless be afforded the necessary protection from such behaviour.

This means that it is important to protect society from illegal behaviour by imposing supervision, discipline and control of young offenders but, at the same time, recognize special needs. Also there must be protection to the young people for their rights and freedoms and a recognition of their assumptions of responsibility.

At the time of writing, the proposed legislation has proceeded through a great deal of consultation with various segments of the criminal justice system but it can not be estimated when it might go before the House of Commons.

Jurisdiction Established by Class of Offence

Under the Criminal Code there are two main classes of offences called "indictable" or serious offences and "summary conviction" offences or lesser offences. These designations are also found in other federal statutes, such as the Narcotic Control Act, the Post Office Act and many others. These classifications are purely statutory and each offence is classified by Parliament in the Code to indicate which court will have jurisdiction.

Indictable Offences. These offences are subject to a somewhat complicated procedure to establish jurisdiction of the court:

(i) In the first instance the accused appears before the magistrate at which time, unless the magistrate has absolute jurisdiction to try the matter with or without the consent of the accused, the accused is put to his election as to the manner of his trial. He may (a) consent to be tried by the magistrate for any indictable offence not within the exclusive jurisdiction of a Superior Court judge; or (b) elect to be tried by a County or District Court judge sitting alone or a Superior Court judge sitting with a jury.

If the accused elects to be tried by the magistrate, a summary trial is held with the accused subject to the penalty provided by the Code. Appeals go to the Provincial Court of Appeal.

If, however, the accused elects either trial by judge alone or by judge and jury, the magistrate holds a preliminary hearing and if he finds a *prima facie* case against the accused (i.e., that it is probable that the accused may be convicted), the judge commits the accused for trial in the court of his choice.

(ii) If the accused has elected to be tried by judge alone, the trial upon commital takes place usually before a County or District Court judge in all provinces except Quebec, where it is a judge of the Sessions of the Peace or District Court judge. In some provinces, Superior Criminal Court judges have concurrent jurisdiction.

(iii) If the accused has elected to be tried by judge and jury, the trial usually takes place at an Assize Sitting of a Superior Court of Criminal Jurisdiction. The trials are conducted by a judge and usually a jury of twelve persons (juries are discussed in detail below). Trials are also conducted by a judge and jury in Courts of Criminal Jurisdiction; i.e., County Court, District Court or Courts of General Sessions of the Peace in Ontario and New Brunswick. These latter courts can not hear trials within exclusive jurisdiction of Superior Criminal Courts.

Summary Offences. Summary conviction offences are those defined and for which procedures are set out in Part XXIV of the Code. As with indictable offences, summary offences are specifically designated. Under Section 722, unlike indictable offences that have varying penalties, a general penalty is provided for such offences, being a maximum fine of $500 or maximum imprisonment of six months, or both. The court having jurisdiction is the Summary Conviction Court, usually presided over by a magistrate, as above defined; but the Code or other enactment may give two or more justices of the peace equal jurisdiction. There are other provincial and local variations.

As mentioned previously, the provincial governments have the power to create offences of a quasi-criminal nature. These and municipal bylaw infractions are generally adjudicated by magistrates or justices of the peace.

Juries

Reference was made above to juries forming part of the trials in indictable offences in County and District Courts and Superior Courts.

The jury is a panel, usually of twelve persons, that sits with a judge of the said courts; its function is to decide the facts in order to establish the guilt or innocence of the accused.

The jury is usually empanelled by the sheriff of the district, from a pool of citizens whose names are on the voters' list of a certain district. In Manitoba, the jury can be mixed, francophone and anglophone; in Quebec the accused can elect to have a jury wholly composed of either French or English members.

When the jury has been chosen from the panel, the accused has the right to offer what are known as "challenges," for the purposes of refusing a potential juror. These vary in category and number. For example, the accused has twenty peremptory challenges if charged with high treason or first-degree murder, twelve peremptory challenges for other offences for which he may be sentenced to imprisonment for more than five years, or four peremptory challenges for all other offences. The prosecutor is entitled to challenge four jurors peremptorily but may have up to forty-eight jurors stood down pending the calling of the whole panel. For instance, there are also specific challenges for cause by the prosecutor or accused: the name of the juror not being on the panel, a juror having been convicted and sentenced to a term of imprisonment exceeding twelve months or being an alien or blind or otherwise incapacitated and unable to perform his duties.

The selection of the jurors results in a jury of twelve, or in the Yukon Territory and Northwest Territories, six. They are sworn to be the jury to try the issues of the charge. That is, to hear the evidence and give a verdict. Upon the verdict being given, they are subject to re-call of jury duty.

A juror may be discharged in the course of a trial if the judge is satisfied that the juror should not, because of illness or other reasonable cause, continue to act. Further in the course of a trial, if a juror dies or is discharged, the jury shall, unless the court otherwise decrees, remain properly constituted unless the number of jurors is reduced below ten.

As stated previously, the responsibility of the jury is to decide the facts and determine the guilt or innocence of the accused.

During the course of their participation in the trial, the jurors must remain together and in the custody of a court officer and must not communicate with anyone other than other jury members or the officer in charge without leave of the court. However, the judge may allow any members of the jury to separate before the jury retires to render verdict.

The jury is provided with suitable and sufficient refreshment, food and lodging until they have given their verdict. If the jury has been given permission to separate, no information regarding any portion of the trial at which the jury is not present shall be published in a newspaper or broadcast before the jury retires to give consideration to its verdict.

To protect the secrecy of jury deliberations, the Code enacts that any member of the jury who discloses information relating to the proceedings of the jury while it is in deliberation is guilty of an offence, unless the information given is to allow for the investigation of an obstruction of justice.

The jury has, with the permission of the court, the right to view places, persons or things outside the courtroom that form part of the trial matter. When the judge is satisfied that the jury is unable to agree upon its verdict and any further deliberation would be useless, the judge may, in his discretion, discharge that jury and direct a new jury to be empanelled or take such other action as is necessary at a future date.

At the end of the trial, the crown prosecutor and the defence counsel make their submissions to the jury on the evidence, and the judge instructs the jury as to the law and how the evidence should be applied in the light of the law. The jury retires in private to arrive at its verdict. This being done, it is delivered to the court and is entered as a court record.

Precedent Law

In the main, Canada is known as a common law country; that is, a country that depends upon law other than that contained in statutes, such as the Criminal Code, based on decisions of higher courts and binding upon the decisions of lower courts. These higher court decisions are known as "precedents." In Quebec, where laws are codified, the precedent applies to decisions of interpretation of the statute laws.

The general rules for the application of precedents over the years have become well defined and are as follows:

1. Each court is bound by the decisions of the court above it. For instance, all the courts are bound by the decisions of the Supreme Court of Canada. The Supreme Court of Canada is bound by its own decisions.

2. Any relevant judgement of any court is a strong argument entitled to respectful consideration.

3. A judgement is authoritative only as to its ground for the decision of the court in a particular case.

4. Precedent is not abrogated nor does it lose any effect by lapse of time.

5. However, very old precedents are not in practice, applicable and followed to modern circumstance.

6. A precedent may be cited from any source the court considers reliable. This refers to the use of the law reports that in time acquire the status of accuracy.

Precedents are used to establish the principles to be followed in the case. The judge applies the facts to these principles and according to his interpretation, makes his decision. The judge is bound by the authority of higher courts concerning his interpretation of how a precedent is applicable to the facts in that case.

The main functions of the judge are to search out and uphold the principles of the law and to ensure the administration of justice. If he can not find a precedent, then he can fall back on natural justice, reason, morality and social ethics.

Sometimes the use of precedents is called "judge made law." This is not exactly accurate, because it is deemed that the law already exists and the judge is merely enunciating it by interpreting the facts in the light of precedents. Besides the facts of the case, the judge would consider, among other things, the social values of the times and environment in which the crime occurred. Therefore, the law is considered to be dynamic, because by interpretation of collateral matters, the court can bring it up to date.

Occasionally, a precedent is criticized because of deficiencies, such as incorrectly reported cases, lack of certainty that the judge considered all relevant authorities, or because it is comment in passing or outside the facts of the case. These problems are more often dealt with by the corrective powers of the legislature and of the Courts of Appeal. Often the main concern is time lag. The courts are criticized for not reacting to social change as quickly as they should; however, as time progresses, there would appear to be a tendency by the courts to lessen the problems created by precedent and to confirm its position as the most desirable method of interpreting and enforcing the law.

From the above, we appreciate that precedent does not create our criminal law nor does it establish the principles upon which it is based. Where precedent does have its effect is in the consideration of how the law in the Criminal Code or any other statute should be interpreted and applied.

The Adversary Principle

The process and conduct of trials in our courts is based upon what is known as the "adversary system." There has developed in recent times considerable criticism of the adversary system of justice, nevertheless it is the system followed by the courts today.

As Rosco Pound said, "It is a contentious procedure." That is, the adversary system envisages the presentation of a trial as much the same as a debate, with the evidence being weighed on the basis of points made by each side, with a difference of application as between the criminal law and the civil law. This difference is established by the principles that in the criminal law the guilt of the accused must be proven beyond a reasonable doubt, whereas in the civil law the guilt for the act, or the responsibility for the act or omission, can be proven by the plaintiff by a preponderance of evidence. In the civil law this can further be refined by the court finding that the defendant may not have been wholly responsible for the damage because the plaintiff may have contributed to the result. The court then makes an apportionment of responsibility.

To function properly, this procedure for resolving legal controversies requires that there be many rules of evidence governing the process. These rules are complicated and have to do with what evidence is admissible and in what way certain facts are to be proven.

Briefly put, the adversary system operates by the prosecution alleging its case by witnesses. Each witness is subject to be cross-examined by the defence for the purposes of discrediting his evidence. Similarly the defence may or may not present evidence to rebut that produced by the prosecution and that evidence too is subject to cross-examination.

It is this element of cross-examination that is claimed to give the adversary system its status of being a superior procedure to that used elsewhere in the world. "It is beyond any doubt the greatest legal engine ever invented for the discovery of truth," said Wigmore.[1]

The Judiciary

For the purposes of this discussion the "judiciary" are the judges, as separate and distinct from the other court personnel and services.

Judges should be and are, on the whole, legally trained and qualified. There are some exceptions. In several provincial jurisdictions, allowance has been made for the appointment of lay magistrates in remote areas; however, in most instances these magistrates have limited jurisdiction.[2]

The prime requirement of the court in the person of the judge is that it function as part of the criminal justice system, completely and distinctly separate from the political and administrative branches of government. Although the judicial appointment is made by the Lieutenant-Governor, it is upon the recommendation of the government in power. To this extent the appointment is political. However, once appointed the judge enjoys absolute independence and in most cases the legislation provides for appointment for life and removal to be made only "for cause." Thus the appointment of judge brings with it freedom from any political intimidation and risk.[3]

The independence of the judiciary is based on the oft-quoted statement of Lord Hewart, then Lord Chief Justice of England, "It is not merely of some importance but of fundamental importance that justice should not only be done, but should manifestly and undoubtedly be seen to be done."[4]

It is this independence that emphasizes the fact that the judiciary is not and must not be in any way related to the police function. Because of this opinion, serious questions have been raised regarding judges functioning as police commissioners. In the past, for reason of designation, criminal courts were known as police courts and judges sitting therein were known as police magistrates. To avoid any possible suggestion of a link between the court and the police, this term has now been dropped almost universally. Most criminal court judges are now designated as judges of the Provincial Court, Criminal Division.

It has been said that the criminal court is the central, crucial institution in the criminal justice system. The function of the criminal court is to administer the criminal law that has been established by society through legislation contained mainly in the Criminal Code. There are two main steps in this function. First, the court must make an assessment and adjudication of the facts; i.e., establish the guilt or innocence of the accused on the basis of the evidence before it.

Secondly, upon a finding of guilt, the court must make an appropriate disposition to sentence the accused.

It is this second step, commonly referred to as the "sentencing process," that has been the subject of most controversy and requires the greatest understanding and appreciation of the function of the court. The aims of this process are to protect society and rehabilitate the accused. The latter aim is referred to as the "process of corrections."

To accomplish such protection of society, the court directs its attention mainly to the principle of deterrence of criminal activity, by imposing a sanction upon the accused that will remove the temptation to become again involved in criminal activity and to impress others similarly tempted not to commit criminal offences now or in the future. The immediate effect is to punish the accused and remove him from society if he is imprisoned.

The court has many alternatives to consider when deciding what sentence to impose, all of which are provided within the Criminal Code.

Once the court has come to the conclusion of guilt, it must decide what sanctions are appropriate. The matters to be considered by the judge are called "the principles of sentencing." These have been established by court practice over a long period and have the objective of obtaining as great a degree of consistency of sentencing as possible. Even taking into consideration the peculiarities of each case, careful adherence to the principles of sentencing ensures some uniformity.

The principles of sentencing have been the subject of many decisions of the court and, while they are not codified, they have been summarized with a degree of particularity, as follows:

1. the degree of pre-meditation involved;

2. the circumstances surrounding the actual commission of the offence, that is, the manner in which it was committed, the amount of violence employed, the employment of an offensive weapon, the degree of active participation of the offender;

3. the gravity of the crime committed with regard to which the maximum punishment as provided by the statute is an indication;

4. the attitude of the offender after the commission of the offence, has this served to indicate to some extent the criminality involved and throw some light on the character of the participants;

5. the previous criminal record of the offender, if any;

6. the age, mode of life, character, and personality of the offender;

7. any pre-sentence report or probation officer's report or any other mitigating or other circumstance that should properly be brought to the attention of the court;"[5] and in my opinion further,

8. the motive of the crime, provocation if any, the family background, the present status of the offender, the mental health of the offender, any reports pertaining to the social behaviour, the relation of this offence to the accused's own life and environment, the relation of this offence to society generally and its frequency, and probably most important what facilities are available in penal institutions or on probation or discharges for the possible rehabilitation of the accused.

The paramount feature of the judicial process that must be clearly understood is that it is founded mainly upon the exercise of discretion of the judge. The responsibility of making decisions is to exercise his discretion reasonably as a result of the reasonable interpretation of the facts and of the law.

In its relationship with the judiciary, it is necessary that the police be seen to function diligently as they pursue their responsibility for the apprehension and preparation of the case against the accused.

The judiciary's attitude toward the police is founded not only on the presence and personality of the policeman in the courtroom but on his professionalism in the accumulation of evidence. There is no excuse or answer for sloppy police work.

The policeman in court is not considered an officer of the court, as is a judge or legal counsel. The policeman appears in court only as a witness. He presents to the court the facts of which he has knowledge concerning the offence with which the accused is charged. Delivery of these facts should be given concisely, clearly and without equivocation. The policeman must come to court prepared with complete recollection of all matter of which he has knowledge. To assist in his recollection, he has the right to refresh his memory from his notes made at the scene at the time and from his full report, prepared for his supervisor immediately after the facts were noted.

Because the court is interested only in the truth, it is imperative that the evidence of the police officer be given in such a manner so as not to suggest or create the impression that the evidence is biased, slanted or purposely incomplete. On direct examination, the evidence must be so complete that there should not be any surprises or undue revelations upon cross-examination that would give the impression of withheld facts.

On occasion the police officer may, as a result of his experience, be qualified to give opinion evidence. This does not occur very often unless he is a highly specialized member of the police department, particularly in the identification branch, and thus is qualified to give evidence in ballistics, identification, chemical analysis, finger-printing and other specific areas.

Generally a policeman will be asked opinion on simple matters based on his experience in the field such as the degree of intoxication. In this case the policeman is able to give an opinion just like any other expert witness. The police officer must appreciate and under-stand that, in spite of his qualification as an expert witness, the court has the ultimate right to accept or reject his opinion.

A crucial event in the process of a trial can be the presentation of a confession or statement made by the accused to a person in authority, usually a police officer, during the course of the investigation. It is important that the police officer be aware of the requirements and method of presenting the evidence concerning the background for obtaining the statement. The judicial investigation during the course of a trial to ascertain whether or not a statement is voluntary is often referred to as a trial within a trial, or more specifically as a "voir dire."

Inasmuch as the primary matter to be established is the voluntari-ness of the statement, the candor of the police officer is most impor-tant. The central line of questioning concerns the actions of the police officers during the course of obtaining the statement. There can be allegations that range from mere intimidation to actual physical abuse. On the basis of the evidence presented by the prose-cution and the accused, if he so desires, the court makes a finding of fact as to whether or not the statement was voluntary.

It is very crucial that at this time the police officer as a witness must be most candid and not create any suspicions concerning the atmosphere or police conduct at the time of obtaining the statement. The court surely will have to make a finding of credibility, and the courtroom presentation of the police officer can have a profound effect on the acceptance or rejection of his evidence with regard to the admissibility of the statement.

As early as possible in his career, the police officer should familiar-ize himself with the basic rules of evidence. He can avoid courtroom conflict and create a much better image if he has clearly established in his mind the rules that govern whether his evidence is legally and acceptably given. It is not expected that the police officer be an expert on the refinements and exceptions to rules of evidence; how-ever, a basic and clear understanding avoids many interruptions, objections and arguments from counsel, which disrupt the process of the trial and the continuity of evidence, and may reflect badly upon the witness and his evidence.

The courtroom appearance and demeanour of a police officer are crucial. If it is his force's regulation that he appear in uniform, he should be properly attired. If, however, he is able to appear in civilian clothes, he should be as well dressed as possible and not casually attired.

At all times the police officer's demeanour should be commensurate with the seriousness of the event. He should not enter into jocularity with the court or counsel, nor should he be argumentative or boisterous. The advice is in all cases to keep his "cool." This has particular reference to cross-examination. How a police officer handles himself on cross-examination and the impression he makes upon the court have a great deal to do with experience.

Experience can be gained by taking part in or watching trials in various courts and for various offences. The efforts of some defence counsel to confuse, to endeavour to have witnesses admit to mistakes, to attempt to discredit the accuracy of the evidence given, are tactics with which a police witness should be familiar. He must also learn how to present to the court an impression that creates confidence in and respect for his evidence, so that his part in the court's search for truth will be accepted.

Today the caseloads of courts are constantly on the increase and dockets are full to overflowing. The whole criminal justice system is frustrated by delays in a system whose goal is to dispense justice speedily. Not the least frustrated are police officers, who view the delays as a challenge to their efficiency. Fortunately the court system in Canada has not become as clogged as that of the United States, but there is the possibility that this could happen and steps must be taken to avoid this event. The role of the police requires close co-operation with the court authorities and the judiciary. All must see to it that investigations are well prepared and not directed to frivolous matters.

Often the results of an investigation will bring to light an offence, culminating in the laying of a charge and the subsequent prosecution. Once the criminal judicial process has been started, it is in the hands of the Attorney General, whose agent is the Crown attorney. Upon his review and discussion of the facts with the accused's counsel, it can often be resolved that not all elements of the charge proposed by the prosecution are present, but there are those that may substantiate another or lesser charge. It is at this point that the defence counsel might admit the true offence and offer to enter a guilty plea to that charge, provided the Crown does not proceed upon the original charge. This process is called plea bargaining, and it is essential that the police officer understand it. It is not only the prerogative of the Crown attorney and defence counsel, but also their duty as officers of the court to enter into this process when appropriate. It is a principle of Canadian justice that a person shall not be convicted of a charge of which he is not guilty, therefore a plea of guilty to another charge, even a lesser one, is a lawful and just act. Only when plea bargaining is used for expediency is the course of justice frustrated, and it may then be rightly criticized.

Plea bargaining sometimes also includes discussions as to the sentence; this is called sentence bargaining. However, there is no assurance that the court is bound to any agreement. In every instance, the court has the ultimate jurisdiction and will never bind itself in secret. The court may be open to suggestions as to limits on which the parties have agreed, but it must be reiterated that sentencing is subject to the court's exclusive discretion.

There exists not only in the minds of the police but in the minds of the public a misunderstanding of the relative positions of the police and the judiciary in the criminal justice system. This has been referred to as the "cops vs. courts" controversy. In a nutshell, there are those who allege that police officers catch the criminals but the courts are too easy on them. There are even some who feel that the court actually impedes the police in their law enforcement activities. In Canada we are greatly influenced by the American media that permeate our daily lives. Much of the controversy is centred around events, incidents, situations and problems that exist only in the United States. In Canada there is a greater appreciation of the responsibilities of the police and the judiciary and their relative function within the system. However, it is most necessary that the police be fully aware of the relative responsibilities of the courts and the police.

How often one hears the criticism by police officers, "I caught him, laid the charge, he appeared in court, the next day I saw him walking down the street—free." Their feelings of frustration are understandable. However, if the police truly understand the laws and the principles concerning the granting of bail, both in the common law and as set forth in the Criminal Code, they will appreciate the judicial function.

There are no hard and fast rules governing the basis for the granting of bail. In all instances, except those covered by the Criminal Code, the judge has the sole discretion to decide whether or not bail should be granted. He must consider the question under broad principles. The matter of bail granting is discussed in another chapter of this book, but I raise it here to emphasize the necessity of appreciating and respecting the function of the judiciary when considering bail.

First of all, under the Canadian justice system no man can be deprived of his liberty unless he is a threat or a potential threat to society. If he is not, then bail will be granted because the court is satisfied that he will appear for his trial and will not become involved in any criminal activity while at liberty. The philosophy of his release is to allow him to remain in the community with his family, to enable him to assist in preparing his defence, and to consult his lawyer with ease. By releasing him, the court has avoided jailing a person who may be innocent, for we must not lose sight of the over-riding principle that every man is presumed innocent until proven guilty. Release on bail also avoids a situation wherein the accused is held pending trial, then receives a sentence of supervised probation and thereby his freedom.

As stated earlier, the courts reflect the changing attitudes of society, and it is not their decisions that are challenging the work of the police. The real problem is that social attitudes are changing, and there is no mechanism by which the police can adapt to these changes at society's speed. Therefore there is a great frustration among police departments and individual policemen, who are required to enforce unpopular laws that are still in force due to the slowness with which legislatures act. The police should understand that the judiciary is bound by the same laws and suffers the same frustrations. It is mainly in the area of sentencing that the judiciary can sometimes reflect changes in social attitudes. It is hoped that we can resolve this conflict and avoid the confrontations that have occurred in the United States, causing the erosion of public respect for all branches of the criminal justice system.

The relationship between the judiciary and the police must be one of mutual respect. Each should be aware of its relative functions, responsibilities, aims and objectives. There should be an atmosphere of co-operation and a confidence in each branch. The police should never speak disrespectfully of the court, though they may criticize its decisions as they relate to the protection of society. However, any criticism should not be of a personal nature or made to reflect on the integrity of the court, so as to undermine its status as the bulwark of our freedom.

The judiciary cannot show bias in favour of the police in spite of their appreciation of the dangers of their work and of their value to society. If the court is to sit impartially and have an open mind, it cannot accept police evidence just because it is the evidence of the police. The court knows that even the police are human and can err. In turn, the police officer should recognize that judges too are fallible. What the police officer must understand is that an error on the part of the judge is readily rectified, and if the error is obvious the Crown will enter an appeal to a higher court.

Having examined the relative functions of the judiciary and the police, it can be readily seen that although each of their functions is distinct and separate, neither operates in a vacuum. Each in its way protects society from criminal activity. But because their immediate aims and powers differ, there is a tendency for conflict to arise. An understanding of the basis for the conflict immediately resolves the problem and engenders the mutual respect that is the foundation of harmonious and united effort to achieve the over-all aims of the criminal justice system.

NOTES

1. Wigmore, *On Evidence*, ed. J. H. Chadbourn. Vol. V, sec. 1367, p. 32. Toronto: Little, Brown & Co., 1974.
2. Manitoba Provincial Judges Act, S.M. 1972, c. 61.
3. *Ibid.*
4. *Rex vs. Sussex Justices* (1929) 1 Q.B. 256, p. 259.
5. *Regina vs. Iwaniw* (1960) 32 C.R. 389, p. 397.

FURTHER READINGS

Gall, Gerald L. *The Canadian Legal System*. Toronto: Carswell Company, 1977.
Greenspan, E. L., ed. *Martin's Annual Criminal Code*. Toronto: Canada Law Book, 1979 et seq.
Guidelines–Dispositions and Sentences. Law Reform Commission. Ministry of Supply and Services. Ottawa: 1977.
Our Criminal Law. Law Reform Commission. Information Canada. Ottawa: 1976.
Report of the Canadian Committee on Corrections. Ottawa: Queen's Printer, 1969.

Chapter 7

The Police and the Crown
Clare Lewis

Perhaps one of the most common misconceptions prevalent in the field of criminal law is that the Crown attorney is the counsel, or lawyer, for the police. While it is certainly true that most frequently the interests of the police and the Crown coincide, it is a grave error to conclude that the Crown represents the police in the manner that counsel for the defence represents the accused.

The functions and responsibilities of the police and the Crown are entirely different and separate. The police role is crime prevention and investigation and, in terms of control of the prosecution, ends with the decision to charge the accused and bring him before the court. The responsibility of the police is to the Police Act, which in Ontario provides in Section 55 that the police are charged with among other things, "prosecuting and aiding in the prosecuting of offenders." The right of police to act as prosecutors is strictly limited to provincial offences such as those arising under the provisions of the Highway Traffic Act, and to summary conviction federal offences, which are of a relatively minor nature. All serious or indictable offences must be prosecuted by the Crown attorney, and the police power in the prosecution is limited to assisting the Crown attorney. The responsibility of the Crown attorney is to the Crown Attorneys Act, which requires the Crown attorney to prosecute indictable offences and, where in his opinion the public interest so requires, prosecute any summary conviction offences.

The Crown attorney is, of course, a lawyer, and his academic training is identical to that of all other lawyers. It is frequently difficult for police officers charged with the responsibility for law enforcement to appreciate that Crown attorneys, as lawyers, have been schooled in a system of law that holds that an accused is presumed to be innocent until the Crown proves him to be guilty beyond a reasonable doubt, and that further maintains a great many safeguards designed to protect all accused from improper conviction. These safeguards are built upon an old legal maxim: "Better one thousand guilty men should go free than that one innocent man should be convicted."

While no fair-minded person would desire the conviction of an

Judge C. Lewis is a Provincial Court Judge, Criminal Division, and was previously an Assistant Crown Attorney for the Judicial District of York.

innocent person, this proposition affords precious little solace to the police officer who day by day encounters the effects of crime, the toll upon its victims, and the uncaring and frequently vicious attitudes of so many offenders—only to find that the rule of law can result in the acquittal of a person whom an officer knows or believes to be guilty.

For it is demonstratively true that our law, in its commendable effort to protect the innocent, does so at the cost of failing to bring a large number of guilty people to justice. The police officer's skepticism all too often evolves into unfortunate cynicism, as he learns that his judgement as to the guilt of an accused may not be that of the court. He is undoubtedly further discomfited when he occasionally finds that his view of the guilt of the accused is not shared by the Crown attorney. The problem, of course, is that the police are interested in actual guilt and the lawyer and the courts can only be concerned with legal guilt.

None of the foregoing should suggest that there cannot be a sensitivity of understanding in the relationship between the Crown attorney and the police. It is probably true that many Crown attorneys and police officers share the view that the contemporary community can ill afford its present generosity to accused persons in its effort to protect the innocent, and that many changes in both substantive and procedural criminal law must be effected to protect the citizens in an ever more sophisticated and permissive society. Nonetheless, we must for now accept the law and its underlying philosophy as it is and recognize that even with such changes the essential roles of the Crown attorney and the police will remain the same, as will their relationship.

Accordingly, it is important to define the position of the Crown attorney in the judicial system. Perhaps the most often quoted statement of the role of the Crown attorney bears repeating in this context, for without mutual understanding of its essence, the Crown attorney and the police cannot properly co-operate in their responsibilities. The Supreme Court of Canada dealt with the prosecutorial function in the case of *Boucher vs. The Queen* (1955); Rand J. stated:

> It cannot be overemphasized that the purpose of a criminal prosecution is not to obtain a conviction; it is to lay before a jury what the Crown considers to be credible evidence relevant to what is alleged to be a crime. Counsel have a duty to see that all available legal proof of the fact is presented; it should be done firmly and pressed to its legitimate strength, but it must also be done fairly. The role of prosecution excludes any notion of winning or losing; his function is a matter of public duty, than which in civil life there can be none charged with greater personal responsibility. It is to be efficiently performed with an ingrained sense of the dignity, the seriousness and justness of judicial proceeding.[1]

It should be noted that in the *Boucher* case the Crown attorney at trial, in addressing the jury, said the following:

> It is the duty of the Crown, when something like that occurs, no matter what, and still more in a serious matter, to make every possible investigation, and if in the course of these investigations with our experts, the conclusion is arrived that the accused is not guilty or that there is reasonable doubt, it is the duty of the Crown, gentlemen, to say so or if the conclusion is arrived at that he is not guilty, not to make an arrest. That is what was done here. [2]

This statement prompted Locke J. in the Supreme Court of Canada to say, among other deprecating comments:

> The Crown prosecutor, having improperly informed the jury that there had been an investigation by the Crown which satisfied the authorities that the accused was guilty, thus assured them on his own behalf of his guilt and employed language calculated to influence their feelings against him. [3]

It is clear from the above that the Crown must stand aloof in presenting his case, and indeed he is an officer of the court, leading a quasi-judicial function in the first instance, and only secondarily is he a prosecutor in its proper sense. Further, it is often said that the Crown never wins or loses, and this statement implies that the Crown represents no party to the litigation. The responsibility of the Crown is to the community as a whole and that community includes the police, the citizens and the particular accused before the court. The police and the citizens have as much right to a fair trial under the prevailing strictures of our law as does the accused, and the Crown is in the delicate position of ensuring that all legitimate interests in the case at bar are preserved. While he performs his duties in an adversarial forum designed to find truth through competing theses, he may only properly apply the adversary process to the issues of the admissibility and interpretation of the evidence and the application of the law, and not to the denial of the protections afforded the accused.

The Crown Attorneys Act of Ontario (R.S.O. 1970, C. 101) provides in Section 9 as follows:

> Every Crown attorney and every assistant Crown attorney, before he enters upon his duties, shall take and subscribe before a judge of the county or district court of the county or district for which he is appointed the following oath: "I swear that I will truly and faithfully according to the best of my skill and ability, execute the duties, powers, and trusts of Crown attorney (or assistant Crown attorney) for the County (or District) of _____ without favour or affection to any party. So help me God."

It will be seen, therefore, that the impartial stance required of the

Crown attorney is imbedded in both statutory and common law.

However, the Crown attorney cannot function without the police and their respective duties require that they work together closely and in some harmony. To that end, an important responsibility of the Crown attorney is in advising the police regarding contemplated prosecutions and those already commenced. In smaller municipalities, the police regularly consult the Crown attorney on matters of evidence required to sustain a prosecution, and on what charges, if any are available and appropriate in particular fact situations. In larger centres, the police forces tend to proceed with both the investigation of offences and the laying of charges without recourse to the Crown attorney in all but the most complex or esoteric of cases. As the criminal prosecution proceeds, the Crown assumes full responsibility for advising as to which, if any, of the charges laid are appropriate for continued prosecution.

While no statute requires the Crown to advise the police, it is considered to be a normal duty of the office. Since the Crown will have ultimate responsibility for carrying the case through to completion, he is normally anxious to guide and assist the police in matters of law, the admissibility of evidence, the charges to be laid, or pressed if already laid and, where possible, to offer a fresh insight into the prosecution.

Indeed, Crown attorneys in Ontario do have a statutory duty to cause charges to be further investigated and additional evidence to be collected by the police when it is necessary to prevent prosecutions from being delayed unnecessarily, or from being dismissed for lack of proof. To be effective in this area the Crown must be briefed fully at an early stage by the police.

Through his advisory function, the Crown attorney develops a close working relationship with many, usually senior, police officers. Throughout, he must be alert to the ever present danger of assuming the perspective of the police. He must, despite the proximity of their duties and goals, exercise and maintain an independent judgement and never be perceived by the public to be an extension of the police. The Crown attorney in Canada does not in this regard resemble the American district attorney, who has his own investigative staff, inquisitorial grand juries and a mandate to ferret out criminal activity as well as to prosecute offenders when they are apprehended.

The Crown attorney provides a further service to the police in many municipalities by advising on general procedural matters. Frequently Crown attorneys attend at police colleges to deliver lectures on matters of law, evidence, and the preparation of cases for trial. Conversely, senior officers consult Crown attorneys to discuss policy matters within their forces, frequently related to budget restrictions and often to particularly sensitive crime problems peculiar to their area. The Crown must be aware of pressures upon the police and responsive to their legitimate needs. For example, since keeping police witnesses in court is expensive and wasteful of investigative man-hours, the Crown must make efforts to see that only necessary officers are subpoenaed and that even they be present in court only as long as reasonably required. Further, the Crown must, where possible, provide senior prosecutors with particular expertise in certain areas such as fraud, morality or organized crime, so that they may be available for advice and as trial Crowns to the specialized police squads that exist in large urban and in federal and provincial police forces.

It is to be noted that lasting friendships often develop between individual Crown attorneys and police officers, by reason of their intimate working relationship, and yet while these are acceptable, they must never intrude on the separate responsibilities of each. A recognition of this rule is found in Ontario, in that whenever a police officer is charged with an offence the local Crown attorneys do not prosecute. Arrangements are made to provide an outside or part-time Crown attorney for the prosecution so that no suggestion of bias can arise.

It is in the area of case preparation that good working relations between the Crown and the police are often tested. While the police have every right to expect diligence in the Crown's preparation and presentation of the facts and the law in every case, so too the Crown expects that the police brief for the Crown be complete and accurate, and that witnesses be properly interviewed and made available to the Crown in advance of trial when reasonably requested. In order to prepare properly a case of any complexity, it is necessary that the Crown have the police brief well before trial or preliminary hearing. Decisions can then be made as to which charge or charges should proceed to trial or to which charges the Crown will be content to accept a plea of guilty, and if such a plea is forthcoming, what the Crown's position as to appropriate sentence will be. In the event that a case is to proceed to trial, the Crown requires some time to consider the strength of the case, what law is applicable, what defences may be available, and specific trial strategy. Time is also necessary so that discussion can be held with defence counsel with the view of narrowing the issues to be litigated, determining what facts will be admitted by the accused without proof by the Crown and in some cases entering into negotiations as to the accused's entering a plea of guilty. Such discussions cannot be commenced until the Crown is in a position to provide the defence with discovery of the Crown's case.

While Crown attorneys tend to become adept at functioning in court with little preparation, having all too often received an incomplete police brief immediately before trial, it can be a harrowing experience, and in a difficult case the Crown's presentation may be, at best, facile. Surprisingly, many apparently simple cases, involving relatively minor crimes, can present difficult legal issues, particularly in an era of accused who are represented by legal aid counsel who can afford to prepare properly an arguable defence. Despite the strain placed upon the police, they simply must assume in all cases that problems may arise and be prepared to provide the Crown with a complete brief as soon as possible.

An unfortunate difficulty in this less than perfect world is that it is the exception that the same Crown attorney will follow a case from its inception to completion. Certainly, in many serious and difficult prosecutions, a Crown will be assigned and take control early in the proceedings. However, the police daily face the frustration of finding, especially in large cities, that their case passes through the hands of many Crown attorneys, beginning with the bail hearing through remands, bail reviews, setting the dates for trial, preliminary inquiry, pre-trial discussions and eventually, trial. Officers require a fair degree of stoicism to tolerate the necessity of discussing a case with yet another Crown attorney and impressing upon him its nuances, when dealing with one person would surely be preferable. And yet this problem will prevail as long as the public is satisfied to allocate such a minuscule proportion of government budgets to the administration of justice. There simply are not enough Crown attorneys in high-crime municipalities to allow continuity of Crowns in any but exceptional cases.

Mention has been made of making discovery of the Crown's case to the defence, and this practice presents an area of concern frequently resulting in friction between the police and the Crown. Police tend to view, and in fact, usually entitle, their briefs to the Crown as "confidential." Traditionally police have been loath to allow defence counsel access to the brief. On the other hand, most Crown attorneys today are anxious to apprise the defence of the whole of the Crown's case as soon as possible. Such production of the Crown's case is done in the conviction that while the accused owes the Crown nothing in the way of discovery as to the defence, nonetheless the Crown, with the possible exception of evidence to counter a spurious alibi, ought not to take the defence by surprise. The late W. B. Common, Q.C., then Director of Public Prosecutions for the Province of Ontario expressed this view before the Joint Committee of the Senate and House of Commons on Capital Punishment and Corporal Punishment, 22nd Parliament, as follows:

> I might say for those members of the Committee who are not familiar with the procedure of trial and I am not going into technical matters, it

will suffice to say this: That in all of the cases, not only in capital cases but usually in all criminal cases, there is complete disclosure by the prosecution of its case to the defence. To use a colloquialism, there are no "fast ones" pulled by the Crown. The defence does not have to disclose its case to the Crown. We do not ask it for a complete full disclosure of the case. If there are statements by witnesses, statements of accused, the accused is supplied with copies; they know exactly what our case is, and there is nothing hidden or kept back or suppressed, so that the accused person is taken by surprise at trial by springing a surprise witness on him. In other words, I again emphasize the fact that every safeguard is provided by the Crown to ensure that an accused person, not only in capital cases but in every case, receives and is assured of a fair and legal trial.

Accordingly, the police have no legitimate ground for withholding evidence from the defence before trial; however, they do have an interest in saving witnesses from harassment and in preventing an obstruction of justice, and to that end the Crown, in appropriate cases, will withhold names and addresses of witnesses from the defence. The Crown is well aware that certain accused will not hesitate to subvert the course of justice and the Crown will act in concert with the police to prevent this from occurring.

If ever Crown attorneys were reluctant to provide discovery to the defence, that day is past now that the federal minister of justice is considering legislation to formalize pre-trial discovery through mandatory procedure. It is generally considered by prosecutors that such legislation as now exists in many of the American jurisdictions is cumbersome, time-consuming and unnecessary. As a result of such putative legislation, the attorney-general for Ontario has instituted experimental pre-trial guidelines for discovery in certain cases and Crown attorneys' offices, particularly that in Toronto, are establishing formalized, though voluntary on the part of the defence, pre-trial discovery procedures at all levels of court. The Supreme Court of Ontario in co-operation with the Crown has established its own voluntary pre-trial system, which usually does not require the intervention of a judge and which has worked to the advantage of all, particularly in shortening trials by defining essential issues.

A matter of great concern to the Crown is the practice of some police, in this age of ever increasing sophistication in investigative techniques, of withholding information relevant to a case from the Crown. As intelligence squads increase reliance upon wiretapping as an aid to investigation, there are frequently hundreds of hours of conversations recorded. It is important that the Crown be informed of the nature of such conversations and the identities of the parties to them, to avoid surprise and embarrassment to both the Crown and the police, and to dispel any suspicion of unfairness. Occasions have arisen in which police have become aware of one crime while wiretapping with regard to another quite different offence involving other parties. In such cases it may well be that the wiretaps do not have to be introduced in a subsequent prosecution to achieve conviction, and occasionally the Crown is not informed of their existence. Little good is done to the administration of justice, or the relationship of the Crown and the police, when a thorough defence counsel raises the existence of the wiretaps, and as a result questions the admissibility of evidence derived from them.

It is not only in the area of wiretapping that police may not fully inform the Crown. Many prosecutions are successful because the accused has given an inculpatory statement or statements to the police. Frequently these are formal statements, typed or written and sometimes signed by the accused, but often they are merely oral utterances of the accused that may or may not be recorded by the officer present in his notebook. Now they most certainly *ought* to be recorded and the Crown should have them in his brief. On occasion, after an accused has testified in his own defence, the Crown will be informed, for the purpose of cross-examination, of an oral statement of which he was not previously aware. Aside from the legal difficulties of using such a statement in these circumstances, it is true that, given the general rule that the accused is entitled to discovery of the Crown's case, such a practice is considered unfair to the accused, and in any event is open to an allegation of impropriety. A Crown faced with such a situation might well refuse to use such evidence. Once again the police must assume that problems may arise, and thoroughly briefing the Crown of the whole of the evidence, and the means of obtaining it, is the best way of preserving the integrity and strength of the case.

Once the Crown attorney is fully briefed, he may enter into an area of great interest and concern to all involved in the criminal process, that of plea negotiation. It appears that many academics and members of the media disapprove of the practice of plea negotiation, and yet it flourishes and serves a valid purpose. To be sure, it ought not to persist as an expedient answer to overloaded court dockets. Further it is an inappropriate practice if it leads the police to overcharge an accused with a view of giving the prosecution scope to offer illusory concessions in return for a plea of guilty to some, or lesser, charges, or if it leads to a belief by the accused that he can exert meaningful pressure on the prosecution to obtain a particular sentence.

On the other hand, the Crown, having been fully briefed, being given a degree of discretion and properly exercising his quasi-judicial function, may then determine what is fair to the accused and required in the public interest. Having weighed the evidence, considered the number and type of charges laid, the character of the accused, the need for deterrence and the interests of the victim, the Crown may then entertain negotiations as to reduced plea and sentence. There are certainly cases that admit of no negotiation and must be prosecuted to the full, or conversely, should be withdrawn, either because the accused is clearly innocent, or more frequently because the evidence available simply does not support the charge. All such negotiations must be conducted with the view of fulfilling the proper administration of justice and they are the sole province of the Crown and not of the police. It would be both rare and exceedingly discourteous for the Crown to finalize plea and sentence negotiations without first informing the police of their course and seeking the police view. Nonetheless, the final decision is the Crown's, and indeed the police should never enter into plea or sentence negotiations with the accused or his counsel, nor should the police accede to a defence request to temper their instructions to the Crown in return for a plea of guilty.

When a Crown attorney has arrived at an agreement with defence counsel on plea or sentence submissions, that decision should be final and not subject to breach. Therefore, the defence has a right to expect that one Crown attorney will respect another's agreement and give effect to it. Once a Crown has taken a position in court, then if he or the police are unhappy with the result, they are bound by it, and cannot succeed in varying the result by the Crown taking a different position in an appellate court. Necessarily then, the Crown must take great care in arriving at any commitment with defence counsel, for once made he will be bound by it.

Through a full understanding of their own and of the other's areas of responsibility and proper needs, the Crown and the police are able to develop a condition of mutual assistance and respect. The proper application of their separate but interdependent duties nurtures a confidence in the community that these two important public bodies provide a service of protection to all citizens. While the police provide the Crown with a sensitivity to criminal threats to the community, the Crown ensures some checks and balances upon the police as required by a free and democratic society.

NOTES

1. *Boucher vs. The Queen* (1955) S.C.R.16, 20 C.R.1, 110 C.C.C. 263.
2. *Ibid.*
3. *Ibid.*

FURTHER READINGS

Ashworth, A. J. "Some Blueprints for Criminal Investigations." (1976), *Criminal Law Review*, p. 594.

Bowen-Colthurst, Judge T. G. "Working Relationships: Crown Counsel, Defence Counsel and the Court," in *Studies in Criminal Law and Procedure: Addresses Delivered at a Seminar Conducted by the Canadian Bar Association, Montreal, August 26/72.* Toronto: Canada Law Book Co., 1972, p. 11.

Branson, Cecil O. D. "Discovery and Criminal Proceedings." (1974-75), 17 *Criminal Law Quarterly*, p. 24.

Ferguson, Gerald A. "The Role of the Judge in Plea Bargaining." (1972-73), 15 *Criminal Law Quarterly*, p. 26.

Grosman, Brian A. *Police Command: Decision and Discretion.* Toronto: Macmillan of Canada, 1975.

Kelly, William and Nora. *Policing in Canada.* Toronto: Macmillan of Canada, 1976.

Klein, Arthur D. "Plea Bargaining." (1971-72), 14 *Criminal Law Quarterly*, p. 289.

Lidstone, K. W. "Policeman's Duty Not To Take Liberties." (1975), *Criminal Law Review*, p. 617 and especially at 628.

Purves, R. F. "That Plea Bargaining Business: Some Conclusions From Research." (1971), *Criminal Law Review*, p. 470.

R. v. Agozzino (1970), 6 C.R.N.S. 147, 1 C.C.C. 380, 1 O.R. 480 (C.A.).

Walsh, Harry A., Q.C. "Discovery in the Criminal Process," in *Studies in Criminal Law and Procedure: Addresses Delivered at a Seminar Conducted by the Canadian Bar Association, Montreal, August 26/72.* Toronto: Canada Law Book Co., 1972, p. 185.

Wilkins, James L. "Discovery." (1975-76), *Criminal Law Quarterly*, p. 355.

Chapter 8

Canadian Police and Defence Counsel
E. L. Teed

It appears there has been a great deal of misunderstanding by the average policeman with respect to the role of the defence counsel. We hope in this chapter to clarify some of these misunderstandings. The first matter for clarification is the duty of defence counsel. The second is the relationship between defence counsel and the police constable.

Under the Canadian system of criminal law the basic rule is that a person is presumed to be innocent until found guilty by a proper legal tribunal, which is some form of court or a judge. The proceedings before the judicial tribunal, which we shall call a court, are normally started by an information. That is a written document in which an informant swears to the truth of facts that appear to constitute a crime. The suspect is then deemed to be charged with an offence, which is the breaking of a law whose violation by statute constitutes a crime.

A person may break a law that is not criminal in character and for which he is not subject to arrest; such a statute forms part of civil rather than criminal law. Violations of a provincial law that constitute offences are commonly classed as quasi-criminal, and for our purposes the same concept of rights to a defence apply.

A person charged with a violation of a law, criminal or civil in nature, is entitled to a full defence and opportunity to appear before the court. This ensures that the proper procedure is followed and sufficient legal, or admissible, evidence is presented to the court to enable it to discharge its function of determining whether or not the accused is guilty. The court does not determine whether the accused is innocent—he is presumed innocent until proven otherwise.

Because most people are unfamiliar with the courts and their procedures and rules of evidence, it has been found desirable to have the assistance of specialists or persons learned in the law, otherwise known as lawyers. Lawyers have a variety of names. Most developed from the particular court where the lawyer traditionally practised.

Eric L. Teed is Chairman of the Canadian Section of the International Association of Penal Law, National Director of the Canadian Association for Prevention of Crime and is Past National Chairman of the Canadian Bar Association.

"Solicitor" has come to mean a lawyer who does not go to court. "Attorney-at-law" has become shortened to "attorney" and in the United States has come to mean a court lawyer. However, the terms that clearly mean court lawyer are "counsel" or "barrister." The first derives from this lawyer's job to counsel the accused.

For Criminal Code purposes, counsel means a barrister or solicitor, with regard to the matters or things that barristers and solicitors, respectively, are authorized by the law of the province to do in relation to "legal proceedings" (Criminal Code, Section 2).

The Criminal Code recognizes the right to have counsel. Section 577(3) states: "An accused is entitled after the close of the case for the prosecution to make full answer and defence, personally or by Counsel." The Canadian Bill of Rights also recognizes the right of any person who has been arrested or detained to retain and instruct counsel without delay. Section 2 of the Bill of Rights provides: "No law of Canada shall be construed or applied so as to (c) deprive a person who has been arrested or detained (i) of the right to be informed promptly of the reason for his arrest or detention (ii) of the right to retain and instruct counsel without delay."

The value of the effect of this provision was brought to public attention by the Supreme Court of Canada in the case of *Brownridge vs. The Queen* (1972) 7 C.C.C. (2d) 417. In this case a police constable refused to allow the accused to consult his lawyer as to whether or not he should provide a sample of his breath for a breathalizer test. The court ruled that this deprived the accused of his right to retain and instruct counsel without delay and thus constituted a reasonable excuse for his refusal to provide a breath sample under the provisions of the Criminal Code. While denial of the right to retain counsel in violation of the Bill of Rights is not an absolute defence, it may be a reasonable excuse for refusal to take a breath test. In other words, if the accused requests the right to contact a lawyer he must be given the opportunity of trying to secure a lawyer. The concept of the right to one phone call is not valid. What is reasonable depends upon the circumstances. If it is late at night and he makes one call and is unable to contact a lawyer, this does not satisfy his right. On the other hand, if it appears the accused is not able to get a lawyer, then the police do not have to wait forever. The right to instruct counsel also means that when an accused is talking to his lawyer, he can do so in private. This applies whether the lawyer is personally present or whether the conversation is by telephone, although an accused must request to speak privately, or else he waives this right.

In breathalizer cases, for example, the right to consult counsel does not mean that the accused is entitled to wait an hour until counsel can attend. As long as he has the opportunity of talking with counsel in private, the provisions of the Bill of Rights would probably be satisfied.

The New Brunswick Court of Appeal has reviewed the position of the lawyer in the case of *Regina vs. Kenny* (1974) 17 C.C.C. (2d) 158. The court stated the Bill of Rights confers on any person restrained by the police the right to consult counsel. One question that arises is the position of the constable who is interviewing a person who requests a lawyer. In law, a party is not required to give any information to the police other than possibly his name and address.[1] If he requests to talk to a lawyer, then, unless he is not under arrest, nor detained, he is free to leave of his own volition. What often happens, in fact, is different. Some police think that a person can be kept incommunicado until an investigation is complete. This is not correct and in theory it would leave the officer open to claims for damage for violation of the person's rights. Canadian police too often adopt American television police methods. These are based on American statutes and are not applicable to Canada.

As peace officers are public officials charged with a public duty, so lawyers are court officers also charged with a duty. As courts are an essential part of our society, so lawyers as officers of the courts can be deemed an essential part of our judicial system. As a court officer, the lawyer has a twofold duty: first, to use his best endeavours to assist his client, and secondly not to deceive or mislead the court. As a policeman may abuse his powers, so a lawyer may abuse his position. Fortunately, for both categories, instances of abuse are rare.

No lawyer must take an accused as his client, unless a court so orders; then a lawyer is bound to so act to the best of his ability. A Supreme Court of a province has an inherent jurisdiction to require its officers to perform certain duties. As a counsel is an officer of the Supreme Court, this court has the right to direct counsel to assist an accused in his defence of any criminal charge before such court, without remuneration. However, an inferior court, such as a Magistrate's Court, has no power to direct counsel to undertake the defence of any accused.

In addition, the Criminal Code has given Provincial Courts of Appeal power to assign counsel to act on behalf of an accused (Criminal Code, Section 611). In some provinces, such as Ontario, Courts of Appeal are separate from the Provincial Supreme Court. In others, such as New Brunswick and Nova Scotia, the Court of Appeal is part of the Provincial Supreme Court. Where the Court of Appeal is part of the Provincial Supreme Court, the authority of the Criminal Code is not needed to enable the court to assign counsel, as he is an officer of such court and subject to its control. However, where the Court of Appeal is separate, then the Appeal Court must rely on the statutory provision.

The question of the right of Parliament to give a Court of Appeal the power to direct counsel or provincial lawyers to undertake defence duties without compensation was argued in New Brunswick in the case of *Regina vs. Happeney* (1970) 5 C.C.C. 353, where it was held that Parliament has such power as incidental to its powers in relation to criminal law.

While the Superior Courts have the power to require their officers (attorneys) to undertake the defence of persons charged with committing a criminal offence who are being tried before such court, the development of legal aid throughout Canada has effectively eliminated the need for this power.

A legal aid program was advocated by the Canadian Bar Association for many years. Its development, while comparatively recent, is a recognition of the fact that there cannot be two types of justice— one for those who can afford to pay a defence attorney, and one for those who cannot. Legal aid schemes were a major subject at the Fifth Commonwealth Law Conference held at Edinburgh, Scotland, in 1977. Statements from various Commonwealth countries that have common law as the foundation for their criminal law included the following principles: (1) Legal aid services have a particular potential for assisting disadvantaged groups and individuals; and (2) in a modern democratic state which adheres to the fundamental concept of the rule of law wherefrom flow the terms equality before the law and equal opportunity, it is being increasingly recognized that justice should be available to all and that there cannot be real equality unless legal advice is available to the poor people in the same manner as to others.

It has been recognized that in our complex legal system the assistance of counsel for a defence is essential to ensure a fair trial. As a result, society has agreed that, in criminal matters, a system of providing defence counsel will be available. The legal aid program has received the support of the federal government, in that it has made grants to those provinces that have devised a legal aid scheme that meets certain minimum standards.

Various provinces have instituted different programs of legal aid, Ontario being one of the leaders before any commitment of funds was made by the federal government; likewise New Brunswick.

There are two basic types of legal aid schemes. Under the first, the province hires public defenders who represent the accused. Under the second, the scheme is administered by the provincial Bar Associations, or by an organization set up to administer it. Both of these bodies are funded basically by the government through grants. Lawyers are chosen from those who have volunteered to act on a legal aid basis, placing their names on a panel. Applications are made by accused for legal aid, who, if he meets the criteria, is given a legal aid referral slip, which he takes to a lawyer on the panel. If the lawyer accepts the case, he will bill the legal aid scheme; he is not authorized or entitled to bill the client. The client in his turn may be required to repay some or all of the funds to the legal aid scheme. The legal aid lawyer's contribution to the legal aid program is acceptance of a tariff of fees of a lower schedule than he might otherwise charge, and the waiver of 25 percent of such schedule.

Applicants are screened to ensure that only those who are in circumstances whereby they would not be able to afford legal counsel can secure legal aid defence attorneys.

At the same time, depending upon funds available, the various Bar Associations operating this type of program have imposed limitations on what cases will be handled. Certainly the more serious crimes, where there is risk of imprisonment, are included, while lesser ones—including provincial offences—may not be.

In addition to the legal aid program, the system of duty counsel has evolved. A lawyer who volunteers to be on a duty counsel panel takes his turn at being present in court and interviewing any persons charged with a criminal offence. The duty counsel is paid through the legal aid scheme at a predetermined discount rate. He is not a solicitor or counsel for the accused, but rather an independent advisor.

If the accused wishes to plead guilty, duty counsel is prepared to give him assistance and speak on the matter. At the same time, if it is a serious offence, duty counsel may recommend that he seek his own lawyer or a legal aid lawyer to act for him. Duty counsel is a byproduct of the legal aid scheme, and is available to any person regardless of his financial status.

In a public defender program, the government will hire a number of lawyers who act as defence attorneys. While this program has some merit in reducing costs, it limits the choice available to the accused, and results in a proliferation of the bureaucracy.

The result of both programs is that a growing number of lawyers are now able to participate and develop competence in criminal law practice. At the same time, all persons are ensured a chance of reasonable advice, at reasonable cost.

For practical purposes, no lawyer today need accept a particular case. It is then necessary to determine on what basis a lawyer may or may not decide to act as defence counsel. He must first ascertain the facts, and from the facts determine whether or not he wishes to defend the accused. The lawyer may decline the case because he does not handle the particular type of offence, has a personal repugnance for the crime committed, or feels he is unable to establish a working relationship with the accused.

However, if he decides that he will undertake the case, then he must do his best, irrespective of his personal views as to the guilt or innocence of the person charged. As one judicial authority has stated: "A barrister on presenting the case of his client, is entitled to make the utmost use of all lawful methods relevant to the proceedings, and to comment even forcibly upon the allegations, facts and evidence."[2]

It is up to the judge or the jury, as the case may be, to determine guilt or innocence. The defence counsel must take the position that an accused is deemed innocent until proper procedures have proven him guilty. There is one stipulation, however, that must be observed by the defence counsel: if his client has related facts from which it would appear that his client has in fact committed the crime, and the client proposes to take the stand and deny these facts, which would constitute the crime of perjury, the defence counsel must decide not to call his client as a witness. Except for this restriction, the client is still entitled to all the benefits of the law.

It is important to appreciate that a person charged with an offence of which he is in law innocent may believe himself to be guilty. Ignorance or a feeling of guilt by association more than once has induced an accused to plead guilty to a charge of which he is legally innocent. For example, a person may be charged with assault. He in fact hit another person and therefore believes he is guilty. He does not realize that his actions were justified as self-defence. Unless care is taken, he may plead guilty to an offence for which he would be found not guilty if all the facts were presented to the court.

In this circumstance, the defence counsel can take two positions. He can let the matter proceed to trial, or he is entitled, if the information is not drawn properly or proceedings are not brought in accordance with the rules and statutes, to make technical objections in an effort to have the matter thrown out of court. Some say this stand defeats the course of justice, and that a trial should be held, but it must be observed that justice can only operate on certain lines and if, for expediency's sake these are broken, society would lose the protection of due process.

We now come to the position of the defence lawyer and the police constable. In theory, the police constable is only another prospective witness in the case. However, his position is in fact akin to that of an expert witness. He presumably is better trained in observation and has a better grasp of what is essential than the ordinary witness. Through his experience in court, he is able to present the factual situation better than the average witness.

There is a general fear that too often police constables will become partisan and in their desire to convict, they will tailor their evidence accordingly—not necessarily in material aspects, but to cover up omissions. Although this does happen on occasion, constables should endeavour at all times to be truthful and accurate. If they have made an error or omission in the proceedings, then this should be admitted.

A quotation from a 1920 edition of a leading textbook on Evidence indicates the inherent danger, felt at least by some at that time:

> With respect to policemen, constables and others employed in the suppression and detection of crime, their testimony against a prisoner should usually be watched with care; not because they intentionally pervert the truth, but because their professional zeal fed as it is by habitual intercourse with the vicious and by the frequent contemplation of human nature in its most revolting form, almost necessarily leads them to ascribe actions to the worst motives, and to give a colouring of guilt to facts and conversations which are perhaps in themselves inconsistent with perfect rectitude.[3]

Defence counsel may defend his client by cross-examination of the prosecution witnesses, or by producing his own witnesses, or by a combination of both.

There are some judicial expressions to the effect that when it is intended to suggest a witness is not speaking the truth upon a particular point, his attention must first be directed to that fact by cross-examination, so that he may have an opportunity of correcting his statement.[4] While this point has not been clearly settled, nevertheless it presents a problem to defence counsel.[5] Therefore defence counsel in most cases will feel it is necessary to conduct a cross-examination of any witness he proposes to show by later evidence is mistaken.

As the police constable may be subject to searching cross-examination, it is necessary for him to understand the procedure. Phipson states that "the object of cross-examination is twofold—to weaken, disqualify or destroy the case of the opponent; and to establish the party's own case, by means of his opponent's witnesses."[6]

Wrottesley proposes three objects to cross-examination: "The first is to elicit something in your favour; the second is to weaken the force of what the witness has said against you; and the third is to show that from his present demeanour or from his past life he is unworthy of credit."[7] In Regina vs. Treacy (1944), it was stated that "All cross examination must be relevant to the issues or to the witnesses' credibility."[8]

It is the duty of defence counsel to treat the policeman the same as any other witness and to endeavour to illustrate to the court that the constable's testimony is inaccurate and should not be accepted. To do this, he will ask many other questions that may seem irrelevant but are designed to demonstrate to the court that the witness's testimony should not be accepted; i.e., the constable is prejudiced, he has a faulty memory, he is making statements of conclusion rather than fact, and other such suggestions as would indicate to the court that the constable is not an independent, accurate witness.

In the case of cross-examination, leading questions may be asked, and must be answered, although it is not permissible to mislead the witness by false assumptions or misstatements. Provided the question is relevant to the matters in issue it need not be confined to the subject matter of the evidence already given by the witness in chief.

There are a number of techniques and procedures used in cross-examination, and the police witness must appreciate that the lawyer concerned is not conducting his cross-examination as a personal attack, but as part of his job, and would do the same with any witness.

Eventually, constables will gain reputations of either being straightforward and accurate or of colouring evidence. Once a police constable has received the reputation of giving concise, correct and impartial evidence, the defence lawyer will normally be reluctant to attack his testimony. However, there are some counsel who take the approach that all constables colour their evidence to suit their own purposes. Fortunately this is not the prevailing practice.

There is a mistaken concept that a witness "belongs" to either the defence or the prosecution. This is completely erroneous.[9] Both defence and prosecution may in fact subpoena the same witness.[10] There is nothing to prevent an attorney from interviewing a proposed witness, but on the other hand, there is nothing to require a proposed witness to talk to an attorney. This rule of law has created much misunderstanding between police and defence counsel.

An accused has an absolute right to call any person as a witness for the defence, including a witness previously called by the prosecution.[11] In one murder trial, the accused wished to call as his witness a person who had given evidence as a witness for the prosecution and had been subject to cross-examination. The trial judge refused to allow the witness to be called on the ground that he had been subject to cross-examination. The Court of Appeal of Alberta allowed the appeal from conviction on the ground that the accused was entitled to call any person as a witness even though he had already been a witness for the prosecution.[12]

There is a general confusion between a person who may be going to give evidence and a witness. Under the Criminal Code, a witness is defined as a person who gives evidence orally under oath or by affidavit in a judicial proceeding, and includes children who give evidence not under oath (Section 107). Until a person gives evidence he is not a legal witness. However, in popular terms, a person who is expected to give evidence is called a witness.

The Criminal Code makes it an offence to obstruct justice; Section 127, sub-section 2 provides: "Everyone who wilfully attempts in any manner to obstruct, pervert, or defeat the course of justice is guilty of an indictable offence." Sub-section 3 continues: "Everyone shall be deemed wilfully to attempt to obstruct, pervert or defeat the course of justice, who in the judicial proceedings existing or proposed, dissuades or attempts to dissuade a person by threats, bribes or other corrupt means, from giving evidence." Therefore a defence counsel who wishes to interview a witness for the prosecution must do so discreetly, to avoid any allegations or suspicion of tampering with a witness.

While an ordinary witness is under no obligation to talk to defence counsel, a police officer, while under no legal obligation, has a degree of moral obligation to apprise the defence counsel of the relevant facts. The police officer who initiated the proceeding leading to trial must have had some grounds for his action, and unless the defence is apprised of such grounds, the accused is unable to make full answer and defence.

It may be that, under departmental rules, police are required not to divulge police business without permission from their superiors. In such cases co-operation is restricted until permission is received. However, there is a distinction between a constable who is involved as an ordinary citizen, and a policeman who is professionally involved in a case. If, for example, an off-duty policeman observes an accident, he would appear to be in the same position as any witness who happened to observe the event. However, should he be actively involved in the investigation and make demands and inquiries of the occupants of the vehicles in relation to his duties as a constable, then this becomes official police business, and he is under greater restrictions. Police constables may be subject to disciplinary procedure if they divulge any information to counsel without permission, but this is entirely a matter of departmental policy.

Generally the police constable should not subject himself to searching cross-examination by a defence lawyer before a court appearance in a case where he was the principal investigator. If there is a prosecuting attorney, he should divulge the general gist of the information to the defence counsel. In any indictable offence, the accused can elect to discover this evidence by way of preliminary hearing. In summary convictions, where a Crown counsel is engaged on a case, very often the defence attorney will advise or request the Crown counsel to indicate who are the witnesses and their proposed evidence. Where the Crown counsel is not engaged, defence counsel will do the same thing with the police officials. In some instances, this is done through a superior officer.

What should be disclosed by a police officer who is being interviewed by defence counsel, either as a witness not actively involved or after permission has been secured from his superiors? The answer is the facts as he recalls them. However, information secured by him from other sources can also be of assistance to the defence. Basically the policeman's position should be that there is nothing to hide. Police should not be concerned with securing a conviction at any cost, but with ensuring that legal justice is done.

The policeman's initial actions were based on what he saw or was informed of and at that time he was satisfied that there were reasonable and probable grounds for believing an offence had been committed. However, when he so acted he did not have the benefit of all the facts. The court has the job of adjudication after Crown counsel and defence counsel have to the best of their ability endeavoured to present all the relevant facts. In some cases, the relevant facts are known to two people, the police constable and the accused, whereas in other situations the testimony of many people may be required in order to obtain all the relevant facts.

If an officer is observant, acts in accordance with the legal procedures, and gives his testimony as to what he saw, heard and did, he will have discharged his duty and been a credit to our law enforcement system.

There is also considerable confusion as to the role of the defence attorney in the Juvenile Court, and in fact there is some misunderstanding of the position of the Juvenile Court in the judicial system. The very word "court" implies that the individual concerned is given the full protection of our system of justice; namely, the right to a fair hearing, the right to be represented, and to have counsel. The Juvenile Delinquency Act was designed to protect the child from being exposed to the experiences associated with the regular criminal courts and to endeavour to rehabilitate the child. The offence of "delinquency" covers all violations of the law—criminal, provincial and municipal. The key words of the Act are found in Section 3, subsection 2: "When a child is adjudged to have committed a delinquency, he shall be dealt with not as an offender, but as one in a condition of delinquency, and therefore requiring help and guidance and proper supervision."

As a result, a philosophy arose that as there is no offence, a lawyer is not needed, and in some courts very loose practices have developed. For example, a child could be interrogated by the presiding judge who would try to help the child by finding him delinquent and then giving help which could not be given if he were not delinquent.[12]

Many persons tend to forget that a Juvenile Court can also deal with adults involved with juveniles, and there is in law no difference between dealing with a person thirteen years old charged with delinquency, and a person thirty-one years old charged with contributing to delinquency. They appear before the same court and the technical procedures are the same.

Recently people have become aware that the Juvenile Court judge has a greater power over a child than the regular criminal court has over an adult offender. In fact, the penalties under the Juvenile Act may be more severe than those in criminal court. The child can be taken from his parents and placed in an institution for the most trivial offences, since the Act does not distinguish between breach of a municipal bylaw and the foulest murder. Both offences constitute delinquency and their remedies at present are the same.

As a result, greater concern has been evidenced over the rights of the child to a hearing in accordance with the law and not on an expediency basis. In fact, there is even a growing concept that the juvenile should have an attorney to represent his own rights as opposed to those of his parents. Legal aid schemes have been of major assistance in ensuring that the child has proper representation.

The defence counsel in Juvenile Court has a double burden. The first, that of providing a legal defence; the second, that of advising a client who may not be old enough or mature enough to fully appreciate the situation. Because there may be a conflict between doing what is best for the child in the sociological sense and doing what is best for the child in the legal sense, the defence counsel in juvenile cases is not in a happy position. However, if one discounts the popular concept that the social worker and the court worker can resolve all problems in the Juvenile Court, then the defence counsel's duty is clear. A child is entitled to the full protection of the law to the same extent as an adult, and although the procedures may be summary in form, the basic principles of the proper application of the rules of law still should be uppermost, to ensure justice is done, not only for the rich and the poor, but also for the young and the old.

NOTES

1. The law in Canada has recently been established by the Supreme Court of Canada to provide that a person who is seen by a police officer committing an infraction of the law is required to give his name and address to the peace officer (*Moore vs. The Queen*, Supreme Court of Canada. 24 National Reporter, Oct. 18, 1978).

However, the general rule is that where a person has not been seen committing an offence, he has the right to refuse to answer questions put to him by persons in authority and to refuse to accompany those in authority to any particular place unless he is under arrest. There are, of course, statutory exemptions, such as requirement to give information under Motor Vehicle Act Legislation and similar type of provincial laws.

2. *Beaulieu vs. Plante*, 37 Revue de Jurisprudence 1. Quebec.

3. Pitt Taylor, *Law of Evidence*, 11th ed., J. B. Matthews and G. F. Spear, Sweet & Maxwell Ltd., London, 1920, Vol. I, p. 66, para. 57.

4. *Peters vs. Perras*, 42 Supreme Court Reports 244, (April 5, 1909).

5. *Regina vs. Minchin* (1914), 18 Dominion Law Reports 340.

6. Roland Burrows. *Phipson on Evidence*, 8th ed. Sweet & Maxwell Ltd., London, 1942, p. 467, Ch. XL.

7. F. J. Wrothesley. *The Art of Examination of Witnesses in Court*, 2nd Ed., Sweet & Maxwell, London, 1926, p. 78. The Carswell Co. Ltd., Toronto.

8. *Regina vs. Treacy* (1944), 2 All England Reports 229, (July 11, 1944).

9. Halsbury, *Laws of England*, 3rd ed., vol. 15, para 484, Butterworth & Co. (Publishers) Ltd. (Canada) 1956.

10. *Ibid.*, para. 776.

11. Peter K. McWilliams, Q.C. *Canadian Criminal Evidence*, Agincourt, Ontario: Canada Law Book Limited, 1976., p. 484.

12. *Regina vs. Cook*, 127 Canadian Criminal Cases 287, 33 Criminal Reports 126 (March 24, 1960).

Chapter 9

The Police and the Correctional Services
J. W. Braithwaite

"The basic purpose of the criminal justice system is to protect all members of society, including the offender himself, from seriously harmful and dangerous conduct. . . . The law enforcement, judicial, and correctional processes should form an inter-related sequence." (pages 11 and 16)

This comment from the *Report of the Canadian Committee on Corrections*, published in 1967, suggests the concept of teamwork. But teamwork comes in many forms. For example, two policemen were recalling their combined experience. The retired member stated that they had constituted a great team. He had done the driving and the fighting; his colleague had done the talking and the loving.

That represents a description of a team relationship. However, that type of relationship, applied to the role of the police in relation to corrections and, indeed, the total criminal justice system, can result in oversimplification, the notion being that the police are there to catch the offender and the correctional staff are there to control and keep him.

Teamwork: Roles and Responsibilities

All elements of the criminal justice system, that is, police, probation, courts, institutions, parole and private correctional and after-care services, should share a common goal. But they should not all play the same role. They should not be the same but symbiotic; they should not be identical but interrelated. On a hockey team, the goalie stops pucks while other team members move pucks and score goals. Together, the team achieves victory.

The police and correctional staff exist to support a Criminal Code that is common throughout Canada. To that end, they share a common concern regarding the criminal law. It has been said that the criminal law not only properly seeks to protect our persons, property and governmental processes from serious harm, but also seeks—unsuccessfully—to guard us from vice and sin.[1]

John Braithwaite is Deputy Commissioner, Communications, for the Correctional Service of Canada. Previously he was appointed the first Deputy Commissioner of the Canadian Penetentiary Service responsible for Inmate Programs.

However, in recent years, certain former offences, such as homosexuality between consenting adults in private, and being drunk in public, are no longer seen as criminal acts. This development and the review of our Criminal Code by the Law Reform Commission are efforts to reduce and improve the work of police, corrections and the total system. They also help to clarify roles and encourage cooperation.

When the average citizen considers the criminal justice system, his thoughts immediately turn to the police, the most obvious representatives of our social defence system. While those in corrections too often subscribe to the stereotyped assumption that the role of the police is merely to apprehend criminals, the police frequently see some of their correctional colleagues as "the offender's friend" and thus "the policeman's pest." But both parties are frequently guilty of ignoring the fact that each attempts to protect society and to prevent crime. Professionals and members of the public are always more conscious of police action that terminates in the punishment of the offender than in police action that results in the prevention of crime. Any police agency that efficiently enforces the law operates as a definite deterrent to criminal activity and therefore contributes in a significant way to the prevention of crime.[2]

Citizens look to the police as safeguards, as the defenders of social values, as the "new centurions." But what is their real role? It is submitted that the prevention of crime, rather than the detection of crime, and a general concern for order within society are the primary roles of any police force.

The goals of prevention and detection of crime can be equated with the protection of society—a goal shared by all elements of the criminal justice system. However, the police and corrections are frequently seen as the two elements of the criminal justice system that are farthest apart, both in their involvement in the system and in their attitudes toward crime and offenders.

Insufficient emphasis has been placed on the unique role of the police in the total criminal justice system. Without the police as enforcers of the Criminal Code, there would be no offenders. In addition, the police, while more obvious, are also more vulnerable. They are identifiable and therefore invite criticism. Moreover, the police are particularly sensitive to the total criminal justice situation in that, unlike other elements of the system, they are deeply involved in the dramatic, and indeed traumatic, events of the crime itself. They see and experience the victims—and their tragedy—and this undoubtedly affects the police perspective.

Another distinguishing element is that the police function is the most active, dramatic and best reported. A crime occurs, the public becomes excited by the events and looks to the police to redress a wrong. Therefore it is no small wonder that the police may be more sympathetic to retribution and incarceration than to rehabilitation and reintegration as the objectives of corrections.[3]

Corrections, on the other hand, takes a more long-range perspective. They receive the offender and are required to take short-run risks in order that he be permitted the opportunity to present evidence of an increased ability to function in a responsible manner. Too often, the released offenders that police encounter are those who turn out to be bad risks. As a result, police develop a distorted view of the risk correctional officials take. Correctional failures—parole and probation violators, inmates who fail to return from temporary absence—add an unwelcome burden to already overtaxed police resources.

The impact, however, of police practices on corrections, while not as obvious and dramatic as the effects of correctional practices on the police, is, nevertheless, important and vital to the ability of the total system to function. The policeman is the first contact with the law for most offenders. He is on the scene. He is "the man," the initiator of the relationship between the offender and the total system. He is also the ambassador and representative of the society and the system he serves. To the extent that the offender's attitude toward society and its institutions will affect his responsiveness to that system, the police in their initial contact may have a substantial, indeed, critical influence on his future behaviour.

Police exercise broad discretion in the decision to arrest and how they exercise that discretion determines, to a large extent, the numbers and the types of individuals who will constitute the correctional clientele. In fact, police decisions may have a greater impact on the nature of corrections and its clientele than legislative decisions relating to the kinds of conduct that are considered to be criminal. Some of the more obvious examples of this are liquor offences, prostitution and gambling, and, of course, control of mass demonstrations, including Grey Cup celebrations.

However, there is another way in which the police make a significant contribution. The policeman, by virtue of his responsibilities, knows his community and its citizens. He knows what resources are available; he knows where traps exist; he knows where potential hopes may lie. He is, himself, a valuable community resource for existing and potential correctional programs. All of this, of course, implies that the police take a view of their function as one of preventing future crime as well as enforcing the existing law and maintaining public order.

One wonders why there is not an expanded and more productive relationship between police and corrections. Indeed, it can be said without risk of controversy that there is much more rhetoric than reality, more discussion than demonstration, of teamwork between police and corrections.

There is a tendency to talk a good line but not necessarily substantiate it with activity. Nevertheless, significant steps have been taken; new areas have been explored and productive activity has resulted. This is not to say that we have achieved all to which we have aspired. But a trend is developing, one that we hope will result in better service to society.

Corrections
Size

What is corrections in Canada? If nothing else, it is massive, mixed and misunderstood.

As an indication of the size of corrections in Canada, one might refer to statistics relating to incarceration and parole. During the fiscal year 1977-78, those incarcerated, by average count, in federal and provincial systems was 10, 185. The province of Ontario alone had in 1977-78, 42,181 on probation and under supervision in the community.[4] To deal with these offenders, there were significant numbers of federal and provincial staff, plus representatives of private organizations, such as the John Howard Society, Elizabeth Fry Society, St. Leonard's Society, Salvation Army, Association of Social Rehabilitation Agencies and other halfway-house organizations.

The figures related above refer exclusively to those adjudicated as offenders and does not take into account the untold number of individuals and organizations who strive to prevent or keep potential offenders from entering the criminal justice system. These include organizations whose aim is to divert selected individuals from the total system: an aim that is desirable, appreciated and supported by those who face the responsibility of dealing with fellow citizens who are adjudicated as offenders.

The expenditure of funds on the criminal justice system is difficult to estimate, but it costs no small penny to provide police, courts, probation, prisons, penitentiaries and parole, plus related costs such as social assistance to dependents. One can only guess at the total financial burden, especially when it is known that the cost of individual incarceration can be as high as $30,000 per year.

Administration

The corrections system is mixed to the extent that it involves the federal government, the ten provincial governments, the governments of the two Territories and numerous private organizations.

Each government exercises a responsibility for maintaining a probation service within its jurisdiction. In addition, each government maintains institutional services, at least of a detention nature, and Ontario, Quebec and British Columbia and the federal government operate a parole service.

Under the British North America Act of 1867, the federal government is responsible for any adult given a prison sentence of two years or more; the provinces are responsible for those sentenced to less than two years. However, there exists between the federal and the provincial governments, with the exception of Ontario and Prince Edward Island, an agreement or contract that permits each jurisdiction to send an incarcerated offender to the other if it is felt that the security or the program available is more suitable.

In relation to confinement, there are significant differences in the institutions. The Federal Penitentiary Service, for example, administers approximately fifty-one institutions in eight of Canada's ten provinces. Of these, fourteen are maximum-security institutions, thirteen are medium-security and twenty-four are minimum-security. The percentage breakdown amongst these institutions is something like 40 percent maximum-security, 46 percent medium-security and 14 percent minimum-security. Institutions range from Kingston Penitentiary, which was established in the 1840s and was visited by Charles Dickens, to units such as the Community Correctional Centre in Saint John, New Brunswick, which occupies a floor of the YMCA, or forestry camps where inmates are employed at the going wage. It is obviously true that prisons are not all stone walls nor iron bars.

This array of federal, provincial and private agencies constitutes the correctional system in Canada. There is no single voice, no single entity that one can address in terms of dealing with corrections. There is a national organization known as the Canadian Association for the Prevention of Crime, which provides a forum for the discussion of all matters related to the criminal justice system, but the system itself is diverse and divided and, in seeking an audience, a representation or a relationship, one must go to several sources.

Philosophy

In addition to the mixed and diverse jurisdictions there is no universally accepted philosophy of corrections. It has been said that the ideology of corrections has evolved through three significant phases, defined by Dr. Daniel Glaser as revenge, restraint and reform, or the three "R's."

Revenge was the foundation of the corrections system until the middle of the eighteenth century. In addition to retribution, penalties had the presumed purpose of deterring others from crime.

Restraint was the product of the classical school of criminology and its basis was incarceration to make the offender penitent. The philosophy of restraint supported the development of probation and parole, in the sense that both these techniques seek to control and, at the same time, assist the individual to succeed within society.

The philosophy of reform has led to a great variety of efforts to "rehabilitate" individual offenders. Whether the means of rehabilitation was through education, vocational training, psychotherapy or some other method mattered little, and these "treatment programs" developed significantly in North American prisons and reformatories during the latter part of the nineteenth century and the early twentieth. Probation and parole programs were fashioned around a rationale of reform in an effort to meet the needs and problems of individual offenders through counselling, job finding, education and other forms of community-based treatment.[5]

It may be said that federal, provincial and private corrections, and institutional and community correctional programs, are an amalgam of these three basic philosophical attitudes, which appear in varying degrees and combinations, depending on the administration. Given these quite different, and frequently contradictory, goals, it is small wonder that those who administer the correctional programs have also been called "managers of a social dilemma," "professional schizophrenics" and "magicians."

Thus, in corrections services, there are diverse jurisdictions and philosophies. Fortunately a common creed is emerging. A statement of objectives and basic principles has recently been developed, originally designed for the federal system but only after consultation with the provinces and the private sector. These principles are as follows:

1. The offender is ultimately responsible for his criminal behaviour.
2. The sentence of the court constitutes the punishment.
3. The community is a responsible participant in the correctional process.
4. Corrections is responsible for the provision of an environment with appropriate measures of security conducive to active participation in program opportunities.
5. Corrections is responsible for the provision of adequate procedural safeguards to protect the rights of the offender.
6. The offender is responsible for earning and maintaining his privileges.

Having stated these principles, there is a need to elaborate on some of them. For example, it is assumed by correctional personnel that the individual who comes within their charge has received an adequate and proper trial and has been found guilty. Moreover, it is also assumed that he is capable of discerning right from wrong. The sentence of the court constitutes the punishment and that punishment refers to some degree of loss of liberty. Correctional personnel are not entitled to add to the punitive element of the sentence.

That the community is a responsible participant in the correctional process is relatively obvious. The individual is a product of the community, and his reformation, rehabilitation and reintegration are the responsibility of the total community, not just corrections. The provision of opportunities for the individual to develop skills and responsibility is shared between the correctional agency and society.

The correctional agency, regardless of where it may operate and its level of governmental responsibility or status, must adhere to a sense of responsibility for the provision of adequate procedural safeguards to protect the rights of the offender. This is necessary because the offender is, regardless of his offence, a citizen of Canada and entitled to all of the benefits and safeguards of any citizen, except for those that are lost through the criminal justice process.

Finally, the offender himself is responsible for earning and maintaining his privileges. If he appears to earn the opportunity for a temporary absence, for example, it is up to him to see that he operates in a manner that reflects positively upon that decision and shows his ability to take on greater responsibilities, such as parole.

The above is submitted as a philosophical foundation for probation, prisons and parole that the public and police might accept as a reasonable working philosophy. In this model, corrections is not a magician, a witch doctor or a therapist. Corrections cannot rehabilitate anyone. The individual must do that. The responsibility of corrections is to provide program opportunities to the offender and protection, through controls, to the citizen. God forbid that anyone be sent to prison for "treatment."

Police Participation in Corrections

In pursuing these principles and goals, corrections should expect assistance from police. Specific examples of how police may assist are outlined below.

Probation. Probation is not new. It began in 1841, when a cobbler in Boston, Massachusetts, decided to take into his home, care for and supervise an offender charged with being drunk and disorderly. However, it was not until some thirty-seven years later that legislation appeared establishing the first official probation officer paid to perform this specific function.

In Canada, probation first appeared in Ontario in 1893, when the Children's Aid Society was empowered to remove delinquent children from home situations where the living conditions warranted such removal, and to place them in foster homes under the supervision of the Society. However, it was not until 1908 that there was enacted a federal Juvenile Delinquents Act, which recognized probation as a legally acceptable method of control of offenders.

Nowhere in the criminal justice system do police and correctional personnel work closer together than within the realm of probation. Police have great discretionary powers. They decide on the intake within the system. Having decided that an individual should be referred to the system and, assuming that the court finds that individual guilty, there is a distinct possibility that he or she may be placed on probation. Indeed, the general and growing trend is toward treatment and control within the community. Out of one hundred offenders, roughly fifty-five will be placed within the community with a degree of supervision. In addition, thirty-seven will be placed in provincial correctional institutions, and eight will find themselves in a federal penitentiary.

Thus, it is obvious that the police and the probation officer have the brunt of dealing with the majority of apparent offenders and serve as screens or sorters for the criminal justice system. The probation officer relies upon the arresting policeman to provide the circumstances of the offence. This is essential to the pre-sentence report required by most courts in Canada today, before deciding on the disposition of the offender. The probation officer has a critical role, and one that cannot be dispensed without the accurate and immediate advice of the arresting officer. The arresting officer can provide the circumstances of the offence but, in addition, if he is a beat policeman with prior knowledge of the offender, he can provide background and family information indispensable to both the court and the probation officer.

Probation and other community alternatives to incarceration are of the utmost importance to correctional personnel. This is true not just in relation to the number of cells available, but also in relation to the significance of control and care within the community.

Correctional personnel are concerned with two basic elements of the correctional process—control and change. The first responsibility is to lend a degree of control, and the second to provide an opportunity for change.

The probation officer requires police co-operation, understanding and information if probation is to be successful. Frequently, the probation officer is not available to the probationer each and every time a crisis arises. Nor is he always aware of the current situation. Frequently, the police officer, knowing the charge, the disposition of the court and the individual involved, will be an invaluable help to the probation officer. Also, the probationer may frequently find himself in situations where he will turn to the police officer for assistance, recognizing the police officer as a source of assistance rather than anxiety.

Probation is not a novelty, a leniency, or an escape from the criminal justice system. Probation, properly administered, is one of the most effective, considered and controlled situations in which an offender can find himself. Probation is not granted out of a spirit of forgiveness or freedom. It involves placing an offender under the supervision of a probation officer for a specific period. Supervision reflects continuing control by the court, through the probation officer. The control is manifestly of a different character than that present in correctional institutions but, nevertheless, it is control.

While probation is based on control, it is like all other elements of the criminal justice system, concerned not only with control but with change, that is, the provision of opportunities for the probationer to involve himself in a better life. In this area, the police can be of significant importance. The police frequently know the probationer's background, his available opportunities and his difficulties in taking full advantage of those opportunities. They can also lend support to his making an effective effort towards change and self-control. All in all, the police, in the presentation of the original charge, in the preparation of the pre-sentence report, in the subsequent control of the probation sentence, and, in the protection of the offender from former criminal colleagues, play a principal role in probation.

A good probation officer encourages, enlists and elicits the support and information of the police. A policeman who is effectively serving the total criminal justice system gives such support, information and advice willingly and responsibly.

Institutions. The bulk of those incarcerated are found within provincial institutions. The more difficult offender, or those requiring a more deterrent sentence, either for themselves or for the presumed message to their fellow citizens in the community, are found in federal institutions.

Institutional personnel, like all others within the criminal justice system, are concerned with control and also with change. Institutional programs are designed to administer the sentence imposed by the courts and to provide opportunities for the offender to prepare himself for a more rewarding, law-abiding role in society. Whether or not the offender takes advantage of the opportunities provided is up to him. The sentence does not impose upon the offender a requirement that he or she necessarily pursue any prescription or program.

With the abolition of capital punishment, incarceration became the last resort for society and the last resource for the offender. When all socialization processes have failed—family, schools, church, community resources and even probation—the offender will end up behind bars.

As a total system, only those who are the more persistent or the more dramatic offenders will find their way to penitentiaries. Also, viewed as a system, one would not expect penitentiaries or prisons to have a glowing record of success with those with whom they have to deal.

The police play a role in the incarceration phase in several ways, which are necessary but often not recognized. Initially, the information provided by the police for the pre-sentence report is of great value in assigning the offender to a given institution or program. Whether the individual is considered to require maximum, medium or minimum security is frequently determined on the basis of police information relative to the offence.

A less obvious but more consistent role is that played by the police in temporary absences from institutions. The fact that the Canadian Penitentiary Service alone permitted some 42,069 temporary absences during the year 1974 is indicative of the requirement for police co-operation. Those temporary absences involved a total of 20,824 offenders.[6] Each offender required the approval of the police in the community he visited to be allowed there. Subsequently he needed police awareness and support during the temporary absence.

To this extent, the police play an effective and essential role in decision making within the correctional institution. Not that the police have a veto power but they do have a contribution to make, one that must be considered by correctional personnel in making effective decisions.

Police involvement in a dramatic hostage taking or riot is expected. Nevertheless, the police have a greater role to play than just conflict intervention. They provide information to prevent incidents but they may also serve as "honest brokers." All offenders have encountered the police and to the extent that they have found the police to be fair, objective and trustworthy, they are prepared to accept and seek their presence in certain crisis situations. Therefore, it is no surprise that police have been invited to serve as negotiators and even monitors during such incidents. Strange as it may seem, the police, because of their professional role, are accepted by many offenders as objective observers of the prison scene. Small wonder, for example, that the Royal Canadian Mounted Police were used as observers during the resolution of a major riot at the British Columbia Penitentiary in 1976.

The police have a larger advisory role also. Individual citizens may complain about the existence or the absence of a specific "treatment" program within an institution, or about the incidence of temporary absences from a given institution to their community, or about the behaviour of staff in relation to inmates. In all of these situations, the police, if called upon and invited to participate as members of an institutional advisory committee, can lend great credibility to its recommendations. They can also serve as a safeguard against programs that are unduly risky or lack appropriate consideration in their development.

In relation to convicted offenders the police have a relationship that is unique and, to the outside observer, almost unbelievable. The police set forth a process that often ends in incarceration. Nevertheless, the inmate may see the police as an objective arbiter or advisor in his current situation. Unfortunately the police and correctional personnel are somewhat reluctant to recognize and develop this participation. This relationship is in keeping with the current trend to greater community involvement and reflects the mutual designation of peace officer shared by the police and institutional personnel.

Parole. Contrary to popular belief, parole is far from the latest concept in corrections. It dates back to the introduction of the "mark system" by Captain Maconochie in Norfolk Island, Australia, in 1840. Marks or merit points could be gained for positive behaviour by inmates, resulting in a shortening of their sentences. At this point, the "ticket of leave" was granted to the offender. The concept was introduced in Ireland in 1853, by Sir Walter Crofton, who expanded upon it by the introduction of a number of grades or classes for inmates, which culminated in release. However, the release involved periodic reporting to designated responsible citizens and the threat of return to prison for those who violated their agreement.

The parole system expanded into England, and private organizations were established with government approval and financial support to supervise men on ticket of leave. Subsequently, the parole system came to North America.

The Ticket of Leave Act was passed in 1899 by Canadian Parliament and a Remission Service was set up in the Department of Justice to conduct the operations of the release and supervision of inmates. The Salvation Army established the Prison Gate section to concern itself with community supervision of offenders and one of its officers became the first Canadian parole officer.

Many years later, in 1959, the Parole Act was passed, replacing the

Ticket of Leave Act and abolishing the Remission Service. The Act established a National Parole Board with exclusive jurisdiction over the granting, supervision and revocation of parole. Today there are twenty-three regular members of the board, including the chairman and three temporary members, whose responsibilities, to a great extent, are allocated on a regional basis throughout the five regions (Pacific, Prairies, Ontario, Quebec and the Atlantic) of Canada.

With the establishment of the National Parole Board, greater impetus was given to the development of private organizations to assist offenders on their return to the community. As provincial probation services developed, they too participated, under contract, in parole supervision. Nevertheless, the Parole Service itself has continued to grow and now private involvement is limited to supervising 12.2 percent of all those paroled.

Ninety-nine percent of all inmates in federal and provincial institutions return to the community. This fact constitutes the most sensitive aspect of corrections to the police. To police, parole tends to be the most obvious and vulnerable aspect of corrections, but it is also an area where police co-operation is both direly needed and greatly desired.

The granting of parole has frequently been construed to cover all types of release from institutions. This is incorrect. Parole has been defined as "the conditional release of a selected convicted person before completion of the term of imprisonment to which he has been sentenced. It implies that the person in question continues to be... in custody and that he may be incarcerated in the event of misbehaviour. It is a measure designed to facilitate the transition of the offender from the highly controlled life of the institution to the freedom of community living. It is not intended as a gesture of leniency or forgiveness.[7]

There are three basic elements within the concept of parole. These include the conditional serving in the community of part of the sentence; the element of contract or agreement between the offender and the paroling authority; and the agreement by the parolee to accept supervision of his activities while he is serving the remainder of his sentence in the community. In short, parole is a social contract into which both the paroling authority and the individual enter willingly.

In this sense, it differs from mandatory supervision in which a portion of the inmate's sentence is arbitrarily served under supervision in the community. Mandatory supervision became effective in early 1972, although it was proclaimed in August 1970. This program provides supervision to the offender to cover that portion of the sentence which has been diminished by the effect of earned remission or what is known as "good time." Since the inmate going out on mandatory supervision has not been granted parole, it is of benefit to himself and the community that supervision is available upon release from the institution. However, it is different from parole in that the inmate, released on mandatory supervision, does not voluntarily seek that supervision. He must accept the supervision or remain inside to serve the remainder of his sentence. As the term implies, the term "supervision" is mandatory. Under mandatory supervision, he is subject to the same provisions and penalties and has access to the same resources as a parolee.

The other form of release that frequently draws criticism from the police is temporary absence. This differs from parole and mandatory supervision in that the offender remains an inmate who, with or without escort, is permitted to spend a specific period of time within the community. An absence seldom extends beyond fifteen days and most frequently is granted for a period of less than twenty-four hours. In addition, the offender may or may not be under escort while in the community.

Recent legislation has given the authority for the decision as to release whether under parole, mandatory supervision or temporary absence exclusively to the National Parole Board. However, because of the volume of decisions, the Board will delegate some of its responsibilities regarding temporary absence to institutional directors. In 1979, 45,320 temporary absences were granted, with 194 failures to return.[8]

In 1979, the National Parole Board considered 4,002 federal parole and 1,763 provincial parole cases. Of these, parole was granted to 1,617 federal cases or 40.4 percent and 901 provincial cases or 51.1 percent.[9]

No inmate leaves an institution by benefit of parole without careful consideration and complete review of police concerns regarding his return to the community. This is not a simple yes or no situation, but rather a consideration of impact on the community. The relationships of the individual with the community, his friends, current concerns, and other relevant matters are all requested and available from the police. No parole or any other release decision is made without input from the police and without the police being informed of the decision.

In addition, parole affords police access to information regarding criminal activity. The individual offender frequently needs assistance to pursue his goal of not returning to an institution and no offender, regardless of his motivation, leaves an institution with a plan to return. Threats and inducements to return to crime are as much a part of the parolee's first days out as is the sweet free air.

Police can assist in supporting the offender in the community by enforcing parole regulations, conditions and, of course, the law, and also by providing advice, encouragement and support.

There are many advantages to release on parole. Supervision offers greater hope for adjustment of the offender, and also greater control. There is a calculated reduction in expensive incarceration. There is also an added benefit to society, in that the offender assumes his responsibilities and makes a contribution to the economic life of the country. Hopefully, it also provides for a reinforcement of his confidence and ability to realize responsibility.

A policeman who contacts the parolee's employer in the work place with questions, endangers the possible successful adjustment of the offender. The relationship between the police and parole staff should be such that, when police wish information, a discreet call to the parole supervisor should provide an appropriate response.

In addition, it is also recognized that supervising authorities frequently are not as fully aware as police of the possibility of further crime. Police occurrence reports can be extremely helpful to all elements of the criminal justice system and, in particular, to parole agents.

During the course of parole, many crises may develop. Frequently, the police are asked for assistance. There may be occasions in which the parole officer, with his knowledge of the parolee and his relationships, including those formed in prison, may request police assistance, surveillance or even apprehension in order to prevent the occurrence of a crime.

The parole officer also relies on general information regarding the parolee's activities. There are certain basic conditions of parole, such as the avoidance of criminal activity, the maintenance of a specific address and, usually, continued employment at a given job. There may also be more specific requirements, such as the avoidance of certain areas frequented by criminals or of former friends reputed to be engaged in criminal activity. Information on adherence to these conditions is available from the police and represents a tangible and mutually beneficial bond between police and parole staff.

In summary, parole is an important control device within the system and its impact, both in the initial granting and in the subsequent program, is reliant upon the police for enrichment and effectiveness.

In 1973, the National Parole Board and the National Association of Chiefs of Police established a joint committee of police and parole officials to develop better means of mutual assistance. This committee subsequently became known as the National Joint Committee of the Canadian Association of Chiefs of Police and the Federal

Correctional Services. The motion establishing the Committee noted that ". . . the effectiveness of the parole system depends largely on the willingness of police and parole to assist each other. . . ."

Police As Community Agents

The police role in the community, as it relates to corrections, is not confined to probation or parole. There is a growing attitude that the policeman is a social agent—not just an enforcer. He knows, or should know, his total community. The community creates its own criminals and the policeman knows their spawning grounds. Thus, he can play a role in the prevention of crime as well as the apprehension of criminals. Indeed, there are strong arguments that the latter is the lesser of his many roles.

In support of this concept, August Volmer wrote: "I have spent my life in enforcing the law. It is a stupid procedure and it is not, nor will it ever solve the problem unless it is supplemented by preventative measures."[10]

Police were not established primarily to be law enforcement agencies. Citizens supported the establishment of local police to provide twenty-four-hour emergency services to all members of the public. Local police agencies have been charged with the performance of service functions such as watching for fires, dispensing relief to the poor, advising their communities on time and weather conditions, assisting probationers and maintaining public order. These responsibilities are consistent with the dictionary definition of police as "the department of government concerned primarily with the maintenance of public order, safety, health and enforcement of law."[11]

As public service organizations, police should be receptive to insuring that functions needed and required by citizens are carried out. To devote police resources exclusively to criminal apprehension ignores the wishes of the majority of those who seek police services and seriously curtails preventive efforts.

If police accept a broader definition of role, more impact could be made on criminal and other activity that is damaging to society. Also, there are a multitude of human service organizations responsible for performing functions that can prevent deviancy and crime if brought into play soon enough. These agencies exist in every urban area, but may be disregarded by arrest-oriented police. Many potential deviants and deviants who are ignored or funnelled into the courts could likely have received assistance that would have prevented the continuation of their behaviour if they had been referred to helping agencies. Close relationships between the police and other human service agencies would increase the social contribution of the police. Crime prevention would be increased; the total role of the criminal justice system would be enhanced; and human resource agencies would achieve greater effectiveness.

"If we believe that people's conduct is motivated at an early stage in life, we must provide programs that will influence the environment where attitudes are developed—the home. And some agency in the community should be responsible for seeing there is a proper delivery of service."[12] Words of a social worker, psychiatrist, politician? No, these are the expressed concerns of a career policeman, Chief Walter Johnson of the London, Ontario, Police Force.

He refers to the family crisis intervention program established by his force and the University of Western Ontario in recognition of the fact that the role of police everywhere is shifting to social problems and 80 percent of a policeman's time overlaps the concerns of mental health. A special training program was developed for his staff to recognize social and family problems. Five consultants from the social sciences are available and located in police headquarters to provide a twenty-four-hour emergency help service.

"When we get a call, the force responds in the first instance with a uniformed officer," Johnson reported in January 1977. "If, in the opinion of the responding officer, the family or the individual concerned can benefit from the involvement of a family consultant, he will call one. The officer then fades out and they take charge, if necessary, bringing in or co-ordinating other services. Many cases can be resolved by their intervention alone."[13]

This is indicative of the move to redefine the police role to emphasize the social or community agent aspect and to promote both crime prevention and community peace.

The police and correctional staff are in key positions to encounter the failures at crime. But, uniquely, the police also encounter those who are highly successful and seemingly immune to the criminal justice system. Because of their perspective and awareness of the forces and factors creating both the unsuccessful and successful offender, the police have a significant contribution to make in total criminal justice planning. This potential contribution is increasingly recognized and correctional and other agency representatives work together with police in what may be referred to as criminal justice planning councils.

In 1973, there developed in Windsor, Ontario, a Community Corrections Council that exemplifies this concept. This Council, with representation from federal, provincial and private organizations, such as the St. Leonard's Society, the John Howard Society and the Salvation Army, provides a means of communication, mutual education and growing awareness. The Council co-ordinates and unifies the existing correctional, diversion and preventative services in the community and plans their future development. It also serves as a means for legal and penal reform at all levels and all areas in the country. As too many societies resort to criminal legislation or prisons before considering other alternatives, more such planning groups and councils are needed.

This type of endeavour has spread beyond the example cited. There are similar councils and organizations in other parts of the country. One of the more significant examples is the presence of the British Columbia Criminal Justice Planning Councils, encouraged and supported by the Attorney General's Department. Indeed, the concept has become international.

The American Correctional Association, in developing standards for correctional agencies, has included in its proposed standards specific essential requirements with regard to mutual co-operation and planning. For example, the standards for Adult Paroling Authorities include the following: "Members of the Paroling Authority meet at least annually with representatives of relevant criminal justice agencies—police, prosecution and courts—to develop means of co-ordinating programs, to undertake joint planning, and to agree on the means of implementing and evaluating such plans."[14]

Conclusion

Bringing about a better working relationship between police and corrections may not be easy. Progress can be made only if both recognize that they are performing mutually supportive rather than conflicting functions. Corrections has been inept in expressing its concerns to police. Police have had difficulty in accepting certain roles expressed here. Closer working relationships must be developed through mutual understanding, and police and corrections should immediately increase their efforts in this regard.

This is not an idealistic "pie in the sky" statement. Assistant Deputy Chief A. C. Bates, in the 1976 Report of the National Joint Committee of the Canadian Association of Chiefs of Police and the Federal Correctional Services, said:

> It has been some two and one-half years since our inaugural meeting and at that time my reaction was: who needs these meetings? What really do we have in common? Subsequently, we have listened to each other and learned that each of our Services have problems. None of us are an entity unto ourselves. We each profess and, indeed, are working for the protection of society. If we are complacent, we become part of the problem. We must have an input into the correctional field and only by top executive support will success be attained at the line level.[15]

The co-operation that results through these endeavours will

greatly enhance the total criminal justice system. For the police, it will ensure more protection for society because of the greater emphasis placed on crime prevention. It will provide a fuller and better police contribution to the supervision of parolees and will build a better liaison with institutional services. Co-operation will encourage and stimulate contacts and involvement with various social agencies in the field of mental health, welfare and private after-care agencies.

For corrections such teamwork will provide essential information for the management of offenders and the selection of individuals for all types of release. It will help to ensure better supervision and security and help in the conversion of offenders to responsible behaviour.

For the offender—who experiences the total system—such co-operation provides significant benefits. These would include a greater access to social agencies and community resources, protection against the undue and improper influence of former criminal colleagues, and demonstrated evidence that the police are there to support and assist as well as to seek out and apprehend.

As former Deputy Commissioner of the RCMP, W. H. Kelly, once said:

> The rehabilitation of offenders is not merely coincidental to the system of criminal justice. It is one of the main purposes of the system. The uncoordinated efforts that now exist are costly in terms of money and effort, and fail to produce the desired results. It is obvious that there is need for better communication between all segments of the criminal justice system. Better communication means better understanding and better co-operation but to reach this point there is need for leadership from the highest level to ensure that the various components work together to accomplish what the public expects from the system. This in turn will attract the full support of the public, which is not forthcoming at present.[16]

This is a time of increased concern regarding effective use of resources. This is also a time of considerable concern regarding criminal activity. Frequently police expression of support for a preventive or corrective program can have a significant effect on the allocation of resources. The police and correctional staff, private, provincial and federal, work with the victims of society, including both the offended and those who offend. Their world is peopled with the unfortunate, the unsuccessful and the unfulfilled. The police also encounter those who seem invulnerable to the system.

Cynicism exists and cynicism is to be expected. But despite such cynicism, the policeman and the correctional worker strive toward a common goal. To make less than a full effort would be to give up, and in so doing, diminish our view of our fellow man and his potential. Each of us realizes that there but for the grace of God or luck go I. We are beginning to realize that we cannot look to police, courts, or confinement for a solution to crime in our society. The answer to that dilemma lies more appropriately in the fields of education, welfare, health and employment services. But the creation of more effective programs in all those areas is dependent upon the combined and concerned voices of correctional employees and police.

The world of corrections needs the input of the police, not just in carrying out more effectively the assigned role of corrections, but more importantly in preventing individuals from coming within the criminal justice system.

NOTES
1. Norval Morris. "The Law Is a Busybody." New York *Times*, 1 April 1973.
2. Robert G. Caldwell. *Criminology*. New York: Ronald Press, 1956, p. 255.
3. National Advisory Commission on Criminal Justice Standards and Goals, *Report*. Washington, D.C.: Corrections, 1973, p. 6.
4. Report of the Minister, 1978. Ministry of Correctional Services for Ontario.
5. R. Carter, R. A. McGee and E. K. Nelson. *Corrections in America*. New York: E. B. Lippincott Co., 1975.
6. Internal Statistical Documents, Operational Information Services, Canadian Penitentiary Service, Ottawa, 1975.
7. *Monograph on Parole*. United Nations Department of Social Affairs, United Nations Educational, Social and Cultural Organization, New York, p. 9.
8. Operational Information Services Inmate Record Systems, Ottawa.
9. Research and Evaluation Section, National Parole Board, Ottawa, March 20, 1980.
10. August Volmer. "Community Co-Ordination," in V. A. Leonard, *Police Organization and Management*. New York: Brooklyn Press, 1964, p. 10.
11. National Advisory Committee on Criminal Justice Standards and Goals, *Report*, Washington, D.C., January 1973, pp. 7–8.
12. Jocelyn Marshall. "London Police Pioneer in Family Crisis Intervention," in *Liaison*, a Monthly Newsletter for the Criminal Justice System. Ottawa: Department of the Solicitor General, Vol. 3, no. 1, January 1977, p. 1.
13. *Ibid.*
14. Standards for Adult Parole Authorities, Commission on Accreditation for Corrections, Standard 1013, p. 3.
15. Report of the National Joint Committee of the Canadian Association of Chiefs of Police and the Federal Correctional Services, Department of the Solicitor General, Ottawa, 1976, p. 1.
16. *The RCMP Gazette*. The Royal Canadian Mounted Police, Ottawa, Vol. 34, p. 9.

FURTHER READINGS

Annual Report of the Solicitor General of Canada. Ottawa: Department of the Solicitor General.

Canadian Journal of Criminology and Corrections. Canadian Association for the Prevention of Crime, Ottawa.

Carter, R., R. A. McGee, and E. K. Nelson. *Corrections in America.* New York: E. B. Lippincott Co., 1975.

The Criminal in Canadian Society. Ottawa: Department of the Solicitor General, 1973.

Kirkpatrick, A. R. and W. T. McGrath, *Crime and You.* Toronto: Macmillan of Canada, 1976.

Liaison, monthly newsletter for the Criminal Justice System, Department of the Solicitor General, Ottawa.

Manual of Standards, Commission on Accreditation for Corrections, Rockville, Maryland, 1976–1977.

W. T. McGrath, editor. *Crime and Its Treatment in Canada.* Toronto: Macmillan of Canada, 1976.

Reports on Courts, Community Crime Prevention, Police and Corrections. The National Advisory Commission on Criminal Justice Standards and Goals. Washington, D.C.: Law Enforcement Assistance Administration, 1973.

Report of the Canadian Committee on Corrections. Ottawa: Queen's Printer, 1969.

R.C.M.P. Gazette (Quarterly publication). Ottawa: Royal Canadian Mounted Police.

Chapter 10

Who are the Criminals?
Michael Mitchell

Most people have definite ideas about what constitutes crime and who criminals are, yet many of their ideas may be based on inaccurate stereotypes. This chapter will try to examine who become criminals, why they commit crimes and how the problem can be dealt with. Although the nature of the analysis will be general, the concept of criminality will be examined to expose as many false assumptions and untruths as possible. Statistics used in the chapter have been taken from the Statistics Canada publication *Crime and Traffic Enforcement Statistics 1975*, because this is the most current source of information.

Defining the Criminal

In Chapter 1, crime was seen as behaviour that is prohibited by criminal law. It stands to reason that a criminal is a person who violates one or more criminal laws. While this appears to be a straightforward, functional definition, it does not cover all possible cases, nor does it allow for various interpretations. The rest of this section will discuss aspects of criminality that lie outside the range of this definition.

In 1975, there were 273,887 adults charged for Criminal Code offences and 71,212 young persons charged as juvenile delinquents. Canadian laws for juveniles differ significantly from those for adults and technically only adults are considered criminals. Therefore, depending on the province, a criminal is an offender over fifteen, sixteen or seventeen years of age.

The age of the offender is only one differentiating criteria. Normally people believe that the thing that separates the criminal from the non-criminal is the illegal act, yet at some point in their lives, most people commit a criminal offence. Does this make them criminals? Perhaps then the criminals are the ones who are caught and charged for violating the criminal law. Certainly the police think that they do not arrest innocent people, even though many accused are found not guilty at their trial. Are the criminals the ones who are arrested or only those who are convicted?

Michael Mitchell is Program Analyst for the Ministry of the Solicitor General for Ontario.

Taken to the extreme, a person could participate in criminal activities throughout his life without being caught, thereby avoiding being labelled criminal, while another person could commit one crime, be arrested and convicted and have to live with the stigma of being a criminal. The point of the argument is that, like the term "crime," the term "criminal" is a relative one, subject to personal interpretation. It would appear that most people distinguish between those who commit criminal acts and those who are actually criminals. A criminal is perceived as one involved in serious criminal acts or in a variety of criminal acts over a substantial period of time.

Another example of the ambiguous nature of the concept of criminality is that it changes over time and can be influenced by factors such as political sensitivity. For instance, in our society, a murder occurs when one person intentionally kills another, and it is seen as the most heinous crime. Yet in wartime, this type of behaviour is encouraged. Similarly when people in communist countries stole airplanes and flew them to Western countries they were known as freedom fighters and acknowledged as heroes. When people started stealing planes in Canada and flying them to other countries they were called hijackers, and special laws and penalties were legislated to prevent this crime.

"Crime" and "criminal" are vague terms relating to behaviour that is deemed undesirable, yet at the same time they are subject to interpretation and alteration. The fact remains, however, that the criminal justice system continues to label increasing numbers of people as criminals and to punish them. It is to these persons who have been defined as criminals that the researchers have turned to determine what causes crime.

The Causes of Crime

Why does a small percentage of the population become labelled criminal? A great number of diverse theories explaining the causes of crime have arisen, and yet none of them have produced substantial information from which a cure can be formulated. At the same time, research has dispelled many false perceptions concerning crime and criminals, and a review of some prominent theories should indicate what has been achieved.

Historically very little attention was given to determining what caused criminal behaviour because it was assumed that people became criminals because of some mental or moral weakness that could be rectified only by punishment or a system of vengeance. In the latter part of the nineteenth century, some researchers began to search for factors that differentiated criminals from other people. They viewed crime as a problem not unlike a sickness and assumed that if they found the cause they could develop a cure. While the factors being examined may have changed, researchers are still searching for clues concerning the cause of crime.

Much of the original research in this area was directed towards a biological or physiological explanation of criminality. It was thought that criminals were biologically inferior or emotionally regressive. While it has been shown that a few criminals may be mentally retarded, have an endocrine imbalance, chromosomal abnormality or some other type of physiological defect, these findings cannot be generalized to include a large proportion of the criminal population. As well, often more than one member of a family may be involved in criminal activity, but this does not prove that crime is the result of heredity. In short, the possibility of a cure for crime being found by medical science is remote.

Psychology has gained importance throughout the twentieth century and psychologists have addressed themselves to the problem of crime and criminals. Psychologists feel that crime is the result of a defect in the personality of the offender. A person becomes a criminal because of stress or a mental or emotional state that finds release through criminal actions. Some criminals do show signs of psychological abnormality; in fact, we have special institutions for the criminally insane. But like the biological theories, the psychological analysis does not apply to a large percentage of criminals. In many correctional institutions, psychiatric facilities are available for the offenders, but it is unreasonable to expect that they will produce a large cure rate.

More general explanations are offered in the sociological theories of crime causation. Rather than study individual criminals, sociologists examine groups of offenders, their backgrounds and environments. They observed that the crime rate in the urban setting was considerably higher than in rural areas. Even within cities the incidence of crime and the number of criminals seemed to be highest in certain areas. This led to the conclusion that crime was the result of a poor environment, and that the solution to the problem was simply redevelopment of the areas with high crime rates or relocation of the families that lived in the poorest areas. This is one of the motivations for public housing and urban renewal. While the intentions of those involved might be admirable, the fact that these studies indicated where the majority of crime and criminals dwelt did not prove that the physical surrounding of these areas caused people to turn to crime. In many cities redevelopment and relocation have not solved the problem, but just shifted it to other areas.

Other sociologists maintain that crime is a cultural problem. They feel that most people in society desire material wealth and they observed that most criminals come from the lower socio-economic groups. This led to the conclusion that crime was the result of poor people being unable to compete for the legitimate means of attaining wealth, and resorting to illegal means of making money. Crime is a behaviour that is learned inasmuch as the individual is taught to value material possessions and then learns to commit crimes to get them.

There is also the suggestion that crime might be the result of conflicts due to culture. When people from different cultures have to live together, animosity can develop and lead to criminal acts. Likewise, people moving from one culture into another may be unaware of cultural differences that are reflected in the laws of their new country. In Canada, incest or sexual intercourse with a female under sixteen years of age are regarded as serious crimes, yet in other countries they may not even be illegal. Thus a person could perform an act that would be permissible in his homeland but criminal in Canada.

Another sociological theory revolves around the concept of a sub-culture. A sub-culture is a group within a larger culture that has distinctive values that sets it apart. It may be ethnic, religious or occupational. In fact, the police are often referred to as a sub-culture. (A criminal would belong to a sub-culture that has crime as one of its differentiating characteristics.) A criminal sub-culture rejects certain of the commonly held social standards and puts a high value on illegal behaviour. From the group, a criminal derives the knowledge, approval, status, help and encouragement that most of us receive from our families or occupations.

Sociological studies have indicated that most criminals come from unstable homes in poor areas. There seems to be a high incidence of criminal and other undesirable behaviour on the part of other members of the family, resulting in inconsistent supervision and discipline. Criminals usually leave school earlier than most children. Finally, it has been shown that there is a higher incidence of crime in urban areas than in rural communities. Although these studies have illustrated correlations between these factors and crime, they do not explain why many people from these types of environments lead law-abiding lives despite all the poor influences. Similarly these factors may only reflect the fact that this type of criminal is the easiest to apprehend and convict, and therefore is disproportionally represented.

As a result of the influence of the psychological and sociological theories of crime causation, emphasis was transferred in the 1950s and 1960s from a theory of punishment and deterrence to a treatment philosophy aimed at rehabilitating criminals. It was felt that a group of professionally trained staff could work with the offender in the institution or the community to turn him into a law-abiding citizen. Because the staff would understand the offender's background and problems, they would be able to influence him to change his behaviour. Although the types of treatment used varied greatly, none produced the expected results, and in the 1970s the concept of treatment and rehabilitation have been partly abandoned in favour of newer theories.

These circumstances have lead to another school of thought called "labelling theory." In this concept, the emphasis is shifted from the criminal act to the process established to deal with criminals. It suggests that the process of getting caught, convicted and labelled separates the criminal from the non-criminal. In this context, a criminal is one who perceives himself to be a criminal or, in other words, one who is convinced this is what others expect him to be.

For those who follow a labelling philosophy, more importance is attached to studying the process through which people are labelled than in studying the criminal himself. The laws and the criminal justice system must be re-examined with a view to limiting, as far as possible, the number who go through the system. The concept of diversion is essential to this philosophy. Because of the many adverse effects of being labelled a criminal, every effort must be made to divert an offender from the process before he is convicted. This includes allowing the community to solve a crime problem, having the police use their discretion to screen cases, settling or mediating disputes before trial, and using alternatives to prison. As well, the consequences of labelling could be avoided if some offences were decriminalized and treated in another manner. For example, drug addiction could be dropped from the criminal law and treated as a medical problem. Greater use of discretion on the part of the police and the courts would be preferable if alternate measures of dealing with the offender were present. These and other solutions seek to control the amount of crime by dealing with the criminal justice process and limiting the number of people who go through it.

Another recent theory of crime causation revolves around economics and is outlined in Chapter 1. Although consideration of this and the numerous theories mentioned in this section can be confusing, they illustrate the diverse nature of crime and criminals and that there is no single treatment method that will work with all criminals. All these factors have some validity and must be taken into consideration when dealing with criminals.

The Amount of Crime

The theories of crime causation are varied and can seem contradictory for a number of reasons. One reason is that the term "criminal" includes so many different individuals engaged in any of a number of activities. Another reason for possible confusion is that crime is a phenomenon that is extremely difficult to measure. Determining the actual amount of crime in Canada is a difficult if not impossible task. Although a great deal of statistical data is collected every year by various police forces and Statistics Canada, how well these figures reflect the true amount of crime is questionable.

The initial problem occurs because a great deal of crime goes unreported for a number of reasons. The offender may in fact be the only one aware that a crime has occurred, as would be the case in an undetected income tax fraud. Even if more than one person is involved, they may be willing partners (for example, in a gambling transaction) and therefore unlikely to report their activity. In crimes where people are aware that they have been victimized, they may not wish to report the occurrence for fear of reprisal from the offender or his associates, or they may wish to avoid the embarrassment and inconvenience involved in investigation and prosecution of the occurrence. Another reason for crimes remaining unreported is that those victimized would rather handle the problem themselves. This is true of institutions such as retail stores or financial businesses where employee theft can cause inconvenience and adverse publicity, so management implements its sanctions of warnings or dismissal. Finally, the discretion used by policemen, and outlined in chapters 11 and 12, may result in some offences not being reported and altering the rate of crime.

Taking into account these limitations on interpreting criminal statistics, it would still appear that the amount of crime in Canada rose drastically during the 1960s and the first half of the 1970s. In 1975 a total of 1,585,805 Criminal Code offences were reported, of which 329,260 were cleared by charge and 209,379 were cleared otherwise. This means that 34 percent of the reported crimes were cleared, indicating that for most crimes there is not even an arrest let alone a conviction. One explanation for the drastic rise in crime in the last fifteen years is the effect of the baby boom. The age group fourteen to thirty seems to be the most prone to crime, and the large number of young people of this age range has led to a great increase in crime since the early Sixties. If this theory is correct the amount of crime should have levelled off and started to decrease in the latter half of the Seventies.

There are a number of factors affecting crime rates that could alter the amount of reported crime. One of the most influential is police activity, which can work to either increase or decrease the amount of reported crimes. It may seem ironic that police work could increase the amount of reported crime, because it has always been assumed that improved clearance rates tend to deter potential criminals from engaging in crime. On the other hand, if a police force increases its efforts directed at a prevalent but seldom reported crime, such as prostitution or gambling, their efforts may lead to an unusual number of arrests in this area and an increase in the number of crimes reported.

Because factors such as these can influence the apparent amount of crime, it becomes important for the police to properly assess if a change in statistical data reflects an actual increase or decrease in the amount of crime. If it does, then they should attempt to discover the cause of the change, so that they can either encourage any decreases or try to counteract any increase.

Conclusion

This chapter has outlined some of the major problems in measuring crime, discovering the reasons for it and dealing with the criminals. The objective of police agencies and the rest of the criminal justice system should be the prevention of crime. As the amount of knowledge about criminals increases this should become easier. At present the police and other criminal justice agencies must deal with crime and criminals on a daily basis making best use of the information that is available.

FURTHER READINGS

Gibbons, Don C. *Society, Crime and Criminal Careers*. Englewood Cliffs, New Jersey: Prentice Hall, 1977.
McGrath, W. T. *Crime and Its Treatment in Canada.* Toronto: Macmillan Co., 1976.
Silverman, Robert A. and James J. Teevan. *Crime in Canadian Society.* Toronto: Butterworth and Co., 1975.
Statistics Canada, Justice Statistics Division. *Police Administration Statistics 85-204*, Ottawa.
Statistics Canada, Justice Statistics Division. *Crime and Traffic Enforcement Statistics 85-205*, Ottawa.

Chapter 11

White-Collar Crime
Royal Canadian Mounted Police

This chapter will supply the reader with a brief insight into that area of criminal activity commonly known as white-collar crime. Fraudulent activities in the marketplace are not new; they are as ancient as society itself. What is new, however, is the sophistication of business procedures and practices which has enlarged the spectrum of operations for the "white-collar criminal."

There is a burgeoning group of professional confidence men and international criminals who apply sophisticated corporate techniques to the age-old art of swindling. Using modern transportation and communication, they perpetrate their schemes with skill and confidence, relying on the many inherent problems created when crimes are committed across a multiplicity of jurisdictions. In fact, many commercial crimes, when viewed in isolation, appear to be bona fide commercial transactions.

All too often we find ourselves anxious to label a questionable incident a civil matter, leaving the complainant to seek assistance from private legal counsel. This approach is no longer satisfactory, as many of the successful prosecutions for fraudulent activities in the marketplace stem from what would appear, at first glance, as unethical but, nevertheless, lawful business transactions.

It is incumbent upon all policemen to have a basic understanding of what constitutes a commercial crime and to be able to recognize the warning signs. It is hoped that this learning process will spark an interest in this challenging specialty, as many a rewarding police career is to be found in pursuing criminals who travel the world divesting honest citizens of their money. To match wits with a capable con artist is to make the acquaintance of an individual who supplies the inspiration for some of the greatest detective thrillers.

Cost of Commercial Crime
The annual cost of commercial crime in Canada is at least several hundred million dollars. In the United States, losses incurred through the actions of white-collar criminals are two to three hundred times higher than in Canada. The impact of such losses is

This article was submitted by the RCMP in the interests of law enforcement.

manifest in two ways. The first is felt in the wallets of all residents. Although individuals are sometimes victimized, more often losses are suffered by governments and corporations. Any losses suffered by the public sector must be recouped through taxation, and the taxpayer becomes the ultimate loser, whether it is at the municipal, provincial or federal level. A loss suffered by a corporation qualifies as a tax write-off. Businesses also anticipate certain losses in advance, and these are built into the prices of their products. Again the cost of commercial crime is borne by Canadians, either through increase prices or through taxation levied to compensate for unpaid corporate taxes on profits that are reduced as a result of commercial crime.

The second impact is on the behaviour of individuals within the business community. If market manipulation and other securities-related offences are prevalent, potential investors will be discouraged from participating in the securities market. This not only affects those involved in the investment trade, but will tend to create an attitude that will discourage rather than encourage national economic growth. Similarly, victims of fraudulent bankruptcies may tend to be over-cautious in extending credit, and in so doing prevent would-be legitimate businessmen from starting up or expanding their operations. Corruption of officials, whether they are in the public or private sector, can only decrease—if not destroy—the confidence of the public in both government and private enterprise. This lack of confidence not only depresses the economy, but leads to mistrust and suspicion of those in power.

Computer Crime

The fact that the use of computers is becoming ever more widespread needs no repetition here. Almost as obvious is that the tasks to which computers are put are becoming increasingly varied. As a consequence, it is probable that the incidence of computer-related crime will also be on the upswing. Crimes involving computers present complex problems of detection and investigation. The investigator of a computer-related crime will require the technical assistance and expertise of computer-specialists.

The simplest type of computer crime is one in which the use of a computer is fraudulently promised to attract customers, for example, "computer dating bureaus." As computers lend credence and respectability to a business by appealing to investors or clients, a confidence man may falsely promise that computer processing is used for certain procedures within a company.

A second area of computer-associated crime is vandalism or mischief. Serious damage, such as occurred at Sir George Williams

University in Montreal in 1969, is relatively simple to prove, but when a disgruntled and skilled employee decides to sabotage a computer operation, he or she can easily wreak expensive damage with little risk of detection. Thefts of hardware or software may also occur. For example, an unauthorized user can clandestinely connect himself to a computing facility and use its services. Such a crime is also hard to detect, and it is even difficult to determine what exact offence has occurred.

The more complex computer crimes include the manipulation of input or output data to assist in committing an offence. Using existing computing facilities, the criminal inputs false information to the computer, producing false results to suit his purpose. To date, this has been the most prevalent type of white-collar computer crime, and includes cases involving the issuing of cheques to false accounts, creation of fraudulent bills, or cover-up of cash embezzlement. Where thefts from companies used to be hidden by false entries in the company's books, they can now be hidden by false entries in the computer system from which the books are drawn up. As computer statements frequently are unquestioned, this activity can easily occur over a long period without detection.

By far the most complex cases of computer crime are those in which the criminal has either programming capabilities, access to the computer, and an intimate knowledge of a corporation's software facilities, or an agent or agents with these qualifications. The criminal can then create original programs or alter existing ones so that additional, undetected functions are performed to his benefit. Banks and other financial institutions are extremely vulnerable to this type of crime. A criminal employee could place a patch in a program so that the computer would automatically transfer into an account controlled by the employee a certain percentage of the funds from other accounts that have been dormant for a specified period. The criminal then simply withdraws the cash from the account. If the patch is removed from the system before detection, and the special account is under a fictitious name, the crime becomes extremely difficult to detect, harder yet to investigate and almost impossible to prosecute successfully. This is only a simple example of software manipulation, but it indicates how complex such crimes can become.

Computers are making crimes easier to commit, more profitable, less dangerous, more difficult to detect, and most important of all, more difficult to prove. Businesses are reluctant to report a suspected computer crime because of the publicity involved, which can lead to a loss of public trust and further damage to the business. Investigative agencies should be aware of the trend to increased computer crime and develop the necessary expertise to combat it.

Stolen Securities

Securities of a value well in excess of $86 million have been reported as lost or stolen in Canada. Statistics from the United States are even more staggering, running to an estimated $55 billion. For the most part, the theft and subsequent use of the securities are the actions of organized crime, which extends far beyond what we call the Mafia or Cosa Nostra. While this criminal organization plays a major part in the criminal activities under discussion, there are a number of other groups, combinations of criminals in a loosely organized confederation, that participate extensively in these crimes. They use systematic planning and co-ordination to steal securities and turn them into cash.

The trafficking of stolen securities is related to other organized crime activities such as gambling, labour racketeering, credit-card thefts and fraud, pornography, smuggling and distribution of narcotics, infiltration of legitimate businesses and a number of other offences.

The crime of stealing securities may begin with a thief entering a building in search of diamonds, gold, furs, etc. In the past, if he came across stacks of securities he would simply ignore them, because as far as he was concerned these were just pieces of paper. Nowadays, the thief has become more sophisticated and knowledgable in the area of finance, and he knows that these securities can be turned into cash. An organized-crime "receiver of stolen goods" knows the petty criminals who are involved in break-and-enter and similar thefts. The receiver can educate the petty thief to recognize valuable securities. The thief, who would normally receive nothing for these securities, is quite willing to sell them to the organization for a very small percentage of their market value.

Organized crime is now becoming more sophisticated in disposing of stolen securities. In the past, some stolen securities were pledged as collateral for loans at Canadian banks; however, this has become very risky for the criminal, as it leaves traces of the crime. Now stolen securities are often taken out of the country, and tracing is difficult, if not impossible. (On rare occasions in the past, counterfeit securities have been pledged to obtain loans; however, this is not a common occurrence in Canada.)

Advance Fee Schemes

Advance fees are monies paid ahead of, and in expectation of, some future service. Collection of such fees is often properly part of normal business practices and becomes illegal only when a person or company is induced to advance fees under a false pretence or as the result of fraudulent misrepresentation.

These schemes appear to surface in cycles, precipitated by a combination of international and domestic factors, such as the high cost of domestic loans, an inflationary economy, an active construction industry, excesses of foreign capital and government taxation policies. More often than not, they are complex and wide-ranging in scope; involve numerous people, some of whom are unaware they are being used; and generally relate to the application for mortgage funds or large corporate loans for which the borrower must pay a finder's fee or advance fee to a broker when making application. The broker is merely a negotiator or arranger who brings together a "borrower" and a "lender," or "principal."

Literally thousands of money brokers operate freely across Canada's international boundaries, most of them legitimately. The borrower may not know who the actual lender will be until a commitment is received. As a result, a borrower is forced to rely heavily on a broker's honesty, integrity and references.

Who gets involved in fraudulent broking schemes? No one particular type of person or company is exempt, not even banking institutions. Victims have ranged from the biggest corporate giants to the smallest independent businessman. For the borrower, or potential victim, the decision to proceed in association with a broker is strictly a financial one. Usually a project is already in the works, and the need for financing is immediate. The borrower may have found himself with a borderline credit situation locally, thus ruling out conventional financing, or the capital funding required on a project as against projected revenues may render it borderline with regard to financial viability. Therefore, he desires to find lower servicing costs in the form of reduced interest rates.

Preliminary negotiations are directed towards finalizing the amount of the fee and loan details. To establish his own credibility with the "client," the broker may emphasize, usually in vague terms, his own and/or the lender's financial stability, may provide names of well-known persons or companies as references and will likely hint at other big deals he has negotiated. Other prospective borrowers will be given as references. If the new client checks, he will be able to verify only that the reference company is in fact dealing with the broker. Quite often, references supplied are in foreign jurisdictions, making them difficult to validate.

Once the preliminaries are settled, the borrower submits a loan application accompanied by the required "good faith deposit," or advance fee. To transfer funds, the dishonest broker uses "shell" offshore companies, overseas-registered offices and improperly registered Canadian companies. After the fee is paid, there will be an appearance of activity: appraisals of property; letters concerning legal matters and technical data; promises of action and of meetings between the lender and the broker. Finally, the broker will likely transmit to the borrower a "vehicle" approval on his loan application. Two things can now happen: approval can be formally documented, or the broker will begin to waffle and proceedings will come to a standstill. Most often, suspicious actions by the broker or non-performance on written agreements are explained away by passing off responsibility to other persons or blaming other companies and their policies for delays.

An advance fee scheme is attractive to victims solely because of the ease with which capital financing becomes available. For the criminal, it represents the possibility of considerable monetary gains at minor expense, and with limited risk of detection. In addition, the scheme's very nature conveys a suggestion of the broker's respectability and commands acceptance in higher social and financial circles. Even if suspected, the accused has available many avenues of excuse and defence and realizes any charges will involve considerable preparation, which delays prosecution.

For an investigator, such a scheme presents an unusual challenge. It requires gathering considerable evidence that certain purported activities did not take place, or that various alleged associations between persons or companies do not exist. This style of enquiry requires painstaking effort to ascertain patterns in the accused's representations and conduct, in order to prove misrepresentation and fraudulent intent. Extreme patience and dogged determination can result in a successful prosecution, coupled with great professional satisfaction.

Pyramid Schemes

A pyramid scheme can best be described as a "multilevel sales organization." It is an offence under the Canadian Criminal Code to operate a pyramid scheme. The defining characteristics of a pyramid scheme, are:

1. It is a multilevel sales organization;
2. The perpetrators of the scheme manufacture and distribute (sell) something to the public and the products are sold by agents who are recruited locally;
3. The sales volume is not important; the question is whether or not, under the scheme, the participant stands to receive a larger amount of money than he paid into the scheme, through the contributions of other recruits;
4. A provision that the organizers of the scheme will buy back the product if asked does not make the scheme legal;

5. Similar fact evidence will be necessary to prove an offence has been committed. Similar fact evidence refers to repetition of a pattern of behaviour.

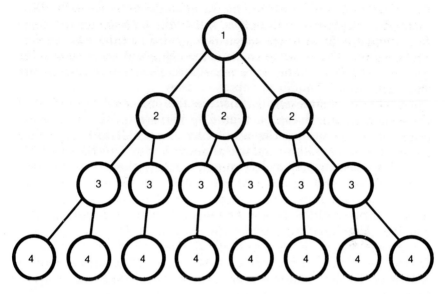

Figure 11 - 1
Example of a pyramid sales organization.

Figure 11-1 shows a pyramid sales organization that has four levels: (1) general distribution; (2) direct distributors; (3) area distributors; and (4) local distributors.

Offshore Banks and Corporate Shells

An offshore bank is one that is outside Canadian jurisdiction and not subject to any Canadian legal authority capable of exercising control over its activities. The term "offshore" is used generally to describe banks in Caribbean countries, such as Grand Cayman and the Bahamas. The term also refers to banks in Lichtenstein and Switzerland.

The countries where offshore banks are located have what are known as banking secrecy laws, which prohibit the disclosure of any information concerning a client's bank account or any transaction he may have made through the bank. The law imposes criminal sanctions against any bank employee who reveals information concerning the banking affairs of a customer to a third party, including police authorities from foreign jurisdictions who are investigating criminal cases.

It is this protection against disclosure that has attracted white-collar criminals to use these banks. This protection has enabled criminals to perpetrate numerous frauds without fear of detection by Canadian authorities. Detection is very difficult, because secrecy laws inhibit the acquisition of evidence required to prove the transfer of certain funds or the existence of certain documents. In many cases, the inability to obtain this evidence can be the difference between a successful or unsuccessful prosecution.

Offshore banks have been used to perpetrate numerous stock market manipulations. Criminals have been able to buy and sell stocks through offshore banks, thus removing the possibility of review of the transactions by Canadian authorities. Offshore banks have also been used to facilitate fraudulent transactions between legitimate Canadian companies and "shell" or "shelf" companies. Shell companies have no assets and are registered in foreign jurisdictions. Through the use of shell companies, monies have been channelled out of Canada to offshore banks. Shell companies are simply held until a transaction is required to perpetrate a fraud. The existence of a shell company is once again extremely difficult to prove.

Market Manipulation

Market manipulation is not new. In the 1920s, promoters used bribery, corruption and price fixing to sell stocks and inflate the market. This led to the development of new regulations in the aftermath of the 1929 Crash. Provincial securities commissions in Canada and the federal Securities and Exchange Commission in the United States were given the mandate of policing the securities industry. Full disclosure of securities transactions was required and people in the securities industry had to be registered. Over the years, market manipulators have developed new strategies to circumvent these regulations, and the stock markets are again being used to turn paper into cash.

The Scheme

Three elements are found in most manipulations: the accumulation of stock, sometimes referred to as a "pool;" a period of promotion, trading activity and public announcements, all intended to induce buying; and, lastly, a period of selling, so that as the public buys, the promoter or insiders will sell.

The promoter is a central figure. Through a network of brokers, lawyers, accountants, geologists and stock distributors, the machinery of selling stock comes into play. Unlike the conventional criminal, the promoter has a right to operate in society. Some provinces even describe the promoter's role in their securities legislation. The point is that promoters, given a legitimate role, can effectively operate their office as a "front." Their legitimate activities may include raising capital, contacting authorities and designing exploration programs; however, the real effort may be toward setting up brokerage accounts, acquiring phony assets, bribing securities salesmen and generally attempting to sell stock.

Formation of a Company

Most jurisdictions govern their corporations by legislation. Companies or Securities Acts are often used by companies as a guideline for the conduct of day-to-day affairs. The promoter, however, sees things in another light. He uses a shell company to create stock; one million shares, for instance, whether they are of any value or not, once controlled and "pooled," become a tradeable proposition. The objective, from a criminal viewpoint, is to acquire control of a dormant company whose shares can be pooled for the purpose of future resale.

This strategy is simple. First, the outstanding shares of a dormant company are purchased, usually for five to ten cents per share. Next, a restructuring takes place, whereby the officers and board of directors are named. In some cases, they can be nominees whose sole function will be to project a respectable or credible image. A retired army officer or a public personality, for instance, might be offered a directorship and be unaware of criminal activities, because negotiations will be carried out by lawyers acting for the interests of the promoter. In effect these "front" people will be buffered from the criminal aspects of the promoter's activity.

Listing on a Stock Exchange

Stock exchanges are places for new companies to raise capital. Shares are offered to the general public through the facilities of a broker, and in most cases the process of listing is negotiated by a lawyer. By this time, the promoter has also hired an accountant to prepare the necessary financial statements necessary to satisfy the regulatory requirements of the stock exchange.

Obtaining an Asset

The promoter now acquires something, such as mining claims, and inflates their value by manipulating the actual and purported prices paid. The prospector who initially staked the property, for instance, will be induced to accept only a portion of the shown price. For example, the promoter offers the prospector $10,000 cash and 100,000 treasury shares of the company. The prospector must agree, secretly, to return these shares to the promoter. The agreements, corporate documents and public announcements will indicate that the prospector received both the cash and shares, when in actual fact these do not represent the true price.

Acquiring an asset adds another dimension to the promoter's objectives. These shares can be later resold at a profit. The point, however, is that the asset, (i.e., the mining claims) has been inflated in value and the agreements and documents from which the accountant prepares the financial statements will reflect that distortion. In other words, the property is not only inflated to serve promotional interests, but by the same token the promoter obtains access to potentially valuable shares.

Taking Out the Offerings

At the beginning of the manipulation certain tactics take place. Brokerage accounts are opened under nominee names in various cities and jurisdictions. At this stage, very little trading activity has taken place, and the price per share has remained relatively low, perhaps in the range of five to ten cents per share. The promoter now places timely purchase orders to indicate a demand. Brokers are led to believe that the company has acquired a valuable mining claim that it intends to explore. The process of placing these timely orders reinforces investor appetite for a possible profit.

The Reverse Split

If a company has, for instance, two million shares outstanding, the idea is to have that number reduced or "rolled back" to one million shares. In other words, the company will ask its shareholders to give up two shares for one, which will automatically double the price and create investor interest. As a corporate strategy, there is nothing illegal about this, but it does serve the promoter's purposes of manipulation.

By causing a reverse split, the promoter learns how many shareholders are still active or alive. If no answer is received, a conclusion may be drawn that these people are neither interested nor concerned about their company, and for purposes of control, from the promoter's viewpoint, it means that the price can be manipulated by means of controlling what is often referred to as a "float." Unexpected sales will not damage the promoter's effort to "run the market upwards."

The Hot Tip

The promoter knows that everyone wants to make money and will strive to get something for nothing. By circulating timely rumours, individuals can be enticed to purchase stock. Brokers, businessmen, lawyers and all sorts of investors are given to understand that they are getting in on the "ground floor," and their investment encourages others to follow. Secondly, by inducing prominent people to invest, the promoter can more easily evade detection; investigations or enquiries may be subtly frustrated by prominent investors who would see themselves in a position of conflict or the target of adverse publicity should the fact of their holding a particular stock issue come to light.

The Promotion

Rumours also induce buying. After the stock has been pooled, strategically placed with various brokers and the price starts moving because of insider buying, the promotion starts to take shape. This involves financial editorials, stock price quotes in newspapers, advertisements, exchange announcements and the submission of a prospectus. The intent is to influence investors to buy the stock. By this time, the mining claims will be projected as a promising ore discovery pending exploration that could lead to the opening of a new mine.

Words with double meanings, sometimes referred to as "window dressing" or "puffing" will be used. For instance, "favourable mineralization" could imply promising ore potential. From a geologist's viewpoint, this term means any plot of ground. A promoter could defend his activities by alleging that no misrepresentation was intended.

Company announcements affect the market price. If the market reacts upwards, the trading activity attracts attention. The promoter tries to coordinate these announcements with increased activity as an inducement to purchase the stock.

Wash Trading

Activity attracts interest and certain methods can be used to create an appearance of active public trading. These phony trades are often called "wash trades" or "matched orders," and are an offence under the Criminal Code (Section 340). The tactic is relatively simple. Accounts are used at several brokerage firms, preferably in different provinces or jurisdictions. At a prearranged time, the promoter will enter orders to buy and sell, to create an appearance of active public trading. No change in beneficial ownership takes place and the effect on the stock market is one of increasing volume. A well-informed investor, by looking at the activity of trading, would naturally ask what's going on.

The Distribution

The promoter has to sell stock to make a profit. If stock were simply offered for sale on the exchange, without corresponding purchase orders or bids, it would create a price decline. Assuming that the price of a share, as the result of wash trading, has risen from ten cents to two dollars, a system must be devised to channel this public buying into the promoter's selling account.

Individuals, known as stock distributors or "hustlers," are recruited to set up these selling systems. They will approach security salesmen and financial institutions with a view to having those people urge their clients to purchase shares of the company under promotion. The incentive is a bribe: whenever the stockbroker generates an order to buy from one of his customers, the distributor will be notified as to the number of shares, the price and the time at which the order will be entered. Given this information, the distributor informs the promoter, who in turn makes available that amount of stock to meet the buy order. In effect, this will be arranged in such a way that only the promoter is able to sell stock into the particular buy order. In this way, the market is not disturbed and the proceeds of selling this stock are in effect guaranteed. The promoter agrees to remit some percentage of the deal to the broker in return for his services.

In recent years, these distributions have taken advantage of international connections. Travel, communication and business have expanded to the extent that these distributions of stock can be centred on, for instance, Europe or the Middle East and calculated on the basis that the authorities will be restricted from investigating beyond their own jurisdiction. This means that foreigners will be induced to purchase Canadian stocks. In the same fashion, these overseas orders can be channelled into the promoter's selling account.

A final calculation will show that by acquiring possibly one million shares at a price of five cents per share and promoting them to a value of four or five dollars a share over a period of eight to twelve months will obviously generate a substantial profit. For this reason, manipulation is a lucrative proposition, particularly for organized criminals who know that white-collar crime is not only safe from the standpoint of detection, but also highly profitable.

A New Variation

A depressed economy has always adversely affected the stock market. Investor interest subsides and the hot tip will be approached carefully. To combat this caution, criminals have developed a new type of manipulation that involves maintaining a false or misleading price. For instance, the majority control of a listed company may be held by one individual or family. As the company experiences economic difficulty, new capital may be sought by the company pledging this controlled stock with a bank or financial institution. Since the value of this stock is directly connected to the loan given to this majority shareholder, it becomes obvious that a stable or "good" price must be maintained.

Accounts are opened with various brokers, preferably in different jurisdictions to avoid detection. If the stock shows no trading activity, buy and sell orders are generated with the intent of showing a volume and maintaining a price. These are fictitious trades, involving no change in beneficial ownership and are designed to mislead the banks or financial institutions, as well as the other shareholders.

If the stock were left alone, without these maintaining trades, the likelihood is that the price would fall. (Trading inactivity makes investors nervous. The first thing that comes to mind is whether or not a market exists for their stock, and the reassurance of a quote, showing volume, in the newspaper would encourage them to keep this stock. The bank manager or financial loan officer is in a similar position. If questioned about the collateral he is holding, the price can always be quoted from the paper to show that a market price exists. As long as a price is maintained with some activity, the scheme can continue.)

A profit strategy may also exist in this type of scheme. Once the money has been obtained, this majority shareholder might then have it transferred out of the jurisdiction to another country, such as Switzerland or the Bahamas. A portion of the money may be used to satisfy the company's capital requirements, but in the long run it may be obvious that the business will suffer and when it fails, going into receivership or bankruptcy, the shareholder is left with the cash while the bank or the financial institution holds onto the worthless stock.

Takeovers and Mergers

Another form of manipulation involves the "takeover" or "merger" technique, whereby company insiders use the market to make profits. For example, the board of directors of Company A must decide on what to do with a large cash treasury, say $10 million. It may propose to purchase or "take over" another company (Company B) whose shares may be listed on the stock exchange at two dollars per share. Company A will confidentially approach the directors of Company B and offer to purchase controlling interest which would, for example, amount to 300,000 shares, at a price of three dollars per share. If all parties were agreeable, then a takeover announcement would be made simultaneous with the purchase of 300,000 shares at a price of three dollars per share at a prearranged date, possibly six months ahead. Since the directors of Company A know that the price of Company B shares will move from two dollars to three dollars, a profit strategy can be worked out. With the use of a nominee account in a foreign jurisdiction orders to buy Company B stock will be placed at amounts beginning around two dollars per share. The accumulation of such stock must be inconspicuous and generally in small amounts. Nevertheless, over a period of six months, a substantial position can be acquired and the profit becomes obvious when the announcement comes out that Company A is willing to pay three dollars per share of Company B. Profits can likewise be channelled back through the foreign jurisdiction to avoid detection. The general public or ordinary shareholders would have no knowledge of such tactics, which clearly favour the insider.

Internationalism

Canada has tremendous resource potential. Many foreigners see this as the last frontier, where profits and fortunes are still a possibility. Promoters realized, first, that a great deal of capital exists in Europe and the Middle East and, second, that Canada is a promotable entity. Its vastness, high standard of living and social stability add credence to a promotional formula.

To promote a Canadian company abroad, shares are purported to represent exploitable resources. Foreign investors are asked to place orders through certain banks or brokers, who have instructions to accept and channel buy orders to another broker who has the promoter's stock available for sale. These transactions all occur on foreign soil. Activity in Canada remains low-key, and may be limited to listing the stock on one of the Canadian stock exchanges.

When the venture fails, the promoter is left with the cash while the investors hold the stock. The promoter knows jurisdictional restrictions will inhibit investigation but, even before the investigative stage, the victim has little if no recourse. Distance and expense will tend to discourage complaints and to whom does the victim complain? Victims may also be reluctant to implicate themselves. Most European countries have tax and currency laws prohibiting citizens from engaging in "offshore" business. In such cases, the mere reporting of an offence could have negative repercussions for the complainant. Finally, the banking secrecy laws will frustrate investigative efforts to the point where it isn't worth the time and expense. Most countries have such laws, particularly against foreign authorities seeking client information. Such activities are detrimental to foreign investment in Canada, and therefore harm all Canadians.

Employee Embezzlement

Embezzlement may be described as an illegal activity that involves the deceitful transfer of an employer's money or property to an employee or another. Closely akin to embezzlement are the offences of "secret commissions" under Section 383 of the Criminal Code, and "rendering a benefit to a government employee" under Section 110 of the Criminal Code.

Businesses such as banks and other institutions whose employees have direct access to cash are most susceptible to embezzlement; however, businesses such as these are generally set up to allow the employer to keep a close check on the activities of employees. Most businesses, however, are fairly loosely run and rely on the assumption that employees are honest. The cost of setting up a system to ensure employee honesty is often prohibitive.

The types of embezzlement are as many and as varied as the number of businesses in Canada. However, there are generally three sources from which a dishonest employee may obtain money or property.

From the Employer

The most common and simplest form of embezzlement by an employee is the outright theft of goods, tools or money from his place of employment. In operations such as a bank, it may be necessary that the employee create documentation to hide the fact that money is missing, because generally there is an accounting at the end of each day, and any cash shortages would be immediately evident. Many companies allow employees to use items such as tools during their shut-down hours in order to curtail thefts by employees. In cases where a company is in the business of manufacturing and selling goods, it will often allow employees to purchase those goods at a reduced rate to deter the employee from stealing directly from the company.

The type of embezzlement in which the employee may become involved depends to a large extent on his duties within the office. For example, A.B. is the loans manager at a bank. He is short of cash and therefore writes up a loan in a fictitious name, forges a signature to it and in that name draws a cheque for the amount of the loan. He then uses a fictitious account at another bank to cash the cheque. When the loan becomes due, he simply writes it off as a bad debt, indicating to the bank's auditors that they are unable to collect on the loan. Or an employee whose job entails the paying of accounts on behalf of his employer may set up a false supplier and place fraudulent invoices in the files in order that cheques may be issued for the payment of those invoices. By setting up a bank account in the name of that company, he can deposit cheques for his own benefit.

These more complex systems of embezzlement often require coercion between one or more employees in a company. An employee in a personnel department may add fictitious names to the employee list and have a co-worker in the payroll department issue paycheques in those names, and then split the proceeds of those paycheques.

From Suppliers

An employee, in return for purchasing goods on his employer's behalf through certain suppliers, may corruptly receive benefits from those companies. For example, C.D. is the purchasing agent for a large department store. As part of his duties, he often purchases men's suits from a certain company. An employee of that company indicates to C.D. that he will give him 10 percent in cash for all the purchases made on his employer's behalf. C.D. accepts this arrangement and later his company becomes concerned that it is greatly overstocked with men's suits.

This practice is contrary to Section 383 of the Criminal Code, if a private individual is involved, and contrary to Section 110 if the employee works for a government department. The embezzler's gain is an indirect loss to the employer, because he eventually pays more for the goods or services than he would ordinarily pay. Large companies are often in receipt of periodic tax rebates or payments from suppliers as a result of discounts, volume purchases, etc. An employee who negotiates the discount, or who processes it at the office, will arrange to have the payment made directly to himself.

From Customers

The methods by which an employee may embezzle funds that should be in the hands of customers may take any one of several different forms. Where the employee has access to goods of another person or company, the embezzlement may take the form of pilfering. For example, E.F. works for a cleaning company that specialized in servicing small businesses and stores. One of the businesses that has a contract with his company is a store selling small radios and appliances. While cleaning the stores, E.F. hides small radios in garbage cans, which he places outside in the garbage. He then returns in the middle of the night and picks the items up.

An employee involved in the receipt of payments from customers (e.g., a clerk in a department store) may overcharge for goods and pocket the difference. The offence may also take the form of misdirection of customer shipments to the embezzler or his accomplice.

A bank employee may take money out of accounts that have been dormant for some time. There may not be much in the individual accounts, but together the withdrawals may add up to a sizable amount. The customer of the bank is often slow to realize that he does not have the correct amount of funds in his account, because he may have not used it for a long while—or even have forgotten he has an account in that bank.

Detection

Crimes of embezzlement are very difficult to detect and quite often the employee's criminal activity will be missed even by company auditors. Even if the activity is detected by the company, the employer will often decide not to inform the police, in view of the fact that he does not wish to cause any adverse publicity. Should an embezzlement be reported, the officer investigating the occurrence must be in a position to spend some time familiarizing himself with the office of the particular company, and especially the function of the employee who is suspect. An investigation of this type can be a long and tedious job, and the police officer is often hampered because much of the evidence must be obtained from individuals who are friends of the accused and have worked with him or her for some time.

Besides looking at the structure of the business itself, the investigator will also have to look into the personal affairs of the suspected employee. This will require a search of his banking records and his home, to obtain evidence to prove that the benefit was received by that particular individual. This evidence may take the form of deposits in a bank account or stolen items in the employee's home. In large and complex cases of embezzlement, the investigator may find that the employee has set up bank accounts in fictitious names either locally or in foreign countries in order to hide his illicit earnings.

Land Transactions

Land frauds involve real property. They vary in nature and frequently concern more than one jurisdiction. It is not uncommon to find land sold to Canadians that is located in another country, such as the Grand Cayman Islands. The sale will involve false statements as to the land itself or may be sold by a person not having title or the right to sell. The land may be nonexistent or used in respect to other fraudulent schemes.

Land frauds involve misrepresentations that are difficult for the purchaser to check, and he can do so only after a considerable sum of money has been given to the vendor. A common example of land fraud is the sale of swampland represented as being liveable with improvements that have not been installed. Or false titles may be used in a sale. This is particularly prevalent in transactions involving land in parts of Tennessee, where a complete title system is not maintained.

In every case of land fraud, an investigator should not become overly concerned with the dollar value of the property. Each investigation should be viewed with an eye to the deceit, falsehoods and other fraudulent representations.

Bankruptcy

Basically, bankruptcy as administered under the federal Bankruptcy Act is a normal civil process whereby the debts of the bankrupt are discharged by court order if he surrenders himself and his property to the control of the court for the benefit of his creditors. Criminals and opportunists with criminal tendencies are quick to find and exploit for their illegal benefit situations where their criminal acts may be camouflaged by civil, company, or commercial law with their complicated jurisdictions and procedures. Bankruptcy provides such situations.

The police interest lies in situations where bankruptcy laws and corporate fronts are used to perpetrate swindles on creditors.

There are four types of bankruptcies.

1. *Legitimate*: In 1979 there were in Canada about 23,500 bankruptcies involving liabilities of about $573 million. It is generally estimated that 1 or 2 percent involve fraud.
2. *Legitimate but with minor offences and crimes apparent*: A previously honest merchant may take the opportunity of a failing business to obtain illegal benefits for himself or his friends.
3. *Corruption of administrative machinery*: Certain creditors or the bankrupt may in illegal collusion with the trustee or inspectors to defraud other creditors. This type of fraud is presently quite rare.
4. *Planned bankruptcy*: Known as "scam" to the underworld, this type of bankruptcy is of the greatest concern to the police.

The planned bankruptcy is a merchandising swindle based on the abuse of credit. It consists of: overpurchasing of inventory on credit; sale or other disposition of the goods; concealment of the proceeds; non-payment of creditors; abandonment of the business, or bankruptcy if creditors seek it. Planned bankruptcy swindles are primarily perpetrated by organized criminal groups with the help of corrupt lawyers, accountants and front men. Occasionally, a previously honest merchant will resort to them to make a "quick killing" before going out of business.

The primary area of operation is in general merchandise, where goods may be purchased in large volume during peak periods, such as Christmas, without attracting attention. One method to perpetrate the fraud is the three-step scam. A business is opened with a bank account. A credit rating is established during the first month by ordering goods from a small group of suppliers and paying the invoices immediately. Cheques are written and cashed to create false activity in the bank account. Confederates may be used to falsely certify each other's financial reliability. The next step is to widen the supplier group, using the first group as credit references. The second group is paid in full, the first only partially. In the third step, a large volume of goods is ordered and disposed of without paying the creditors. The business is insolvent and abandoned.

The one-step scam is preferable, since it requires a shorter time span. This involves the silent purchase or coercive takeover of an existing business with an excellent credit rating. The change in ownership or control is concealed from creditors and credit-rating agencies. Large-scale purchases are made on credit by telephone, personal visits to trade shows or correspondence with distant suppliers. Purchases include anything that can be obtained without regard to previous line of business. The goods are disposed of, the proceeds hidden and the business closes its doors.

An alternative to the last method is the same-name scam. A business is opened with a name purposely similar to that of a successful concern in the same locality, to induce creditors to believe they are shipping the orders to a reputable enterprise. Here again speed is a crucial factor.

Criminals are attracted to schemes of obtaining goods on credit, quickly converting them to cash while planning all along to abandon the fake business and disappear or to rely on the apathy of creditors or the delay and complexity inherent in bankruptcy proceedings to escape criminal liability.

What Is the Cause of White-Collar Crime?

According to sociologists, as freedom increases, so does crime. Canadians have a great amount of individual freedom, which has given rise to increasing social deviance. It would appear also that rapid increase or slowdown of economic development breeds crime. Crime is also an essential feature of a developing society and a predictable byproduct of rapid social change. It seems that outbreaks of crime occur when sudden prosperity or quick technological development unleashes "overwhelming ambition." Expectations rise to unreasonable heights and, in the economic stampede that follows, some people move ahead legitimately while others trample on the rules.

It would appear that a slipping morality has emerged in the wake of the abandonment of traditional values and restraints. Plain high-living is one of the main causes of white-collar crime; people turn their resentment against society when they can't have everything they feel they're entitled to. Materialism, social upheaval, lack of moral leadership, all permit criminals to take advantage of the system. Canadians have the criminals they deserve.

The White-Collar Crime Investigator

The primary skill required by a commercial-crime investigator is proven investigative talent. He must be able to assemble pertinent facts while tossing out extraneous ones. He must be able to analyze financial information and contractual arrangements and interrelate a myriad of information developed during the investigation of a complex matter. He requires not only good common sense, but must possess a high degree of mental acuity to understand fully the situation he is investigating and to be able to quickly comprehend the evidence collected during the course of his enquiries.

A commercial crime investigator must be aggressive and not back away from the hostility he will encounter from lawyers, accountants, and others in the business community. At the same time, he must be able to conduct himself in a professional manner and earn the respect of the senior people in the private sector with whom he is dealing.

The commercial crime investigator must obtain at least an elementary knowledge of business law, accounting, the securities industry, use of the computer and the various statutes applicable to white-collar crime. These include the Criminal Code, the Bankruptcy Act, the Bank Act, the Securities Act, the Combines Investigation Act and several other provincial and federal statutes.

FURTHER READINGS

A Handbook on White Collar Crime. Washington, D.C.: Chamber of Commerce of the United States of America, 1974.
Campbell, Det. Sergeant D. "Investigating Fraud," *The Police Journal,* Chichester, Sussex, England, St. Richard's Press Limited, January–March 1971.
Bloom, Murray Teigh. *Rogues to Riches.* New York: G. P. Putman's Sons, 1971.
Croft, Roger. *Swindle.* Toronto: Gage Publishing Co., 1975.
Gage, Nicholas. *Mafia, U.S.A.* New York: Dell Publishing Co., 1972.
Gosch, Martin A. and Richard Hammer. *The Last Testament of Lucky Luciano.* Waltham, Ma.: Little, Brown & Co., 1975.
Hutchinson, Robert A. *Vesco.* New York: Praeger Publishing, 1973.
Kwitney, Jonathan. *The Fountain Pen Conspiracy.* New York: Alfred A. Knopf, 1973.
Raw, Charles, Bruce Page and Godfrey Hodgson. *Do You Sincerely Want To Be Rich?* London: André Deutsch, 1971.

Chapter 12

Discretion in the Application of the Criminal Law
B. J. Saxton

A young factory worker on night shift was found asleep at his work station by the supervisor on duty. Clearly the worker was breaking a company rule for which he could be instantly dismissed. The supervisor took the young man into his office and considered the situation carefully. He knew that the subordinate was normally a conscientious worker. He was also aware that the man had two noisy preschool children who often made it difficult for him to get his sleep prior to night shift. The young man apologized for his lapse and promised that it would not happen again. After a moment's deliberation of all the circumstances involved, the supervisor severely reprimanded the man, warned him that any future sleeping on the job would probably result in his dismissal and sent him back to work. The supervisor had exercised his discretion in applying his own sanctions rather than invoking the company rules. In other words, he had taken the liberty of using his own judgement in deciding on a course of action that he felt would have the necessary salutary effect.

This case demonstrates what discretion is and how it can be exercised in the application or adjudication of rules. After all, in that particular factory under the conditions of employment with that company, the rules are laws. The worker has broken one of those laws, and the supervisor has a responsibility, by virtue of his position of authority, to enforce them. The similarities end there, however, in comparing this situation to a criminal case. One major ingredient is missing: public reaction.

Canadians live in a democratic political system, which means that the criminal law is public law, legislated in Parliament by elected representatives. Criminal laws reflect the values of Canadians. They are added to, amended, or rescinded by way of interest aggregation within the constitutional framework, to meet the values, attitudes, needs and expectations of society generally. Laws are made for the protection of Canadian society as a whole, and it is

Barrie Saxton is the Co-ordinator of the Law and Security Administration Program at Humber College, Toronto and previously served twelve years in the police service.

expected that they will be enforced in a fair and impartial manner upon all the people. It therefore follows that discretion in the application of criminal law by its practitioners will have many far-reaching implications. Equality before the law is deemed sacrosanct in a democracy; therefore to deviate from total enforcement raises many issues and concerns in terms of fair play and justice. Yet the apparent inequities of the justice system as it works raises many questions for those unfamiliar with its reality.

Why would the police charge one person with theft and merely caution another? Why are some people allowed to get away with breaking the liquor laws or narcotic laws? Why are some accused persons allowed to plead guilty to reduced charges? Why are there obvious inequities in sentencing practices? How can a person be sentenced to life imprisonment and be out of jail in ten years? Answers to these questions can be obtained only by looking closely at the day-to-day interactions of the system and society.

Would society really want a cold, impersonal, objective justice system that would enforce every law to its ultimate extent and punish every miscreant in the same way regardless of mitigating circumstances? For example, in law, two teenagers experimenting with marijuana and passing a joint back and forth are just as guilty of trafficking, according to the Narcotics Control Act, as the professional criminal who sells a kilo of heroin. It would be administratively impossible to draft and pass legislation to cover every contingency; consequently there is a large grey area in law. Likewise, it would be impossible to process everyone who broke the law through the system without enormous cost to the taxpayer. Police, courts and correctional resources are at present strained to the maximum in order to deal with the existing input.

The Canadian Committee on Corrections in its report on the purpose of the criminal law said, "Discretion in the application of the criminal law should be allowed at each step in the process: arrest, prosecution, conviction, sentence and corrections."[1]

The Police

The criminal justice system can be compared to a gigantic filter. Of those who commit crimes, some are not caught; some are caught but not arrested; some are arrested but never tried.[2] The ones who have most contact with crime and do most of the filtering for a multitude of reasons are the police.

In Britain, it has long been an accepted tradition that the police have the right to decide whether or not to prosecute. There exists a formal warning system, complete with records of statistical data maintained nationwide. In 1962 the Royal Commission on the Police said that one of the main duties of the police in England and Wales was to decide whether or not to prosecute persons suspected of criminal offences. The Court of Appeal had an opportunity to comment on the issue in *Regina vs. Metropolitan Police, ex parte Blackburn*. Lord Justice Salmon said that "of course the police have a wide discretion as to whether or not they will prosecute in any particular case." The court, however, found it unacceptable that the commissioner of the Metropolitan Police should issue a policy order that no action should be taken against gaming clubs.[3] In other words the Court of Appeal confirmed the right of the police to use discretion based on individual circumstances, but police administrators must not publish policy orders not to investigate or prosecute certain criminal offences. The implication of such a policy order is, in effect, that certain behaviour becomes legal in that police jurisdiction.

In the United States, the police have no legal right to exercise discretion in any formal way. By virtue of the fourteenth amendment to the Constitution, discriminatory enforcement of the law is perceived as a denial of equal protection before the law.[4] On the other hand, the President's Commission on Law Enforcement and the Administrators of Justice said, "Police must not only exercise discretion, but must assume a risk in doing so;" and so the paradox is perpetuated.

In Canada, many police administrators are reluctant to issue any formal orders with respect to discretion because of the possibility of allegations of unfair enforcement practices and the fear of police corruption. Who can blame them, in the light of two recent cases in point? In 1970 allegations were made that some Toronto police officers (both senior and junior) were exercising discretion in favour of certain citizens with respect to impaired driving and other traffic violations. I hasten to add that all of the officers involved were subsequently exonerated of any wrongdoing at a board of commissioners inquiry. In its conclusions, the report of the commissioners said in part: "This commission will not discourage the use of discretion by any officer, when it is believed that a citizen of this community is deserving of consideration." However, it also cautioned that "extenuating circumstances given as a basis of recommendation for withdrawal of a summons is not acceptable. The officer in charge of the summons bureau must ensure that there is sufficient documentation on record to satisfy any question as to why a summons has been withdrawn. It was obvious during the enquiry that not enough attention was paid by personnel to existing procedures and this must be corrected."[5] So that although the officers involved were cleared, a great deal of adverse publicity was generated by the enquiry and the commission criticized in part some of the discretionary procedures being practised.

Conversely, the Niagara Regional Police came under fire for following the letter of the law too closely in the 1974 Landmark Hotel raid. On that occasion a number of RCMP and Niagara Regional Police officers raided the Hotel in Fort Erie, authorized by a search warrant for narcotics. During the course of the raid some forty-five female patrons at the Hotel were "strip-searched" in the ladies' washroom by two female police officers. Because of a public outcry as to the aggressive nature of the raid and the very small number of charges laid, a Royal Commission was held. After a lengthy hearing into the circumstances of the Landmark raid, the Commissioner His Honour Judge Pringle said in his conclusions: "The actions of the policewomen were, on a literal interpretation of the law, strictly correct. On the whole of the evidence, in respect to the search of the female patrons by causing them to disrobe and subject themselves to a cursory glance of their buttocks and genital areas, I am satisfied that there was not a shred of evidence to support a suspicion that any of the female patrons had concealed heroin or any like substance on their persons prior to the search. In this sense the wholesale search was foolish and unnecessary, as not one female was ever seen with a known heroin or other drug trafficker."[6] In this situation, the police were criticized for their actions, even though those very actions were legitimate and within the boundaries of the law. As one senior police officer put it: "You can't win when it comes to discretion. Take a rock concert, for example. If we were to bust kids for smoking dope in that situation it would probably cause a riot which could result in thirty or forty kids and policemen being killed or seriously injured—then what would people say? On the other hand, when we don't do anything we get criticized for allowing kids to flagrantly defy the law." The citizen by and large does not acknowledge police discretion as a ubiquitous feature of police work. Despite the unacceptability of full enforcement and its high financial cost, the public maintains a limited view of police discretion.[7] Nevertheless, the police do exercise discretion, both formally and informally.

Formal Police Discretion

Of major concern to any police administrator is the effective deployment of human resources. Thousands of calls for assistance pour through police switchboards daily and have to be responded to. There must be sufficient officers on patrol to meet demands for police services. Most often staff utilization is determined by population, crime rates and calls for assistance. It is not unusual on Friday and Saturday nights in large urban areas for police dispatchers to "stack" calls of a less serious nature because units are busy dealing with more serious matters. Similarly, staff assigned to special investigation squads (break and enter, fraud, morality, drugs, etc.) can be spared only in limited numbers. Serious crimes such as murder or rape will warrant more man-hours for obvious reasons, but on the other hand minor crimes of theft or property damage, where there is little hope of detecting the offender, will receive no more attention than filing a report. By the same token, if there is public or political outcry about some particular problem, (e.g., body-rub parlours in the community), additional enforcement resources will be ordered by senior officers. Some municipalities have established detoxification centres where drunks arrested by the police can sober up rather than being processed through the courts.

Another safe area for formal discretion to be exercised is in the handling of juvenile offenders. Most larger forces have established youth bureaus composed of officers who receive additional training and education in dealing with juvenile delinquency. Youth bureau officers investigate all juveniles involved in criminal activity and usually have a fairly broad discretionary mandate in individual situations. In most instances, the case will be disposed of by cautioning and counselling the juvenile in the presence of the parents. Records are kept of juvenile contacts, which include details of the offence and its disposition. A second offence may be dealt with by referral of the offender to a social agency; repeating offenders will be referred to juvenile court usually by way of summons rather than arrest. In exceptional circumstances, it is feasible that a juvenile could be taken before the juvenile court for a first offence, depending upon the gravity of the charge and attendant circumstances.

In less serious matters, such as traffic violations, some police forces have written policies giving guidance to their members. Directives are issued that officers give motorists forty-eight hours to report to a police station with the appropriate repairs made for such offences as a headlight not illuminated or a noisy exhaust system. Other forces have warning tickets for the many and numerous types of parking violations. The latter are usually issued by individual officers at their discretion, depending on the circumstances surrounding the offence. It may not be appropriate, for example, to issue such a warning in the downtown area of a large city during rush hour if the offending vehicle is obstructing traffic.

Informal Police Discretion

Detectives and plainclothes officers have always seemed to enjoy a greater latitude for using their own discretion, to the point where the practice has become a tradition. Perhaps because they are not in uniform, and therefore somewhat anonymous to the public, they can ignore certain crimes without fear of repercussions. For example, the average detective will often turn a blind eye to prostitutes soliciting in return for information on more serious crimes. Similarly, plain-clothes officers involved in the investigation of narcotics offences will ignore offences of possession of drugs or even minor trafficking and make a deal with the petty offender for names, addresses or other information on the bigger dealers. This type of informal nego-tiating is an accepted part of police technique the world over, and has been practised by generations of police officers. Occasionally detectives will charge an accused with a lesser offence, even though they have sufficient evidence for a more serious one. Let us take, for example, a situation where someone is caught entering Canada at a border crossing in possession of a small amount of narcotics. Technically that person has committed the offence of importing a narcotic into Canada, which carries a minimum sentence of seven years' imprisonment. This particular section of the Narcotics Control Act is obviously meant to be a deterrent and is aimed at the criminal element involved in the wholesale importation of drugs to be dis-tributed in Canada. Our hypothetical offender does not seem to fit into that category, with his small amount of drugs obviously for personal use. Under such circumstances, most investigators would lay a charge of possession or perhaps possession for the purpose of trafficking. Such action in fact allows the court to hand down a more realistic sentence to fit the circumstances of the offence.

Cold Canadian winters make life uncomfortable for the ardent football fan, and a majority will take along the traditional "mickey" of liquor to repel the chill. It would be an impossible task for the police to arrest everyone who drinks liquor at a football game. Some people might question the validity of certain liquor laws altogether. But unfortunately there are always a few unruly types who will get drunk and start fighting or disturb other people and encroach upon their rights. The police method for handling these affairs usually involves utilizing a number of uniform officers on visible preventive patrols, and some plainclothes officers mingling in the crowd. The latter will conduct selective enforcement summonsing potentially troublesome individuals and seizing their liquor. Some plainclothes officers are so skilled and unobtrusive that they are rarely ever seen performing their duty by the average football fan.

The backbone of any army is the front-line soldier, and the back-bone of any police force is a well-trained efficient uniform branch. Unlike in other, more bureaucratic organizations, the lowest-ranking member of the police force exercises wide discretion over how his task is to be performed. It is this individual police decision that defines the limits of law enforcement.[8] The uniform branch of any police force is always the largest arm of the organization in terms of manpower. They are the shock troops who deal with all and every type of call for assistance that the Force receives from the public and it is at this level where discretion is exercised most frequently.

Every police officer starts his career in the uniform branch and some never leave it throughout their career. The new recruit is generally inclined not to use much discretion in his early days on the streets. His training has been conducted in a fairly black-and-white situation, whereby he has been taught how and when he can legally arrest, how much force he can use, what his authority to search is, and what evidence is required for a number of the more common offences he is likely to encounter. His head is full of law and procedures, but no one has really spent much (if any) time teaching him about discretionary enforcement. His attitude toward the police role is influenced by a number of factors, among which are: a newfound sense of power and an eagerness to test it out; a desire to do well in his new vocation and impress his supervisors; the knowledge that he is a probationary constable and subject to dismissal if he does not meet the required standards; and a lack of knowledge as to what alternatives are available. Consequently the young police officer will tend to use enforcement of the law rather than other means of reconciling situations. This overenthusiasm often earns the badge-happy recruit the nickname of "hot dog" among older and more experienced officers. Gradually he will learn the norms of his colleagues, community standards and resources available to deal with the variety of problems he is called upon to resolve.

Ask the average experienced police officer why he has decided not to prosecute and invariably his rationale will make good sense. Hardly a night goes by when he is not faced with a domestic assault, a borderline impaired driver or a questionable sexual encounter in the back seat of a car. The warm summer weather brings a preponderance of noisy parties, disorderlies in parks and other public places, nude bathing and illegal drinking. In many such situations, the policeman will adopt a "peace-keeping" role and exercise his discretion in response to community norms and force guidelines, giving warnings and reprimands rather than resorting to prosecutions.

Shame and embarrassment are two factors the policeman considers when he is deciding how to deal with an offender. The housewife caught shoplifting or businessman found in a common bawdy house will probably have suffered enough shame at the conclusion of an investigation to deter them from such behaviour ever again. The embarrassment of being caught in some deviant act is probably one of the foremost preventers of crime. The senior citizen with a weak bladder who urinates in a public place, or the cripple who shouts obscenities at an inconsiderate driver, will receive a humanitarian caution from most officers.

Of course, there will always be the few constables who use discretion as a means of avoiding becoming involved in writing reports and going to court. These fellows can be a source of frustration to both their peers and supervisors. As one police officer put it, in reference to a lazy colleague: "The only work he does is draw his pay and draw his breath." Conversely, some police officers with a strong motivation for upward mobility perceive full enforcement as a means to promotion. This officer has his goals set on either the criminal investigation department or a supervisory position, and tends to go overboard charging everyone and anyone who breaks the law. He is usually notorious within the community and unpopular among his peer group. It is difficult for a supervisor to criticize this type of individual, because he can rationalize his aggressive work habits by saying that he is just doing his job.

The federal Law Reform Commission, in its "Working Paper on Diversion," has recognized that discretion is not a new function for the police.[9] The commission is advocating formalization and broader powers of discretion not only by the police, but at other levels in the justice system. It also contends in the same document that if constraint in the use of the criminal process is to be successful at the police level, society must reward the police for making screening decisions. Police forces are judged on their "clearance" rate (how many charges are laid).[10] It must also be remembered that, for the individual policeman, making a good arrest is rewarded by compliments from supervisors and peers. Some recognition should also be afforded the police officer who uses sound judgement and is able to make amicable arrangements for the disposition of criminal matters without invoking the whole criminal process. After all, is this too not good police work?

Recently some scholars have attacked on ethical grounds the unequal enforcement of criminal law. They argue that if society cannot or will not enforce a rule fairly and completely, it should abolish the rule, and strip the behaviour of its criminal label.[11] This paper has attempted to show that not only is this proposition impractical in view of the many variables involved in police work, but it would be realistically impossible for the system to cope with full enforcement. Any attempt to confine police discretion within rigid rules is doomed to failure, for no matter what the rules, or supervision, effective police work will continue to depend upon the individual exercise of discretion.[12]

The Prosecutor

A second major area in the criminal justice process where discretion is exercised is at the pre-trial stage. After the police have laid an information against an accused person, the case is handed over to the Crown attorney, and it is recognized that he has the right to: decide whether to proceed; what charges to proceed with; the form of the charge; whether to charge several offences jointly or separately; and whether to charge several accused jointly or separately.[13] For our purposes, it will probably be most appropriate to examine the circumstances under which the Crown attorney decides whether to charge, and what charge to proceed with. If the prosecutor decides not to proceed with a case, this is known in legal terms as withdrawal of the charge. In effect, the case is dropped altogether and the accused may not be prosecuted again on that charge. This discretionary decision made by the prosecutor is limited in practice to two general situations: withdrawal for compassionate reasons and withdrawal for police investigatory purposes.[14] Compassionate reasons could include a situation where a man has been charged with a first offence of indecent exposure. Since the time of the commission of the offence he has commenced taking voluntary psychiatric treatment and a criminal conviction may jeopardize his employment. Police investigatory purposes could cover a situation where the victim of a crime has perhaps moved out of the province and cannot be traced, or for some other reason insufficient evidence is available to proceed with the trial.

Discretion at the pre-trial stage is probably most prevalent with respect to what charge the prosecutor will proceed with. This practice is usually carried out in the form of plea bargaining, involving negotiation between prosecutor and defence lawyer for a guilty plea to a lesser charge. Because plea bargaining is often carried on in a hallway outside the courtroom, comedian Lenny Bruce was prompted to say: "In the halls of justice the only justice is in the halls."[15] In terms of court time, plea bargaining certainly speeds up the process. If every accused pleaded not guilty and had to be tried, the courts could never handle all the cases on the calendar, even if they sat twenty-four hours a day. However, it has been noted through a number of studies conducted in the courts that on many occasions plea bargaining has not always ensured that justice has been done to either the accused or the community; not to mention the severe frustration of police officers who may have spent endless hours building a sound case.

The pressure of large caseloads has made the whole judicial system encourage plea bargaining, and perhaps neglect due process.

The range of inducements available to the police, the prosecution and the defence counsel to encourage a plea of guilty clearly raises the spectre of an accused pleading guilty with the false hope of some benefit that may not be forthcoming. The inducement may also lead to the risk of an untrustworthy plea. Considerable pressure may be put on the accused by his own defence lawyer.[16]

There is also a financial consideration that can influence defence lawyers. A guilty plea to a lesser charge results in a quick proceeding, a satisfactory result for the client and more time to handle other cases. A study of plea bargaining practices in the United States showed some similarities to the Canadian scene. State and defence attorneys conspire to expedite the process and adapt a similar attitude towards the accused person. Criminal law practice is far less lucrative than other fields of law and in the U.S. many public defenders were found to come from poor economic backgrounds, had poor training and extreme difficulty in starting a law practice.[17]

Offenders who have been before the courts previously are extremely knowledgable regarding the system and are prepared to manipulate it to obtain the best deal they can through plea bargaining. This perspective engenders little respect for the administration of criminal law and creates correctional and rehabilition problems.[18] It can only be perceived as a cost to the system. Nevertheless, plea bargaining will prevail for better or worse as long as the criminal justice system continues to be overloaded.

The Courts

Discretion does not end at the pre-trial stage. The presiding judge is given a great deal of latitude to use his discretion. Very few sections of the Criminal Code prescribe minimum sentences. Generally speaking, legislation stipulates the maximum sentence for the offence, but leaves the determination of any lesser sentence to the discretion of the judge. The result often is discrepancy in sentencing practices (even for like offences), depending on many variables, but mostly on the attitude of the judge toward the behaviour involved. Some judges believe in using probation for certain offences, while others will resort to prison sentences for the same crime. On the other hand, some judges may rely heavily on fines or suspended sentences to dispose of cases. These haphazard sentencing practices do of course encourage "judge shopping" by astute defence lawyers and accused persons familiar with the system. In his study on sentencing behaviour, Hogarth found a high level of consistency between judges' perceptions of their environment and sentencing behaviour. One cannot understand sentencing without examining the particular ways in which magistrates respond to their social environments.

Sentencing is not a rational, mechanical process and is subject to human frailties.[19]

In recent years, many Canadian judges have started handing down some rather novel alternative sentences. Guilty persons who would normally be receiving a short sentence in prison may be required to serve their time on weekends. The rationale is that if the accused has a steady job he will be able to carry on working to support himself and his family, rather than throwing an additional financial burden upon the community. At the same time, he is obliged to pay his debt to society by being deprived of his own recreational time. In a recent case a Kitchener, Ontario, man who was convicted of indecent assault on two juvenile girls was sentenced to three years' probation by Judge Donald McMillan. The conditions of his probation order were that: he should vacate his present apartment (presumably the victims were neighbours); he is forbidden to converse with children under the age of sixteen who are not accompanied by adults; and he was also ordered to take psychological treatment for his aberration.[20]

Absolute discharge is also being utilized as a viable alternative sentence where the judge considers that the embarrassment of a public court appearance without the lasting stigma of a criminal record will deter the accused person from further trouble.

Corrections and Parole Services

If an accused is found guilty and sentenced to a term of imprisonment, one would assume that his or her situation would be somewhat arbitrarily controlled, but this is not so. Within the correctional system there are discretionary variables. After sentencing, whether it be to a federal penitentiary (for a two-year sentence or more) or a provincial reformatory, the prisoner is usually sent initially to a reception and assessment centre. He will be kept there for a short period and a decision will be made as to the type of institution in which he will be incarcerated, depending upon the gravity and type of the offence, previous record of violence or escape attempts, mental attitude, etc. The alternative types of institutions where he may serve his sentence could vary from a maximum, medium, or minimum security institution, depending upon the decision of the assessors. Likewise, after serving part of his sentence, the prisoner could earn and be granted a day or weekend pass at the discretion of the warden or superintendent. Temporary absence programs, which allow trusted inmates to work in the community while still serving their sentences, are also administered according to local discretion.

Very few persons serve the full sentence imposed by the court.

An inmate may be considered for parole when he has served one-third of his sentence or four years, whichever is the lesser.[21] (There are exceptions to this rule for persons serving life imprisonment.) A person whose sentence is less than two years must apply for parole, whereas individuals serving more than two years will sometimes be reviewed for parole independent of the inmate's application.[22]

Several factors are taken into consideration when the board is considering paroling an inmate: his behaviour while serving his sentence, the crime for which he was convicted, his attitude towards rehabilitation, job potential upon release, and where and with whom he will live. In 1969 of all prison inmates who were eligible for parole (8,792), slightly over half were actually granted parole.[23] The 1975 statistics tell a different story; of the 17,000 inmates eligible, only 5,000 (36 percent) were granted parole.[24] This discretionary tightening of the use of parole is probably accounted for by an increased number of parole violations and a general hardening of public attitude toward parolees.

Conclusions

It is apparent that in the process of applying the criminal law many levels exist whereby those who are caught in the flow of the justice system can be filtered out for a variety of reasons. In its many and various forms, the use of discretionary judgement is practised either formally, with some kind of legal sanction, or informally as an individual choice of alternative action. Although discretion has inherent dangers in terms of the whole concept of fair play and justice, it can be seen that without discretion not only would the system break down through overload, but many marginal offenders would be hurt by "overkill."

The human element in the application of the criminal law is an integral aspect of the concept of justice; but because of the human element it will never be ideal. As the saying goes, to err is human; but there seem to be enough checks and balances throughout the system to address the problems which arise when mistakes are made.

In comparing Canadian society with other nations, the citizens of this country enjoy a secure lifestyle under a fairly sound legal and political umbrella. If discretionary enforcement is part of the reason the system works, then it must be intrinsic to the process. However, nobody has been able to formulate rules to fetter discretion. The reason is obvious: discretion means the freedom to break the rules.[25]

NOTES

1. *Report of the Canadian Committee on Corrections.* Ottawa: Information Canada, 1969, p. 16.
2. Lawrence M. Friedman. *Law and Society: an Introduction.* Toronto: Prentice-Hall, 1977, p. 130.
3. *Regina vs. Metropolitan Police ex parte Blackburn* (1968) 2 Q.B. 118.
4. *Bargain City U.S.A. Inc. vs. Dilworth* (1960) 29 U.S. Law Week 2002.
5. Metropolitan Toronto Police Board of Commissioners, Report on an Inquiry into Allegations Made Against Certain Members of the Metropolitan Toronto Police, 1976, p. 94.
6. *The Royal Commission on the Conduct of Police Forces at Fort Erie on the 11th of May 1974,* pp. 68-9.
7. Wexler, Mark, N., "Police Culture: A Response to Ambiguous Employment," in *The Administration of Criminal Justice in Canada.* Toronto: Holt, Rinehart and Winston of Canada Ltd., 1974, p. 141.
8. Brian A. Grosman. "The Discretionary Enforcement of Law," in *The Administration of Criminal Justice in Canada.* Toronto: Holt, Rinehart and Winston of Canada Ltd., 1974, p. 85.
9. Law Reform Commission of Canada, Working Paper 7: *Diversion.* Ottawa: Information Canada, 1974, p. 7.
10. *Ibid.,* p. 8.
11. Friedman, *Law and Society,* p. 130.
12. Grosman, "The Discretionary Enforcement of Law," p. 92.
13. Law Reform Commission of Canada; Working Paper 15: *Criminal Procedure Control of the Process.* Ottawa: Information Canada, 1975, p. 13.
14. Brian A. Grosman. "The Prosecutor: Discretion and Pre-trial Practices," in *The Administration of Criminal Justice in Canada,* p. 192.
15. David Capolwitz. *Consumers in Trouble: A Story of Debtors in Default.* New York: Free Press, 1974, pp. 218-19.
16. Grosman, "The Prosecutor: Discretion and Pre-trial Practices," p. 195.
17. F. Diamond. Lecture given at York University, 12 July 1976.
18. Grosman, "The Prosecutor: Discretion and Pre-trial Practices," p. 196.
19. John Hogarth. "Towards a Model of Sentencing Behaviour," in *The Administration of Criminal Justice in Canada,* p. 225.
20. Toronto *Sun,* 14 August 1977.
21. D. F. Cousineau and J. E. Veevers. "Incarceration as a Response to Crime: The Utilization of Canadian Prisons," in *The Administration of Criminal Justice in Canada* p. 245.
22. *Ibid.*
23. *Ibid.*
24. *Ibid.*
25. A. F. Wilcox. *The Decision to Prosecute.* London: Butterworth & Co., 1972, p. 112.

FURTHER READINGS

Bard, Morton and Robert Shellow. *Issues in Law Enforcement.* Reston, Virginia: Reston Publishing Co., 1976.
Boydell, Craig L., Grindstaff, Carl F. and Paul C. Whitehead. *The Administration of Criminal Justice in Canada.* Toronto: Holt, Rinehart & Winston, 1974.
Manning, Peter and John Van Maanen. *Policing: A View from the Street.* Santa Monica, Ca.: Goodyear Publishing Inc., 1978.
Niederhoffer, Arthur and Abraham S. Blumberg. *The Ambivalent Force: Perspectives on the Police.* Waltham, Mass.: Ginn & Co., 1979.
Vincent, Claude L. *Policeman.* Toronto: Gage Publishing, 1979.

Chapter 13

Police Discretion and Public Attitudes
J. W. Cooley

The maintenance of law and order is a function of the police, who, in criminal and quasi-criminal violations, are responsible for taking the first action against the citizen-offender. This first contact with the citizen is crucial, for the manner in which he is dealt with by the police may have considerable bearing on his subsequent behaviour and attitude toward the administration of justice.

Increased mobility and communication within the modern community have brought about a corresponding increase in police-citizen contact. The vibrancy of a changing and growing society has increased the need for regulatory laws and the demand for more policemen to enforce them. Provincial traffic laws may be cited as an example of regulatory laws greatly increasing contacts between citizens and the police at the formal level.

The police must have the support and co-operation of the public to maintain order, prevent and solve crimes. This can only come through citizen respect for the law and those who enforce it. There is, therefore, a very real responsibility resting with the police to deal effectively and fairly with citizens who violate the law. Common sense and good judgement must prevail, qualities that exist only when policemen have developed that sense of knowing the right thing to do, and when to do it.

There are those who believe that policemen are not required to think or use their judgement in making decisions. They claim that the police are given a set of laws and it is their duty to enforce them to the letter. Those who oppose that view believe that indiscriminate enforcement violates the spirit of the law, engendering a feeling of persecution that destroys the very feeling of justice the rule of law is supposed to foster and uphold. Whether policemen must always arrest when they have authority to do so, and whether they must always charge suspects when they have reasonable and probable grounds for doing so, are central issues involved in the question of discretionary police powers.

The exercise of discretion by the police is not a new phenomenon.

J. W. Cooley is an Inspector with the RCMP Detachment in Campbell River, B.C.

Policemen have made decisions on whether to arrest and charge offenders since the inception of the first organized police force. Yet the established and apparently accepted fact of discretionary law enforcement has raised questions of its legal, ethical and moral propriety. Although the police do resort to the use of discretion, there is an air of controversy and uncertainty as to whether or not they should. There is no clear-cut answer to the question: Do the majority of the public and the police believe that discretion should be exercised in the field of law enforcement?

Police departments maintain that they use discretion, but there is very little empirical evidence or police policy available to substantiate their claim. The public may be in favour of discretionary enforcement practices, but again, empirical evidence is lacking.

Police and the Law

> I solemnly swear that I will faithfully, diligently and impartially execute and perform the duties required of me as a member of the Royal Canadian Mounted Police, and will well and truly obey and perform all lawful orders and instructions that I receive as such, without fear, favour or affection of or towards any person. So help me God (2).

This is the oath of office taken by all applicants who are sworn in as members of the Royal Canadian Mounted Police. It is similar to the oath taken by most Canadian policemen. New members swear that they will enforce the law with diligence and impartiality, and without fear, favour or affection toward anyone. Policy statements such as the following show that the oath is open to interpretation as to the manner in which the law should be enforced: "A policy of firm enforcement should be followed but not so rigid as to suggest persecution" (21); when enforcing traffic laws "... written warnings may be issued for minor infractions in justifiable circumstances" (21). These two statements imply that to conform to the oath of office it is not mandatory that the law be enforced each and every time that it is violated. They seem to imply fairness and a common-sense approach to the task of enforcing the law, and that policemen be given the opportunity to use their discretion.

Laws are not legislated to be violated, they are enacted to be obeyed. They represent rights and privileges that the public deems necessary for the peaceful enjoyment of life and property. To encourage obedience, those who would disobey are threatened with punishment. To effect this punishment the public chooses from among them a group of fellow citizens to police the laws for them. Policemen are given limited extra powers to enforce the law, apprehend violators and prevent crime.

Enforcing the law is not an easy task. It is a common belief that the law specifies what a violation is. Those who would support that belief fail to recognize that the act that constitutes the offence becomes a violation only because of the interpretation placed upon it. The act does not come carrying a violation label spelling out all the details. If every offence was committed under identical circumstances, and if those circumstances were spelled out in the law, the problem of identifying the violation would be a relatively simple matter. These conditions, however, seldom if ever exist. The police must examine the circumstances of each case to determine if the act is in fact a violation.

The interpretation of the law evolves around its intent. The law seeks to preserve and guarantee the personal rights and freedom of the citizen, and it is important to realize that this protection could not be achieved unless the fundamental rights and freedom of all are respected. Hence the law cannot be preserved as an absolute order; it cannot be arbitrarily and blindly imposed so as to restrain and contain behaviour within the narrow limits of absolute goodness. It must be looked upon as rules of conduct designed to guide behaviour so that rights and freedoms may remain inviolate.

With this view of the law, the police function is not to sit back and wait for the rules of conduct to be violated and then seek out the offenders. In the minds of many, this has been the common view of the main function of the police. The law is best enforced, its aim is best achieved, when the prime responsibility of the police is the prevention of violations. The following statement identifies the objective that all police agencies should be working toward:

> There was a time when the number of convictions the policeman obtained was the criterion of his efficiency. Today the absence of crime in his area or on the beat is the yardstick of his success. Prevention as it is studied, practised and lived, is already paying dividends, and while there is a great need for active public support... police forces are committed to this modern practice (3).

Dedication to programs designed to prevent crime does not mean that the detection and investigation of crime should be relegated to a position of secondary importance. Detection is vital and so is successful investigation of crime committed. It does mean that charging the offender may be seen as the last step available to the policeman. If the ends of justice are best served by taking the offender to court, the officer has no choice but to ensure that court action is instituted.

If laws are rules to guide human conduct and the police function includes crime prevention as well as detection and apprehension, the objective is to ensure that the spirit of the law, rather than its letter, remains inviolate. This requires the police to make decisions as to the best course of action to be taken in any given situation. In a nutshell, policemen must understand the general intent and purpose of the law and analyze the details of each case as it comes before them, including the nature of the offence, the particular complainant and violator, and the general welfare of the public. Having done this, a decision is made on the course of action that will likely best ensure that the rights and freedoms of society (including the offender) are protected.

Considering the amount of law that exists to control today's society, it would be impossible to expect the police to charge everyone in violation, for as Jackson states:

> Policy about prosecution has in fact to keep within reasonable limits. A chief constable who decided to prosecute every ascertainable breach of the law would exhaust his force, overload officers of the courts, and be an appalling nuisance. If he decided to not prosecute any thieves at all, that would be so extreme as to be a dereliction of duty. It is a matter of degree (12, p. 50).

The awareness that prosecutions have to be kept within reasonable limits and that to do so requires the police to adopt discretionary police practices, marks one of the primary issues involved in arguments for and against the exercise of discretion in police work.

If the police are too effective, or overzealous in their efforts to protect the person and his property through enforcement of the law, they may infringe upon the very principles the law is supposed to protect. The public expect the police to be efficient, but at the same time they rebel against authority and infringement of personal freedom. They display an attitude of wanting the law to be enforced but not over-efficiently. For the police, this means striking an acceptable balance, if they are to obtain and maintain the respect of the public. For example, consider the remarks made by Selznick when discussing this critical issue:

> Do we need or want agencies of control so efficient and so impartial that every actual offence has an equal chance of being known and processed? . . . When considering this point, we should bear in mind that offences of all kinds are probably very much more numerous in fact than in record. I am concerned that we do not respond too eagerly and too well to the apparent need for more effective mechanisms of social control. In the administration of justice, if anywhere, we need to guard human values and forestall the creation of mindless machines for handling cases according to set routines (22, p. 84).

It is suggested that the police function has positive and negative roles. The protection of person and property by police presence and preventive measures are considered non-restrictive and positive; enforcement of the law, including restraints initiated by the police and courts, are considered restrictive and negative. In other words, the "helper" and "enforcer" images of the police may contradict each other. The pleasant part of police work relates to the helper image, where policemen are involved in such things as settling family quarrels without charges, locating lost children, and preventing crime in general. Unpleasant duties relate more to the enforcer image and include necessary responsibilities such as investigating fatal accidents and charging those who caused them and, in general, depriving citizens of their freedom through arrest and charge.

This dual role of the police has always been part of the police function and in earlier days presented no particular problem to the police. The enormous growth of regulatory laws during the past forty years has increased police-citizen contact to such an extent that the positive and negative counterparts in law enforcement frequently become intertwined, creating a dilemma for the policeman.

In considering the bulk of the law and the variety of behaviour it is intended to control, Jackson raises the following questions:

> Do all offences (from speed limits to murder) come within the single category of crime? If they do, are the problems of the enforcement of, for example, speed limits, any different from those of enforcing older and traditional criminal prohibitions against murder, robbery, burglary and so on? If they do not, so that we have separate categories of real crime and prohibitions that are not truly criminal, what effect may this have on the problem of enforcing the law? (12, p. 6)

The public may not be aware of what constitutes a criminal or non-criminal offence, but they are aware that some offences are serious and others are minor, and when they violate the law they expect to be treated according to the nature of the offence. The police also appreciate this difference and the public's expectation as to treatment. They are faced with the problem of effectively enforcing the law, and at the same time, satisfying the expectations of the public. This dilemma is primarily related to the enforcement of minor, or regulatory, laws.

The acceptance of police methods in handling minor offences is of vital importance, for to maintain law and order and to cope with serious criminal behaviour, the police need the co-operation of the public. If a policy of full enforcement of all minor laws were followed, public support would soon be lost and a state of lawlessness would evolve. LaFave, in his study of police discretion, supports this contention in stating that:

> If every policeman, every prosecutor, every court, and every post-sentence agency performed his or its responsibility in strict accordance with the rules of law, precisely and narrowly laid down, the criminal law would be ordered but intolerable (14, p. 72).

Police Discretion Defined

Discretion is the "ability to make decisions which represent a responsible choice for which an understanding of what is useful, right or wise may be presupposed." This is a typical dictionary definition. In relation to law and law enforcement, Roscoe Pound defines discretion as:

> An authority conferred by law to act in certain conditions or situations in accordance with an official's or an official agency's own considered judgement and conscience. It is an idea of morals, belonging to the twilight zone between law and morals (17, pp. 925-6).

Both definitions indicate that the use of discretion involves the making of decisions in choices of alternate procedures. Not to react in the usual way because one sees an alternate action that seems likely to enhance the possibility of attainment of a goal involves a discretionary decision. If one is denied that choice, he is also denied discretion. In law enforcement, the exercise of discretion is essentially the exercise of a power that results in the differential treatment of offenders.

There are four stages in the legal process where the police may resort to the use of discretion: non-enforcement of a particular law; non-recognition of a particular violation; non-arrest of a particular suspect; and non-charge of a particular suspect. Included are the issuing of warnings rather than charges, and the laying of one charge in preference to another. At whatever point discretion is exercised, the end result is always the same—differential treatment of offenders.

Authority for the Exercise of Police Discretion

Reviewing the literature on the use of police discretion, one finds that considerable attention has been given the subject by writers and those concerned with the administration of justice in the United States. This has taken place without any consensus being reached as to its legal propriety, or its moral desirability. On the one hand there are well-documented studies dealing with the legal issues involved, expressing opinions favourable to the exercise of police discretion (13, 14, 19, 20). There are also studies, equally documented, questioning the right of the police to use discretion (10, 11). With careful examination of this literature, the impression is that the Americans are hesitant to allow their police the power to make decisions that would constitute their using discretion. This has not, however, prevented them from doing so, for those who have studied law enforcement methods in the United States have produced ample evidence that discretion is exercised.

In Great Britain there is a more favourable attitude toward police resorting to the use of discretion. The right of the police to exercise discretion has been formally recognized by the courts on several occasions. Their attitude is reflected in the case of *Arrowsmith vs. Jenkins* (8). An advocate of nuclear disarmament, Ms. Arrowsmith was prosecuted under the Highways Act for obstructing the highway by permitting the audience she had attracted while speaking to remain standing on the road. She was asked to call the crowd in closer so as to leave the road clear, which she did. The people still partially blocked the highway and consequently, after a lapse of approximately twenty minutes, the police charged her and she was subsequently convicted.

On appeal it was argued that the police had previously permitted partial obstruction of the road, and had been present to clear an opening for traffic as it came along. The chief justice said that he could not concern himself with what had happened at other times, saying that the police could not prosecute every obstructor, and that it would be proper for them to exercise a wise discretion when to prosecute.

Little has been written on the subject of police discretion as it pertains to the Canadian scene. The *Report of the Canadian Committee on Corrections* (Ouimet Report) has one chapter dealing with various aspects of the police function (4, pp. 39–90). Only two pages (44–46) relate to police discretion and that in very broad terms. Nevertheless, the committee supported discretionary police practices, saying that:

> ... the element of the exercise of police discretion cannot be separated from law enforcement and that its complete elimination would not advance the ends of justice. We think that the decision not to prosecute and merely give a warning may best advance the ends of justice in some circumstances (4, pp. 45-6).

In a speech to the Canadian Association of Chiefs of Police in 1970, former Minister of Justice John Turner made the following statement when speaking in favour of police discretion:

> There is a widespread assumption that the police are not involved in making policy decisions but merely carry out neutral administrative functions of law enforcement. That's not so. You know that the police are involved in making policy decisions every day. One example where the police do make policy decisions is in the area of selective enforcement: when do you enforce and when do you not (24).

This is certainly support for the exercise of discretion by Canadian policemen.

In a study of the Metropolitan Toronto Police in relation to handling juveniles, Gandy (9) found ample evidence of discretion being used. He also found that many policemen regard the matter of using discretion as an individual decision each policeman must make. He failed to locate any clear policy on the exercise of discretion in general, and the manner in which police agencies (including the Metropolitan Toronto Police) expected their members to use their discretion.

Like Great Britain and the United States, Canada has no legislated authority covering discretionary police powers. While there are sectors of solid support for its use, the question of whether the police have the right to or should make discretionary decisions is not without controversy. The Ontario Police Act carries a section that states:

> The members of police forces ... are charged with the duty of preserving the peace, preventing robberies and other crimes and offences, including offences against the bylaws of the municipality, and apprehending offenders, and laying informations before the proper tribunal, and prosecuting and aiding in the prosecuting of offenders . . . and are liable to all the duties and responsibilities that belong to constables (16).

Watchorn sees this as a mandate for full enforcement of the law. He contends: "Nowhere have the police been delegated discretion not to invoke the criminal process in a situation which calls for its invocation" (25, p. 50). One could suggest that deciding which situation "calls for its invocation" and which does not is itself a question of discretion.

In referring to a matter involving the same Ontario Police Act, former Ontario Crown Attorney Peter K. McWilliams expressed a contrary view. He was critical of the Metropolitan Toronto Police Commission enquiry upholding discretion by senior officers in respect to laying charges (15). McWilliams explained that the commission's report supported the practice of senior officers dictating when, and under what circumstances, charges should be laid. To him this was ". . . a misconception of the power and the authority of a senior police officer or chief constable over a police constable." He explained that the jurisdiction of a police constable is an original jurisdiction that existed before the organization of disciplined police forces.

Police Discretion—A Canadian Study

As a policeman, the author was particularly aware of the controversy surrounding police use of discretion. Even among policemen, it is sensitive and not talked about, leaving one with the impression that although the police may properly exercise discretion, it should not be advertised for fear the public or perhaps another policeman may become aware of it. Police departments have been hesitant to admit that they advocate such practices, suggesting that the use of discretion when enforcing the law is considered a personal matter between the individual officer and the offender.

While policemen do use discretion in the performance of their duties, and while it could be assumed that the public expects them to do so, there was a lack of empirical evidence to substantiate such a statement. The attitudes of the Canadian public and police were really not known. This prompted the author to choose police discretion as a thesis topic while attending the Centre of Criminology, University of Ottawa during 1970–72 (5).

The survey was carried out within the boundaries of the city of Ottawa, Ontario, during the latter part of December 1970, and the first week of January 1971. Two randomly selected populations were used, one consisting of one hundred citizens and one comprised of one hundred policemen, the latter number being divided equally between members of the Ottawa City Police and the RCMP. The survey was accompanied by personal interviews and the completion of a questionnaire by the respondent at the time of contact.

Both the public and the police agreed that the use of discretion should vary with the circumstances of the case. Responses revealed that 82 percent of the public and 83 percent of the police disagreed with the statement that the police should charge everyone who commits an offence, regardless of the nature of the offence and other circumstances surrounding it. The question was repeated in slightly different form in order to compare the respondents' responses to what they felt was the public attitude. Responses were almost identical, with 80 percent of the public, and 85 percent of the police stating that they did not believe the public would want the police to charge everyone under the circumstances noted above. The similarity in responses suggests that the favourable attitude to the use of discretion is not necessarily a reflection of personal feeling, but is conceived of as reflecting the attitudes of the general public.

The responses to the questionnaire also revealed that discretion should come into play when charges are being considered. Very positive responses were made to the statement that the police should have the right to issue a warning rather than lay a charge when they felt a warning would best serve the purpose, with 94 percent of the public and 88 percent of the police agreeing.

The classification of offences into categories of serious and minor influenced attitudes toward charging all offenders; 91 percent of the public and 90 percent of the police contended that offenders should always be charged when serious offences were involved. When the offence was a minor one, only 17 percent of the public and 13 percent of the police favoured invariable charging.

A review of the literature and the analysis of the survey data resulted in the following conclusions:

1. Those in Canada responsible for the administration of justice favour discretionary practices.
2. There is no legal authority for the police use of discretion excepting the police powers of arrest under the Criminal Code.
3. Both the public and the police favour the exercise of discretion by the police. Its use in relation to the question of charges in serious offences was close to being evenly split, for and against, for both sample populations.
4. Both populations realized that the use of discretion necessarily discriminates in the type of treatment that will be afforded one offender as compared to another, but both did not regard this as undesirable. It is considered the natural outcome of discretion rather than discrimination.
5. The public were more in favour of the police use of discretion than were the police. Although the preference was only slightly pronounced, it is an interesting finding. It questions the often heard statement that the police favour discretion but are afraid to use it because the public are opposed to such practices.
6. Individuals in the public and police populations did not expect differential treatment for themselves when in violation of the law. They were aware of the division of offences into minor and serious categories and expected offenders to be dealt with accordingly.
7. In the case where discretion was expected to be used, both populations wanted the police to look beyond the narrow confines of the evidence to the total circumstances of the case. They indicated that it was the circumstances surrounding the violation which often affected its classification as serious or minor. The police were more inclined to consider circumstances than were the public. For example, given an offence and a minimum description of the circumstances, the public showed a marked preference for the issuance of warnings, whereas the police were noticeably in favour of deferring their decision until they were aware of all the circumstances. The public made a final decision while the police held back. This is regarded as an important finding, for it is not uncommon to hear the remark that policemen see things as either black or white and have no concern for the grey area in between. Police responses to various questions in the study seemed to refute such an assumption.

NOTES and FURTHER READINGS

1. Banton, Michael, (1964). *The Policeman in the Community.* London: Tavistock Publications, 1959.
2. Canada (1970). *Royal Canadian Mounted Police Act.* Revised Statutes of Canada, 1970, C.R.9, S.15.
3. Canada (1952). *Law and Order in a Canadian Democracy.* Ottawa: The Queen's Printer.
4. Canada (1969). *Report of the Canadian Committee on Corrections.* Ottawa: The Queen's Printer.
5. Cooley, James W. *Police Discretion: Law and Equity.* Ottawa: University of Ottawa Centre of Criminology. Unpublished M.A. Dissertation, 1972.
6. Courtis, M. C. *Attitudes to Crime and the Police in Toronto: A Report of Some Survey Findings.* Toronto: University of Toronto Centre of Criminology, 1970.
7. Cressey, Donald R. "What Can Be Done," in Gresham M. Sykes and Thomas E. Drabek, *The Law and the Lawless.* New York: Random House, 1969, pp. 271-282.
8. England. *Arrowsmith vs. Jenkins* 1963, 2 Q.B. 561.
9. Gandy, John M. *The Exercise of Discretion by the Police in the Handling of Juveniles.* Toronto: University of Toronto School of Social Work. Unpublished Ph.D. Dissertation, 1967.
10. Goldstein, Joseph. "Police Discretion Not to Invoke the Criminal Process: Low Visibility Decisions in the Administration of Justice." *Yale Law Review,* 69, 1960, pp. 543-94.
11. Hall, Jerome. "Police and the Law in a Democratic Society." *Indiana Law Journal,* 28, 133-77, 1953.
12. Jackson, R. M. *Enforcing the Law.* London: Macmillan Company, 1967.
13. LaFave, Wayne R. "The Police and Non-enforcement of the Law." *Wisconsin Law Review,* Part 1, 104-37, 1962.
14. LaFave, Wayne R. *Arrest: The Decision Not to Take a Suspect into Custody.* Boston: Little, Brown and Company, 1965.
15. McWilliams, Peter K. "The Need to Screen Charges by the Police." *Globe and Mail,* Toronto, 6 November 1970, p. 7.
16. Ontario (1970). *The Police Act.* Revised Statutes of Ontario, C.351, S.55.
17. Pound, Roscoe. "Discretion, Dispensation and Mitigation: The Problem of the Individual Case." *New York University Law Review,* 35, 925-26, 1960.
18. Quinney, Richard. *Crime and Justice in Society.* Boston: Little, Brown and Company, 1969.
19. Remington, Frank J. "The Law Relating to on the Street Detention, Questioning and Frisking of Suspected Persons, and Police Arrest Privileges in General." *Journal of Criminal Law, Criminology and Police Science,* 51, 386-94, 1960.
20. Remington, Frank J. and Victor Rosenblum. "The Criminal Law and the Legislative Process." *University of Illinois Law Forum,* 12, 481-99, 1960.
21. RCMP. *Royal Canadian Mounted Police Policy Manual.*
22. Selznick, Philip. "Foundations of Theory of Organization." *American Sociological Review,* 13, 82-92, 1948.
23. Turner, John. "The Police in a Confrontation Society." *Royal Canadian Mounted Police Gazette,* 32, pp. 3-8, 1970.
24. Turner, John. *The Police in a Confrontation Society.* Speech to the Canadian Association of Chiefs of Police, London, Ontario, 4 September, 1970.
25. Watchorn, D. J. "Abuse of Police Powers: Reasons, Effect and Control." *Faculty of Law Review,* University of Toronto, 24, pp. 48-69, 1966.
26. *Webster's Third International Dictionary of the English Language.* Springfield: G. and C. Merriam Co., 1963.
27. Wilson, James Q. *Varieties of Police Behavior.* Cambridge: Harvard University Press, 1968.

Chapter 14

Specialized Police Response to the Juvenile: the Ottawa Police Force Youth Liaison Section

Golden Leeson and Arn Snyder

The subject of this chapter is the Police Juvenile Section. Specifically, it will deal with the Ottawa Police Force Youth Liaison Section (YLS) and will discuss its *raison d'être*, philosophical base, organizational structure and relationship with the force and with other agencies. The various responses employed by the section toward the juvenile offender will also be examined.

In reading this chapter, it should be realized that there are, within the police milieu, numerous approaches used by police forces to deal with juveniles and that employed by the Ottawa Police Force is only one of these. This approach is found to be the most effective within the situational context of the Ottawa Police; however, other police forces may find that certain aspects of this method are not relevant or of value to their particular situation.

This not withstanding, it is hoped that this chapter is read with the perspective that it is through the exchange of ideas and approaches that the police function will become more efficient and effective in servicing the community.

The Formation and Philosophy of the Youth Liaison Section

In recent years in Canada, the interaction between the various components of the criminal justice system and the juvenile offender has become a topic of concern. As a result of this increased interest, innovations have been introduced in several areas. One such area is the police field, where during the late Fifties and early Sixties many police forces established specific sections within their organizations

Golden Leeson is a Staff Sergeant with the Ottawa Police Force and has spent fifteen years in the Criminal Investigation Division. He is presently assigned to the Morality Section.

Arn Snyder is a Sergeant with the Ottawa Police Force and under the Criminal Investigation Division is presently assigned to the Youth Liaison Section and the Morality Section.

The authors would like to thank Chief Leo J. Seguin and Deputy Chief Thomas E. Welsh for their comments and assistance.

to deal with the juvenile offender. The Ottawa Police Force was one of these. In 1964 it established a section whose role was that of a liaison between the juvenile offender and the multitude of criminal justice and social agencies.

Originally the youth section was established when it became apparent that certain needs, with regard to the juvenile offender, were not effectively being met. Basic to this realization was the growing awareness felt both by the public and the police that the police agencies should expand their role in the area of juvenile crime prevention and rehabilitation.

Subsequently it was observed that to function effectively in this field it was necessary for the police to increase their knowledge of juvenile delinquency in the region, to respond in a consistent and purposeful manner to delinquent behaviour and to use effectively the resource agencies of the area. To facilitate this, a section was established whose responsibility was:

1. to co-ordinate the force's activities in relation to the youth of the city;
2. to operate a central file and index system to allow for the study and analysis of delinquency;
3. to develop and maintain liaisons with the network of social agencies and professionals;
4. to determine the disposition of a juvenile who comes in contact with the force;
5. to establish appropriate responses to juvenile delinquency problems.

Presently these aims still represent the *raison d'être* for the section.

Although the YLS was established as a separate section, it operates under the same philosophical principles as other sections within the force. A youth officer remains a policeman and must view his primary role as protection of society and perceive that all individuals, regardless of age, be held accountable for their actions. Police officers, regardless of their functions, are aware that inherent in the protection of society principle is the integration of an effective law enforcement approach with a meaningful crime prevention program. They recognize that to establish and maintain a safe society, it is necessary that police action be based not only on the detection of criminal activity, but also on the prevention of opportunities and conditions that assist in the development of criminal behaviour. A police officer transferred to the YLS does not become any less a police officer with regard to this goal.

Under the Juvenile Delinquents Act, however, a differentiation has been made, based on age, concerning the manner in which an individual accused of an offence is handled. This procedural differentiation is viewed as the basis for the police use of discretion in dealing with juveniles. Discretion is a key element in police-juvenile interaction. The act does not specifically present directions to the police as to the method by which a juvenile is to be treated. However, it offers general principles to guide the police in their handling of the juvenile. These principles can be found in Section 3(2) and 38 of the Act:

> Section 3(2). Where a child is adjudged to have committed a delinquency he shall be dealt with, not as an offender, but as one in a condition of delinquency and therefore requiring help, guidance and proper supervision.

> Section 38. This Act shall be liberally construed to the end that its purpose may be carried out, namely that the care and custody and discipline of a juvenile delinquent shall approximate as nearly as may be that which should be given by its parents, and that as far as practicable every juvenile delinquent shall be treated, not as criminal, but as a misdirected and misguided child, and one needing aid, encouragement, help and assistance.

The concepts expressed in the above passages are interpreted as reflecting general principles of procedure to be employed when a juvenile becomes involved with the criminal justice system. They are not viewed by the Ottawa Police Force to be in contradiction to the police role of community protection, but rather as complementing this role. This position is supported in the book *Juvenile Justice Administration*, published in 1973 by the International Association of Chiefs of Police:

> The police are usually the first official representatives of society to take action when the behaviour of a youngster is contrary to public welfare. It is the policeman, then, who, on behalf of the people, steps in to stop the offending behaviour and take control of the offender so that he will ultimately be required to answer for his transgressions. The policeman functions as a public agent of discipline and order. He performs *police* functions—functions which must be carried out regardless of the age of the offender.
> The difference is in the method rather than the objective insofar as juvenile offenders are concerned.
> His conduct is no less antisocial because he is a child. Nonetheless, because of his immaturity and because there is hope that the plasticity of youth will permit correction and reform, public policy has dictated that he will not be treated as an adult criminal would be for the same offence.[1]

Here also, the policeman's role as a member of the network of social agencies within the community can be seen to be a function of this philosophy. The position is supported by the Ottawa Police Force:

> The police have a responsibility to bring to the attention of other youth-serving agencies situations that fall within their proper jurisdiction. They have a responsibility to seek information from and to

encourage close co-operation with these other agencies. Of course, the
converse is also true. Police department policies, therefore, must be in
harmony with those of the juvenile court and other youth-serving
agencies.[2]

Therefore, although the YLS is viewed as functioning under the
same philosophical umbrella as the other sections of the force (i.e.,
protection of society), the YLS has been assigned added tools as
expressed in the *parens patraie* principle (state assuming the
responsibilities of the parents). This principle is found in both the
federal Juvenile Delinquents Act and provincial child welfare legislation. John Gandy, a Canadian police researcher in juvenile delinquency, acknowledges this situation.

> Although the police must make disposition decisions in the case of
> violations by adults as well as juveniles, two factors operate to give
> dispositional decisions more visibility and a character quite unlike
> that of decisions when adults are involved. First, police discretion in
> the handling of juveniles, despite its questionable legal basis, has been
> sanctioned by police and court practices. Secondly, the range of
> actions available to the police in their handling of juveniles who
> violate, or are alleged to have violated, the law is greater than that for
> handling adults suspected of, or who have committed, comparable
> offences.[3]

Structure and Position Within Force

At the conception of the YLS, three officers comprised the total
personnel. Approximately fifteen years later this figure has grown
to seventeen officers, consisting of an inspector, a staff sergeant, two
sergeants and thirteen constables. As it can be seen in Figure 14-1,
five constables are engaged in the school safety-patrol program and
two constables in the children's safety-village program. The remaining six constables are responsible for the processing of juveniles who
come in contact with the section.

The inspector is responsible for the overall functioning of the YLS
and two other sections within the criminal investigation division.
The responsibilities of the staff sergeant encompass the administration of the YLS, and he is responsible for the final decision as to the
juvenile's disposition. The two sergeants co-ordinate the activities of
the thirteen constables and are available for consultation regarding
serious or complicated cases.

The five school-patrol officers are authorized to co-ordinate the
school patrol system consisting of approximately 4,000 school
patrols within 118 schools. Since its establishment in 1946, there has
not been a single child fatality at a location assigned to a school
patrol. These officers give bilingual safety lectures in such areas as
pedestrian safety, bicycle safety and the block-parent programs.

The two officers assigned to the children's safety village are responsible for presenting films, lectures and demonstrations on a year-round basis to all school boards of the region. The village is separate from the station and consists of model buildings, streets, traffic signs and lights. Here students from nursery to Grade 6 can actually take part in safety demonstrations.

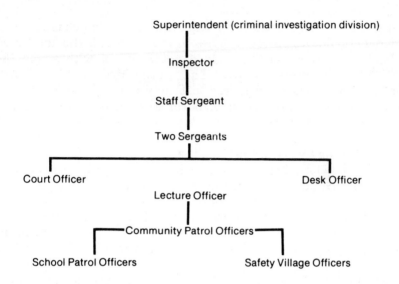

Figure 14 - 1
Youth liaison section.

The six youth patrol officers—five males and one female, working two shifts—are responsible for: liaison with juvenile court; maintenance of the social-history card-filing system; processing of juveniles coming in contact with the section; operation of various preventive programs. Although the YLS is under the criminal investigation division (CID), it is not responsible for investigating a case; that is, determining whether or not there are grounds for a charge. This specific responsibility has been assigned to the actual investigating sections, the detective or morality branch, as the case may be. The question as to whether a section dealing with juvenile offenders should be responsible for investigating cases has been debated over the years, and it is apparent that there are advantages and disadvantages for both sides. The Ottawa Police feel, at this point, that it is more beneficial for the community, the juvenile and the police that the investigative function of the police role be assigned to a separate section. It is felt that the youth officer can communicate and deal with the juvenile more effectively and openly if he is not viewed as the investigating officer.

As a result of this separation, it has been necessary for the YLS and the investigating sections to maintain a close and harmonious relationship. This has been successfully achieved, partly, it is felt, as a result of the in-service training programs that have given the youth officer an opportunity to explain the objectives of the youth section to members of the CID.

A good working relationship with the uniform branch is also considered crucial. As various studies have shown, it is the uniformed police officer and not the trained youth officer with whom the majority of juveniles interact.[4] The youth officer deals only with those juveniles who have filtered past the uniform officer. According to one Canadian study, this would be three out of every eight juveniles reported to the police.[5]

Several methods have been established to assist in maintaining and improving this relationship. First, all the youth officers work in uniform, therefore there is a visual identity with the approximately three hundred uniformed officers. Secondly two "community" cars were established, whose basic purpose was to develop and maintain a liaison with community centres of the city. The personnel (eight police officers) for these cars were drawn from the uniformed contingent but they communicate on a daily basis with the YLS. In this way, a link was established with the uniformed men. Thirdly, candidates for the YLS are drawn primarily from the uniform members to relate on a personal basis to the YLS officers.

However, basic to this discussion of the relationship between the youth section and other sections is the concept that, within the Ottawa Police Force, every police officer, whether uniformed or not, is considered a youth officer. The police officers in the youth section are not seen as having a monopoly in the handling of juveniles. Further, the youth officers working in uniform are readily identifiable to both the adult and juvenile community and interact and respond effectively to their needs.

Selection and Training of Personnel
The selection of a youth officer is made by the chief and his executive officers and is considered a serious decision. It has been expressed that within the majority of police forces the youth section has not achieved a high degree of acceptance and status; however, within the Ottawa Police Force that is not the case.[6]

Specific attributes are looked for in the candidates so that they will become effective youth officers. First, the officer must have at least five years' service on the force. This position is taken for two reasons.

One is to allow for the development of all facets of police work in the individual: The Ottawa Police Force perceives its police officers as "generalists" and to transfer an individual into more specialized area without that individual having experienced general police duties would be detrimental to that officer and to the force over-all. Secondly, to maintain the crucial rapport with the uniform section, it is necessary that the youth officers be respected, and this can be achieved more easily if the members of the uniform section and youth section have known each other personally through working together over a period of time.

Another attribute required is an interest in the field of police-juvenile relations. Both on-duty and off-duty activity with juveniles is examined with this in mind. A third aspect is the ability to interact socially without becoming easily frustrated. It is recognized by the police force that the youth officer is frequently placed in situations where patience is required.

Orientation and the initial training stage for the novice officer are co-ordinated by a senior youth officer. Further, the novice is required to submit a brief on any topic dealing with police-juvenile relations. The content of the brief is then discussed with his supervisors, with the purpose of making this process a learning experience for the novice.

After gaining experience with the section, the youth officer can be chosen to attend specialized courses at either the Ontario Police College in Aylmer, Ontario, or the Canadian Police College in Ottawa. Here specific courses on juvenile delinquency, drugs, lecturing techniques and police administration are given. Further, the Ottawa Police Force supports the youth officer attending related courses at the community college and university level. In this area, the Ottawa Police Force perceives the importance of combining police experience with knowledge of the existing literature on juvenile delinquency. For example, one member of the YLS has recently completed his masters degree in criminology, with a specialization in police-juvenile relations.

Operation of Youth Liaison Section

In 1977 there were 3,969 YLS juvenile contacts recorded; of those, 1,831 involved the alleged commission of an offence by a juvenile, while the remainder could be classified under the broad label of the child welfare concept. The method of operation strived for within the YLS is one that can effectively respond to all the varied demands made upon it by the community.

As the YLS is viewed as an information and referral center rather than an investigative or counseling body, the maintenance and updating of the social-history card-filing system is a crucial part of the operation of the section. At present, there are approximately five thousand cards on file, which are constantly being reviewed so that they will be currently valid and to purge the files of individuals who have gained adult status.

A juvenile's name is placed on the social-history card as a result of a police report being submitted, indicating an involvement in an offence (federal, provincial or municipal), or indicating that a juvenile requires some form of assistance. Juveniles who appear in police reports as witnesses, however, would not be placed on a social-history card. Other information placed on the card includes such particulars as date of birth, address, school and parents' names. If the juveniles were accompanied by friends who were also involved, their names are placed on the card. Further, the reason for the contact with the police is noted, and when the appropriate cause of action is determined it is placed on the card.

The social-history cards are not part of the criminal records system but are considered a completely separate filing system. The social-history cards are filed in the YLS office itself, which is located on a different floor from both the criminal records section and the investigative section. Philosophically, the social-history card is viewed as an element of the *parens patraie* concept rather than a legal record. That is, the purpose of the social-history card is to provide information to the youth officer in order that he can determine the most appropriate action to take, according to the philosophy expressed in the Juvenile Delinquents Act. The youth officer's access to knowledge of a juvenile's past behaviour is considered one of the main criteria in determining a disposition, and therefore the social-history card is viewed as a very important element.

In addition to examining the juvenile's past behaviour, the youth officer also explores other factors of the situation that are seen to be relevant in deciding an effective disposition. These are:

1. Attitude of the juvenile toward such areas as the offence, the law and his guardians;
2. Attitude of the guardians toward such areas as the juvenile, the offence and the law;
3. Type of offence, degree of sophistication, personal injury and property damage;
4. Age of the juvenile;
5. Juvenile's behaviour and social interaction in situations both in the home and outside the home;
6. Range of referrals available at the time.

Where a juvenile is accused of an offence and the facts and circumstances are sufficient to substantiate a charge, the youth officer has a choice of two courses of action. These are: charging the juvenile with the offence and proceeding through juvenile court; or deferring action (DA), not exercising legal proceedings and relying on the youth officer, the guardians and/or a social agency to handle the problem. To assist the youth officer in determining whether a juvenile should be charged with an offence, the Ottawa Police Force has established several guidelines to be considered at the time of the decision. These guidelines are not seen as rules to be rigidly followed, but rather as general working principles. Decisions as to disposition can and do vary from those indicated in the guidelines. The guidelines are:

1. Involvement in offences against persons where there has been violence or personal injury will result in juvenile court proceedings;
2. Involvement in offences where there has been serious property damage or financial loss will result in juvenile court proceedings;
3. Involvement in offences where there has been an assault on a police officer or other person in authority will result in juvenile court proceedings;
4. Involvement in criminal code firearm offences, including possession and threatened use, will result in juvenile court proceedings;
5. Involvement in offences where a weapon was used or threatened to be used against another will result in juvenile court proceedings;
6. Involvement in serious group activity where violence or intimidation has been a factor will result in juvenile court proceedings;
7. Involvement in a Criminal Code offence when at the same time the juvenile is or has been active with the court, for example, probation, case pending, will result in juvenile court proceedings;
8. Involvement in a Criminal Code offence when there have been two previous Criminal Code contacts with police, where deferred action was taken, will result in juvenile court proceedings.

These guidelines do not in any way affect the accused juvenile's right to choose to proceed through juvenile court if there is a disagreement as to the legal facts of the case. The juvenile, like the adult, has the right to take his case to court. In addition to the guidelines, the YLS maintains a close liaison with the Crown Attorney's Office, communicating frequently with this office concerning dispositions and referrals to be taken by the YLS. The decision to proceed through juvenile court is viewed very carefully and it not considered lightly. Statistics for 1977 showed that only 399 offences out of 1,831 proceeded to juvenile court.

To avoid further discriminatory handling of a juvenile, an aspect that John Gandy refers to in his study of one Canadian police force, "quality control" is present through the youth officer's consultation with his sergeants and staff sergeant.[7] As the YLS does not contain a large number of personnel, it is possible for the supervisors to become familiar with and to assist in the decision-making process. When there is a problem as to the nature of the decision made, the youth officer can outline his reasons for deciding upon a certain course of action and discuss them with his supervisors.

In deferring action, the youth officer has determined that the situation can be handled by the police, parent(s) and/or social agency. It is by this method that the majority of juvenile contacts with the YLS are handled. In 1977 1,432 chargeable offences out of 1,831 were processed by deferred action.

Deferred action can extend from the simple reprimand of the juvenile and a conversation with the guardian to a more in-depth examination of the juvenile's situation, involving home and office interviews and communication with various social agencies. An example of the reprimand and release to parents is found in shoplifting

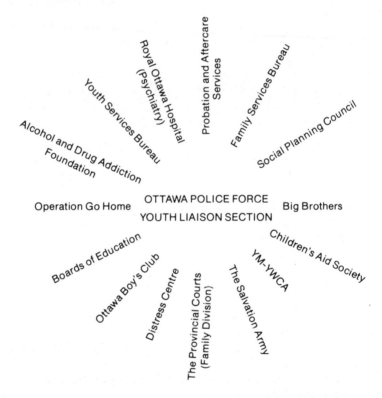

Figure 14 - 2
The PIP Program.

occurrences. The majority of these are first offences, the amount taken is minor and is recovered, and both juveniles and guardian express the idea that this behaviour will not occur again. In cases such as these, to proceed either through the juvenile court system or attempt to involve a social agency would only serve to clog an already over-burdened system.

However, the YLS does become involved in situations where some form of social assistance is required, and it is at this point that the youth officer's intimate knowledge of the various social agencies within the community is of crucial importance. In 1977 this section made numerous referrals to various agencies and the YLS is aware that referral to the appropriate agency represents a saving in time, money and human discomfort. It is for these reasons that the YLS is active in representing itself as a resource for the network of agencies, requesting advisory positions on the governing bodies of the agencies. Personal contact by the youth officers with line workers of these agencies is actively encouraged.

To discuss the working relationship between each individual agency (see Figure 14-2) would be, it is felt, too cumbersome; however, one program that has been instituted on an experimental basis for one year will be discussed.

The program is the Preventive Intervention for Juveniles at the Pre-Court Level (PIP), which was established on December 1, 1976, between the Ottawa Police Force and the Ontario Probation/Aftercare Services. The program was established:

> . . . to divert . . . from the juvenile court first-time juvenile offenders. Underlying this purpose was the assumption that alternative methods to involving such youngsters in the court process and the juvenile justice system were needed. Furthermore, it was the belief of police, probation/aftercare staff and others working directly with children that there should be avenues through which community services would be available to the child and his/her family without immersing them in the court system.[8]

The objectives of the program are:

1. To intervene in a preventive way at the pre-court level;
2. To curtail ongoing delinquency;
3. To mediate on behalf of the child with parents and other interested individuals or agencies;
4. To provide the family with support and reassurances, in light of their obvious anxiety;
5. To expose the juvenile justice system to the child, as opposed to exposing the child to the system;
6. To provide the family with the basic information—namely, a network of resources available within the immediate community;

7. To prevent the type of conditioning that would appear prevalent with the "one more chance" concept;
8. To offer police and PACO staff a better insight and understanding of the other's responsibility;
9. To complement the already established preventive program at the elementary and high school levels respectively.

A further aspect that the YLS perceives to be crucial is the idea that the program is voluntary, and PIP is not suggested until deferred action has been taken. The purpose of this is to avoid any feeling of coercion on the part of the persons involved. As the PIP program is still experimental, a complete evaluation is not available; however, the YLS has found it to be a viable avenue for referrals. Since its inception, 101 individuals have been accepted by PIP, (two other cases were rejected) and twelve cases have appeared in juvenile court subsequent to participating in PIP.

The YLS's utilization of the various social agencies in the community such as the probation/aftercare services in the PIP program can be viewed as an activity established to respond to specific problematic situations. To have effective programs such as these is obviously essential. The YLS also strives to develop programs aimed at alleviating the potential for trouble.

An example of this approach is the enforcement of the curfew regulations found in the Child Welfare Act of Ontario. Although these regulations were in effect since 1964, their enforcement was informal. The YLS proposed that a formalized program enforcing the curfew be instituted, as indications emerged that juveniles were becoming victimized and exploited through their involvement in the commission of offences during the late evening hours. A system was established whereby juveniles found to be "loitering" after 10 p.m. are instructed to return home. Their guardians are subsequently notified by letter of this contact and a copy of the regulations indicating what further action could be taken is also included.

Indications at this time would appear to point in a positive direction. The public, it would seem, supports the program, as only one complaint has been recorded. The juvenile population, many of whom perceived it as a direct harassment tool to be used by the police, mellowed in their opinion when the mass media and actual police behaviour indicated that discretion would be employed and a broad interpretation given to the term "loitering." For the YLS, positive support for the enforcement of the curfew was found when the number of chargeable offences involving juveniles over a two-month period prior to the formal curfew enforcement was compared with the same two-month period during the enforcement. It was found that the number of chargeable offences had decreased by 39 percent. Although it is recognized that there is no actual direct correlation, it is felt that a portion of the decrease can be attributed to the curfew.

A second example of taking positive action is the "youth and the law" lectures that each youth officer is responsible for presenting. The objective of these presentations is to convey to the juveniles an idea of the role of the YLS and the legal system under which it operates. It is hoped also that the consequences and seriousness of becoming involved in the criminal justice system will be considered and be effective in preventing further illegal behaviour. The YLS also establishes "specific subject" lectures to be presented in response to particular problem areas or to be given to selected audiences. Lectures on such areas as shoplifting, drug and alcohol abuse are examples of this approach. By developing in this direction the YLS's objective is to retain flexibility in responding to the youth milieu.

Conclusion

In any discussion of the concept of a youth section, a characteristic that emerges quite distinctly is the changing relationship and interaction between the police and the juvenile. The legal system, the police and the juveniles themselves are all experiencing pressures for alterations within their milieu.

A police officer will find that the element of change is the rule rather than the exception. As the establishment of a youth section is a relatively new phenomenon in Canada (with the majority of Canadian police forces establishing youth sections in the Sixties), there is much exploration and experimentation occurring at present. Programs and policies are being tested by the various police forces in an attempt to find the appropriate response to their situations.

Further, the basic structure on which the police function—the law—is presently undergoing analysis for possible changes. As the Juvenile Delinquents Act (1929) was originally established under a social welfare philosophy, with little concern for legal concepts, present proposals have been put forward recommending a more amenable union of social concern for the juvenile and the legal elements of the juvenile's situation. This process is presently occurring and the result is that the police officer, although functioning under this perspective, is also mindful of the merging points of view as seen in the proposed new legislation.

Thirdly, the police are not only functioning in a relatively new organizational context, under a changing philosophy and policy, but also are relating to a population that is constantly changing. The modern-day youth's rapid acceptance and rejection of various values and behaviours add further complexity to police-juvenile relations. This situation necessitates that the police be receptive and responsive to these varied lifestyles and attitudes.

To facilitate the development of a more effective and efficient response, the police community must be constantly examining and evaluating their programs and be open for suggestions for improvement from outside sources. In addition to acquainting the reader with the Ottawa Police Youth Liaison Section, an added purpose of this chapter is to present various concepts and approaches, in order that they can be evaluated. By doing this police-juvenile relations can be improved to the benefit of the community.

To stimulate discussion the authors pose the following questions: what is the future direction of police in the urban environment and what is the dominant issue facing the juvenile officer in the next five years?

NOTES

1. Richard Kobetz and Betty Bosage. *Juvenile Justice Administration.* International Association of Chiefs of Police, 1973, pp. 112-3.
2. *Ibid.*, p. 113.
3. John Gandy. "The Exercise of Discretion by the Police as a Decision-Making Process in the Disposition of Juvenile Offender," *Osgoode Hall Law Journal*, Vol. 8, No. 2, 1970, p. 329.
4. Arn Snyder. *The Street Policeman's Perceptions of the Juvenile Criminal Offender.* Ottawa: University of Ottawa, 1977, M.A. Thesis, p. 17.
5. John Gandy. *The Exercise of Discretion by the Police in the Handling of Juveniles.* Toronto: University of Toronto, 1970, Ph.D., Dissertation, p. 94.
6. Frank L. Manella. "Exploding the Myths About Juvenile Delinquency," *The Police Chief*, June 1975, p. 61.
7. John Gandy. *The Exercise of Discretion by the Police as a Decision-Making Process in the Disposition of Juvenile Offender*, p. 343.
8. Ken Kealey and Pierre Deschamps. *Program Bulletin* (PIP) (Ottawa: Probation and Aftercare Services of Ontario, 1977).

FURTHER READINGS

Hagan, J., "The Labelling Perspective, The Delinquent, and the Police—a Review of Literature." Canadian Journal of Criminology and Corrections, 14, 150-65, 1972.
Kobetz, R. W. and B. B. Bosage. *Juvenile Justice Administration.* Gaithersburg, Maryland: International Association of Chiefs of Police Inc., 1973.
Moyer, S., Doob, A. and V. Stewart. *The Pre-Judicial Exercise of Discretion and Its Impact on Children: A Review of the Literature.* Toronto: University of Toronto, 1975.

Chapter 15

Culture, Values and Policing Minority Groups
A. S. Lussier

The advent of television was supposed to mark a new era of understanding in Canada. People were now to view programs of other countries and note the harsh realities. Canadians were also to learn about themselves. Unfortunately, few Canadian content programs truly reflect the history and culture of minority groups in this country.

Few documentaries really describe the culture of a minority group. To define French-Canadian culture as being able to speak French is hogwash. One must also learn to think and value certain things the way a French Canadian does. The same can be said about Pakistanis, West Indians, Doukhobors, etc. When it comes to knowing anything or learning anything about minority groups in this country, Canadians are downright ignorant. I would add also that few Canadians (in proportion to the population) know anything about the history of their province or other provinces. The reason is simple: we are all too content with our lot. If troubles or conflicts arise, it is the other person or group's fault. *They* will not conform.

Police officers can oftentimes be classified as individuals who know very little about those with whom they are going to deal. Granted that is a very broad generalization, but unfortunately there have been too many cases of police–minority group conflicts in which minorities have claimed a lack of understanding on the part of police officers to state otherwise.

This paper then, is an attempt to develop some insights into the problems of policing minority groups. Native people will be used as an example in trying to develop an understanding of minorities. Details on culture and values of minority groups will form a good part of this paper, since it is vital that one understands one's position in relation to others.

The term culture can best be summarized as the total way of life of a group of people. It should be noted that culture is contemporary and in constant flux. Culture is not static.

Everyone in this country supposedly belongs to the Canadian

A. S. Lussier is Chairman, Nature Studies Department, Brandon University and previously taught at the Canadian Police College in Ottawa.

and/or North American culture. Minority groups in this country tend to cling to elements of their heritage and thus promote the concept of multiculturalism, claiming themselves to be unique within the Canadian mosaic. That in itself is one of the major problems of our country. The point I am trying to make is simply this: people tend to confuse heritage and culture. Thus one oftentimes has to contend with an individual who wishes to attach himself to a romantic past and calls it his culture.

Canadian "culture groups" are unique in that some of them base their way of life on religious beliefs (Hutterites, Doukhobors); language (French, Ukrainian); economic conditions (Indian, Métis); etc. Because of these differences in their cultural traditions, such "culture groups" or "minority groups" develop value systems that are different than the Canadian norm. The police officer who has to deal with any of these specific groups should be well aware of the values he will be confronting.

Values are the most important element of a culture. All people have a set of values that has developed within their immediate milieu. Since culture is determined by one's immediate environment, the impact of which are immeasurable, it follows then that one's values reflects one's upbringing in a particular area.

A nun once told me that she could tell whether our drinking cups at home were made of plastic or china by the manner in which I drank from any cup. I thought it absurd, but I now see her point. One can judge others by such trivial idiosyncracies.

Returning to minority groups, one can note then that Hutterites would value single-parent pregnancy as deplorable, but the "outside world" now accepts single parents. Twenty years ago society "forced" the girl and boy to marry. Values change depending on the basis on which they are held and also on the homogeneity of the minority group.

As a society we have both negative and positive values. A negative value would be incest—we deplore it. A positive value is keeping our lawns clear of dandelions. These two examples demonstrate a source of conflict.

Look at yourself. You are a twenty-eight-year-old constable in Police Force A. You are educated, white, have a middle-class home, a car, you know your neighbour to say hi, have a bank account, Grade 12 education, you are a good policeman, enjoy dining and dancing when you can afford it, etc.

You also probably hate welfare recipients because you were brought up under the "God helps those who help themselves" and "Idle hands do the devil's work" syndrome.

You also probably can't stand Indians, Pakistanis, Hindus,

Doukhobors, etc. Why? Any reason would suffice your ego. You, my friend, represent the protection of the citizen and yet you have "wild" ideas about each of the minority groups mentioned. Why? You probably learned them at home, at work, on the street, etc.

Those ideas of yours, coupled with your values (as defined by your upbringing), could very well create insurmountable problems for you should you tangle with a minority group whose values differ drastically. I will use an hypothetical example to illustrate my point.

We have all seen the dilapidated old car on an Indian reserve or Métis community. We have all passed judgement respecting the value of keeping such a wreck in front of the house. Here then is a *possible* conversation between a policeman and the native inhabitant:

Policeman: Why do you keep that old wreck with its broken windows and lack of a motor?

Native: My children play in it; it serves as a recreation area.

Policeman: Don't your neighbours complain?

Native: Why should they, their kids play in it.

Policeman: If I were you I'd get rid of it soon—it smears the community.

Native: That is the trouble with you policemen, you don't understand. What you white people would do with it if I did decide to scrap it would be to take it to the scrap metal joint, bend it out of shape, paint it and place it in front of the University of Manitoba and call it a work of art costing about $20,000 and a work of art which a few ladies would look at and wonder what kind of a mind could have developed such an ingenious thing?

One can infer from such a conversation that people oftentimes see the same thing from different concepts of values. The problem that can come out of this is the possibility of the native person moving to the city with values accumulated on the reserve or Métis settlement. For instance: when I moved to X I was told by my neighbours that they were expecting an Indian from India to move in. The previous owner had informed them that I was a professor of Indian extraction. Many of them did not even consider the possibility of a Canadian native being educated. Such being the environment, I proceeded to discuss with my wife the possibility of testing their diehard, bleeding liberalism. Keeping in mind that people in the city love their lawns to be green, flowerbeds for flowers, houses painted and gardens at the back of the house, I proceeded to convince one of my neighbours, in April of that year, that I was growing corn in my flowerbed under my picture window. At the time tulip bulbs were coming out of the ground. One can imagine the conversation that went on when I was assured that the individual was convinced of my intentions.

"What are you trying to do to the neighbourhood?"

Said I, "Nothing. I'm paying taxes for this lot and since corn grows so high it would create shade for the rest of my garden, I've decided to grow it in front, under my picture window."

Well, it didn't take more than half a day before everyone knew of this diabolical plot. Fortunately my phone was unlisted at the time. However, people sit outside in the summer and it didn't take long before racial verbiage was shouted in my direction from across the street.

"What do you think this is, you damn aboriginee—the reserve?" was a mild one. All along I sat back and laughed at their ignorance. Eventually the tulips came out and they then realized they had "been had," so to speak.

Discussions followed and I informed them as to why I had done it. Suffice it to say that their attitudes changed not necessarily because they now loved natives but merely because I hadn't grown corn in my flowerbed. The questions that remain in my mind are: What would have happened if I had grown corn in my flowerbed? What would have been the consequences? It is obvious that city people have a different value system, *depending on where they live in the city*. How do I know that one of my neighbours is not a landlord who owns homes in the core area where values are altogether different?

Problems oftentimes occur in cities simply because of value conflicts and they do not necessarily have to involve minority groups. People who come in from rural areas frequently find themselves in conflict situations because of their own priorities.

What would happen if I moved next door to you, a policeman, and did such things? You would also get upset and do and say exactly the same things that some people said and did. But what is the point of it all? Simply that people who do not live in an urban area develop a different attachment or value to their possessions as compared to people in the city. Native people, especially those on reserves, may very well see their house as a shelter instead of an investment. Upon arrival to the city, that same value persists, the results of which lead white people to say: "They are going to make a ghetto out of our area;" "More of them will come," etc. Unfortunately it is sad to note that urban people do make judgements about outsiders based upon urban values. Few urbanites accept native newcomers at face value; instead they want them to change. On the other hand, how many whites are willing to change to the native lifestyle when they are requested to teach or police on an Indian reserve or Métis community? Few if any.

As a police officer you must always be aware of your shortcomings and prejudices. Policing minority groups is not an easy task. Learn about their values, their culture, their raison d'être. Get involved with them.

More importantly, inform the people about your job and the responsibilities that go with it. Oftentimes, minority groups are as ignorant of you as you are of them. Be aware that many immigrants who have come to our great country have often left countries that are best characterized as police states. Hence these people, in all probability, view you as an arm of government instead of as protectors of society. Minority groups also need to understand that policemen do not make the laws. This is a common misconception that needs to be rectified, and you as a policeman have a responsibility to the general populace to make this fact not only known but understood. Minority groups need to understand police work. A carefully planned public relations job is needed for this to come about. It is not enough to go into school classrooms; you must reach the community. You would then not get such comments as I have heard from different segments of society that 50 percent of cops have piles and the rest are perfect you-know-whats. Get out of your car—participate on hockey teams, baseball, football, whatever is your pleasure. Let people see you out of your uniform once in a while. Remember that as protectors of society you are not above it—you are part of it.

In the past few years the provincial and federal governments have established Special Band Police Forces. Noting the high crime rate among native peoples, both levels of government have attempted to do something about the problem. Originally the attempts had problems, since special constables were oftentime hired by band councils. The problems were those of jurisdiction and also that when the band council was defeated in elections, the new council would hire a different person for the job. Eventually through training at the RCMP Depot in Regina many special constable positions became more stabilized, since most now answered to his NCO and not the chief and council. Fears were expressed, however, that perhaps such native constables would become their own worst enemies, vis-à-vis their own people. Statistics had shown that the American experience with black cops had proved this to be true.

Fortunately, aside from a few incidents, this has not been the case in Canada. Nonetheless, the native constable working in his own community is in a rather precarious position. Unlike other officers who are sent here, there, and everywhere, these men are sent to their respective communities. To date, no data exist to show whether they are respected in their community as policemen, or as J.B. the native policeman, or simply as J.B.

After a shaky beginning, the program has proven itself very beneficial for all concerned. Let us hope it continues to grow, while becoming a vehicle for educating the non-native policeman about an old Indian saying: "Never judge a man until you have walked a mile in his moccasins."

Chapter 16

Personality Development and Human Relations
Victor Szyrynski

In dealing with people, one should understand how personality functions. Currently, we understand human personality in a dynamic way. It means that everyone is constantly adjusting to his surroundings and his inner conditions. All the time, people have to cope with different types of stresses occurring in their environments or in their organisms. On the other hand, people differ from one another in the way they respond to different situations. The modern science of human personality developed by psychologists, psychiatrists and other research workers analyzes the factors responsible for human behaviour and predicts different behaviour patterns and, in some cases, controls certain behaviours, such as preventing abnormal and antisocial responses, changing disturbed behaviour and correcting sick or antisocial patterns.

All people who deal professionally with other individuals in whatever capacity, such as doctors, psychologists, personnel officers, teachers, clergymen, policemen, nurses, need to develop skills in three particular areas: understanding human personality and human behaviour; mastering basic principles of effective communication; developing empathy with other human beings, whether they are normal, abnormal or antisocial.

Dynamic Understanding of Human Behaviour
A dynamic understanding of human personality postulates: the existence of basic driving forces that stimulate everyone to act to fulfill his needs, appetites and goals; the existence of universal psychological mechanisms that enable an individual to cope to varying extents with obstacles encountered in the fulfillment of his needs and appetites; and the operation of the above factors on the conscious or unconscious level of human personality.

Dr. Szyrynski is presently Professor of Psychiatry and Psychology at the University of Ottawa and formerly Professor and Chairman of Psychiatry and Neurology at the University of North Dakota. For the last twelve years he has been teaching RCMP officers at the Canadian Police College in Ottawa and has published four books on psychiatry, neurology, psychology and criminology.

The immediate practical result of recognizing the above factors is the acknowledgement of limitations on "free will." Different factors operating within the human personality control human behaviour with a varying influence on decision making. We recognize that many acts are not the outcome of a deliberate decision, but may result from the dynamic forces operating on the unconscious level of the personality. The simple "pleasure-pain" principle, whereby people seek pleasure and avoid pain, has a complex effect on many everyday situations.

Personality and Its Determinants

One may define personality as the sum-total of everything that distinguishes one individual from another. Every individual has his own unique personality, his own physical and psychological traits organized in a certain manner that influences the individual's responses.

An important and still largely unsolved question is the relative influence on the development of personality of biological heredity and social upbringing. Some scientists, such as Franz Kallman,[1] emphasized the significance of heredity in determining normal or abnormal human behaviour, throughout an individual's life. According to this theory, most people are born with strong tendencies to display some personality traits and to behave in a certain manner. The opposing point of view places emphasis on the impact of training, of social learning, on an individual. J. B. Watson[2] even maintained that if any child is subjected to a carefully planned program of training, he may be turned into either a saint or a criminal. Quite recently, the science of ethology suggests possible inheritance of particular behaviour patterns without the underlying somatic features.

For convenience, one may divide human personality into three basic factors: intelligence, temperament and character. Intelligence varies according to the properties of the brain; some brains label an individual as a genius, others as mentally defective. Intelligence is a permanent trait and remains essentially constant during a lifetime. It determines a person's ability to learn, whether through formal education or experience. More intelligent children do better at school, study more easily and may reach higher educational levels. Measuring intelligence through intelligence tests helps to guide people toward different occupations, increasing satisfaction and preventing frustration. A less intelligent individual finds it difficult to cope with complex responsibilities, while a more intelligent one will more quickly develop boredom and frustration at unchallenging and routine occupations. Marked differences in intelligence may lead to marital maladjustment. Leadership in different social groups will be more easily accepted from more intelligent individuals. However, if the difference is too great, the highly intelligent leader may be rejected, due to difficulties in communication.

Intelligence develops naturally to about the age of fifteen. Afterward, it remains unchanged for some time and then begins to decline with differing speeds in different individuals. Education, life experience, and acquired knowledge will obviously increase beyond that point, but the pure mental alertness does not.

It has been suggested that decline of intelligence may be delayed by intellectual exercise, in the same way that physical exercise delays the reduction of physical fitness. With proper exercise, many older people retain high physical efficiency. With continuous studying and a keen interest in the world, many people will retain strong mental alertness into old age. On the other hand, all the factors that injure the human brain, such as over-indulgence in alcohol, drug-taking, vitamin deficiency, unsuitable diet or physical injury speed up intellectual decline.

A frequently asked question about the relationship between general mental alertness and particular abilities has been dealt with in the two factors theory of C. E. Spearman.[3] He distinguished "general intelligence" (the G factor) from a great number of "special abilities" (S factor). He also recognized different relationships between these two factors. In Figure 16-1, we see that some S factors, for example administrative ability, are highly correlated with factor G, general intelligence. Others, for example, writing poetry, would still require an adequate level of factor G. On the other hand, some special abilities, such as drawing or modelling, may be found even in mentally defective individuals.

In dealing with any person, it is always helpful to know his level of intelligence in order to select an appropriate level of communication.

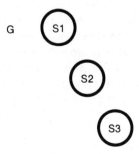

Figure 16 - 1
Relationship of S factors to G factor.

Antisocial or criminal acts are committed with different degrees of recognition by mentally defective and more intelligent people.

The second factor in personality may be called "temperament." People differ in their degree of emotionality, their speed of reaction, their cheerful, serious or miserable dispositions. It has been found that the temperamental makeup of different individuals can be traced to hereditary influences and remains markedly independent from environmental modifying forces. This does not mean that upbringing has no serious impact on the total personality; it simply suggests that some people may find it difficult to develop more agreeable temperaments than others.

The influence of the social environment is, however, primarily responsible for the formation of individual character. We usually define character as the social aspect of human personality. Consequently, one may evaluate character by saying that someone has a good character or an antisocial or criminal one. Some people respect the social values of their culture, while others follow a system of values generally condemned by their society. Such choice of "good" or "bad" values depends only partially on individual preference. To a large extent, it results from the total social experience of a developing child, who follows the examples of his parents and other significant people in his life.

Importance of Early Childhood

It is generally agreed that the earliest periods of child development are of particular significance for the formation of personality. In fact, one may consider that overlooking this principle is the main mistake of the North American parent. Early neglect can hardly be corrected. One should remember that the influence of the parents is the greatest during the earliest weeks, months or years, when children are very dependent on them, accept their judgement unquestioningly, and derive much satisfaction from following their requests. It is with the onset of adolescence that children become more critical and distrustful—perhaps even hostile—toward their own parents, often looking to other models in shaping their personalities. It has been observed that even the more severe contemporary crises of adolescence, like alienation, dropping out of school, drugs, etc., are more easily resisted or overcome after a short period by young people subjected to more solid and efficient upbringing during the early childhood stages.

For the proper growth of the child, love, security and communication should be provided by the parents. Love should be steady and healthy. An excess or deficiency of love may be equally harmful; one creates unrealistic expectations, the other diminishes self-confidence and self-acceptance. Security depends on predictable behaviour by parental figures and an essential agreement on expectations and values between parents. Communication requires that an adequate amount of time be spent with children, introducing them patiently to the problems of living in the world.

To develop frustration tolerance, a child must receive an adequate degree of discipline. Life is full of restrictions and limitations. Over-indulged children often discover these suddenly at the beginning of adolescence. Unable to cope with frustration, they try to escape into the instant happiness produced by drugs and other indulgences. Unable to face reality, they drift into neuroses, psychoses or delinquency. Proper limitations within a balanced disciplinary code help the child to develop sufficient endurance to face life's obstacles.

Work requires effort, concentration, persistence and patience. Those traits should be developed early in the child's life. Paradoxically, many exceptionally intelligent and talented children suffer from inadequate working habits. Faced with programs that are too easy for them, they go through primary and secondary education on their intelligence alone, without adequate challenge. Meeting with the necessity to start working hard at the college or on a job, lacking adequate working habits and with a low frustration tolerance, such young people get easily discouraged and drop their studies or work.

The problem of discipline is often discussed in connection with the upbringing of children. The current research tries to evaluate the relative merits of the authoritarian and the more liberal, permissive approaches. One thing appears certain: that both approaches, without an adequate amount of love, security and communication, produce harmful effects on the personality. If those essential ingredients are present, each approach has its merits. The liberal approach develops more initiative, independence and better interpersonal skills; the authoritarian approach produces a dependable, efficient and perfectionist personality.

Young children are often disturbed when faced with a choice between different desires and temptations. They will easily identify with the adult who helps them find a solution; they learn in this way to make decisions, to put their foot down in different situations. Children have a keen instinct for justice and just punishment helps them feel more secure.

Adolescence

Many volumes have been written about adolescence; this period is recognized as a particularly important and difficult stage of development. Some children go through adolescence with relatively little turmoil; others suffer from more serious, occasionally very critical personality disorders. Among many other factors, this largely depends on their early upbringing. A well-organized childhood protects children from the perils of adolescence.

Physical development in adolescence is often erratic and this makes it difficult for teenagers to accept themselves. Psychosomatic and neurotic symptoms indicate serious conflicts within the personality. Adolescents have to abandon childhood play and fantasy to face reality. Their ties with parents are often at the breaking point, they are grasping for support in a broader social environment, and they are difficult to understand or to communicate with.

It is helpful to remember that, in general, an adolescent behaves differently when alone from when he is with a group; he is likely to adjust his behaviour to the perceived norms of the group to obtain peer acceptance. A hostile and resentful teenager when approached individually may turn out to be a shy, insecure, dependent, intelligent and co-operative individual. When first approached, he may present resistance to a closer relationship and deeper communication, but with sufficient patience and understanding, a more open and constructive personality may surface.

Adolescence is an important step in developing a mature personality. Certain definite goals should be achieved at that time. Among different classifications, L. S. Hollingworth[4] enumerated the following four items:

1. development of one's own life philosophy—determining the main goals of existence and the hierarchical system of values;
2. occupational choice—selecting preferred occupational goals with proper planning and effort to achieve them through education, training, etc.;
3. weaning away from home—gradually acquiring greater independence from parents, greater freedom of choice and decision-making, without developing feelings of guilt and hostility toward the family, which are often complicated by neurotic symptoms or juvenile delinquency;
4. sexual enlightenment—with objective evaluation of the role of sex in human life, in keeping with adopted moral standards and free from pathological disturbances, which in our culture often complicate the process of sexual maturation.

All the above goals should be properly balanced and may be used for planning appropriate guidance programs for teenagers; however, if such balance is disturbed and only one particular item taken out of context is given excessive preeminence, the resulting one-sided program may be misleading and harmful.

Understanding the Family and Its Functions

The family, the basic unit of human life, creates an environment where many essential needs of both adults and children are gratified. In most countries, the child develops physically, mentally and socially in a family environment, and it is here also that adults can feel some social and emotional stability. For not only do children need parents, but certain parental needs are gratified by caring for children. Family relationships should satisfy "the need to be needed," and the needs to be loved, to feel secure, and to be able to communicate. Other social needs, such as recognition, response, security and new experience, should also be satisfied. There may be complications when growing children reject parental help, when parents acquire too much independence from each other, or when basic needs are not satisfied. Parents or grandparents who feel no longer needed may try to slow the normal development, maturation and attainment of freedom of their children by forcing them to be emotionally and economically dependent on them.

Achieving a deep understanding of family life is a very difficult task. Interactions between the conscious and unconscious factors within individual family members should be considered. However, contemporary research into family functioning stresses that a family unit is not just a sum-total of its members, but is a unit run under its own dynamic forces. This means that while some clinicians try to remedy family disorders by treating individuals, helping them understand and manage conscious and unconscious motivating forces, others feel that the whole family should be treated as a basic functional unit, and they work with all family members in each treatment session.

The family helps the child develop ego strength and coping skills. Self-love and self-acceptance help an individual to face the challenge of living and give him the energy to promote his self-actualization. People with this drive have been usually accepted in early childhood by parents who taught them to think well of themselves and others. Children deprived of love, security and communication in the early stages of development lose interest in life and care little for their own existence. Frustration tolerance, good working habits, positive response to reasonable discipline and proper self-control are the results of an upbringing that exposes the child to reality in the earliest years.

A triad of frustrated biological and social needs, impaired communication and hostility are responsible for family disorders and also explain violence in the family. Individuals with accumulated hostility are often unable to talk openly about why they are tense, and are more inclined to blow up against family members. This may be further increased by low intelligence, immaturity and bad learning experiences in the individual's own violent early family environment.

Healthy individuals are capable of being free and independent, and of existing alone without the need to lean on or depend upon another. Too much dependency leads to enslavement and deprivation of freedom, resulting in possessiveness, neurotic clinging to another, mistrust, jealousy or an exploitation of children to gratify parental dependency needs. Maturity implies control of emotions by reason, a lack of selfishness, an ability to make free decisions based on strong self-discipline, high frustration tolerance and not running away from or denying the existence of conflict by submissiveness and blind obedience.

Happy marriages are full; empty marriages lead to unhappiness. Young people who get together should be able to fill their lives with mutual interests, ambitions, plans, projects and worthwhile pleasures. They should pursue interesting and exciting goals, being able to help one another in such undertakings. They should take part in community life and take some responsibility for the happiness of people around them. At the same time, they should maintain a special interest in one another that is reminiscent of the excitement of courtship and engagement.

Children are happiest in a home where parents love one another and invite the children to participate in their happiness. In many unhappy marriages, children are often used as unfortunate substitutes: a mother, frustrated with her husband, demands excessive love and affection from her son. An unhappy father with a hostile, inadequate wife may try to secure excessive care and attachment from his growing daughter. Children often feel oppressed by an excess of affection, and become hostile, trying to free themselves from these suffocating ties.

Young people planning marriage should try to foresee their lives in the years they will be together, imagining themselves in middle and old age. Many youngsters avoid planning for the future, forgetting that clear goals make life easier: they think only about the present. If their eyes were open, in time they would probably decide to break off an unsuitable partnership. Many counsellors often remark how some young couples planning marriage are reluctant to discuss the realities of married life. They prefer not to talk, not to hear, and not to think about what marriage actually is.

Psychoanalytic Understanding of Personality

The teachings of Sigmund Freud helped man to understand better the development of the personality. He maintained that human personality consists of three basic elements called the id, the ego, and the superego.

At birth, an infant is subject to essential biological needs: hunger, thirst, bodily comfort, and also some basic pleasurable experiences that come from close contact with his mother and later on with other significant people in his environment. When these basic drives, or instincts, which are totally self-centred, are gratified, the child is relaxed and happy. When they are not fulfilled, the child becomes upset and angry; he cries and kicks. A little child is totally selfish. This part of the personality Freud called the id.

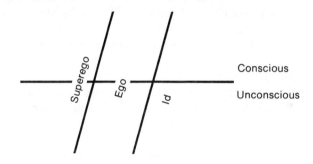

Figure 16 - 2
Freud's analysis of the personality.

In growing up, a child learns to observe certain "rules of the game." He learns that he can more easily obtain love and security from his parents if he behaves in a certain way. When he breaks the rules, the parents become angry and withdraw their love and benevolence, so that the child feels rejected.

If the parents present a consistent pattern of expectations, and the father and mother agree on what is "good" and what is "bad," the child develops a clear-cut system of values, feels comfortable when he follows the rules and anxious when he breaks them. This anxiety may be called guilt; people become quite disturbed and uncomfortable when they are burdened with severe guilt feelings. This part of the personality that dictates to an individual the norms of behaviour and produces guilt feelings Freud called the superego. Technically, he claimed that the superego develops through introjection—taking into one's own personality the system of values represented by the parents, and later on by the other significant people in the child's environment, such as teachers, clergymen, policemen, youth leaders, etc. Throughout a lifetime a continuous battle is fought between the moral, socially oriented superego and the amoral, self-centred id. In our culture, there are two particularly strong drives emerging from the Id and strongly censored by the Superego that most commonly produce guilt feelings. They are sex and hostility, or aggression. When such conflicts become particularly severe, some people develop various psychoneurotic or psychosomatic disorders and possibly even mental illness (psychosis).

The third element of the human personality is called the ego, which plays the important role of maintaining the balance between the appetites of the id, the demands of the superego and the reality of existence. In helping a man to face reality, the ego also employs the so-called mechanisms of adjustment, which help him to cope with frustrations, conflicts and physical or psychological stress. When the ego is functioning well, when it is strong, a person may face life and function efficiently. When it gets weak, being undermined by physical or psychological disturbances, an individual may collapse or break down in the face of obstacles. The ego also gets its strength from the healthy relationship of a child with his parents or an adult with his social environment. Here again, an adequate amount of love and security strengthens the ego, while poor interpersonal relationships, particularly in early childhood and adolescence, make the ego weak and unable to formulate healthy goals and ambitions and to pursue them constructively. People suffering from neurotic or psychotic conditions, as well as many drifters, people who cannot accept responsibilities, suffer essentially from weakness of the ego. Friendly support or the influence of a strong group may improve ego strength. Psychiatric treatment known as psychotherapy improves ego strength by removing the so-called complexes and providing an individual with a new, well-balanced and constructive social experience.

Psychoanalytic theory claims also that the personality consists of the conscious and unconscious. Quite often human behaviour cannot be understood unless one considers the existence of different tendencies based on past experiences accumulated in the unconscious. Such forgotten experiences, which have a strong emotional content and are removed from conscious memory by the mechanism of repression, are known as complexes. They may also account for an individual's special sensitivity to certain situations that they tolerate poorly.

Freud suggested that human life is governed by two principles: the pleasure principle and the reality principle. Numerous needs and appetites require fulfillment; however, the cold reality of life is often very frustrating. When the ego is weak and the intensity of such appetites quite forceful, the individual may escape from reality into fantasy. It may be innocent daydreaming; it may be an overindulgence in the movies or fantastic books; or it may go so far as to carry an individual into a psychotic illness in which he loses contact with aspects of reality in varying degrees. The stronger the ego, the easier it is to maintain a firm grasp on reality. For instance, healthy people take objective criticism of themselves in a constructive and grateful manner; people with weak egos respond with violent emotions whenever their unrealistic self-image is threatened.

Maturation, Fixation and Regression

Some people are considered more mature than others. Some display mature behaviour in their teens; others act in an immature way throughout their lifetimes. While small children are self-centred, easily prompted by their emotions and quite dependent on others, the mature individual is more altruistic, concerned also with the welfare of society. He controls himself through his reason rather than being at the mercy of his emotions, and he can function in an independent, free and responsible way. Maturity goes along with ego strength and both factors can be influenced by the very sensitive balance between an individual and his environment.

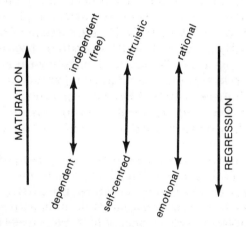

**Figure 16 - 3
Maturity and regression.**

It helps to understand this delicate situation by imagining that everybody carries within him a little boy or a little girl. Under the influence of stress, the shell of maturity may break down and the child within may spring to action. An apparently serious and well-balanced man stopped for speeding may begin justifying himself like a child facing his strict father or the school principal, or may become very agitated like an upset little boy. In a situation that reminds one of a difficult childhood experience, such regression easily occurs. In a similar way, a grown-up person faced with serious frustrations may constantly complain, telling everybody his miseries in search of a dependent relationship.

General maturity is closely linked with sexual maturation. During normal development a child grows and identifies himself as a man or a woman. Confidence in one's sexual role helps in developing good ego strength. In some people, any threat to sexual identity undermines their adjustment. That is why many people are particularly sensitive to suspicions or accusations of sexual deviation or inadequacy. Here again, regression may occur under the impact of some severe frustrations, or sexual development and maturation may not reach its perfect goal but may be arrested (fixated) at the level of early childhood or adolescent patterns; for example, excessive attachment to or dependence on the parents, particularly tender and dependent friendships with people of the same sex, etc.

Personality and System of Values
Throughout life people are exposed to different choices and they have to make decisions. Someone once described human beings as "decision-making animals." Decisions are made easily if a person recognizes clearly his own individual system of values. A healthy adolescent will be able to define the purpose of his existence, his personal goal in life. Research has shown that juvenile delinquents, so-called "alienated youth," demonstrate much greater confusion in this respect than better-adjusted young people. Developing an individual philosophy of life, choosing an occupation, gaining independence from home and achieving a sexual identity are the four main goals of adolescence. Gardner Murphy[5] claimed that the individual personality is best understood in terms of a "hierarchical system of values" whereby each person clearly recognizes his main purpose of life, followed by other values in a descending scale of importance. An individual who builds such a pyramid of values finds it much easier to resist temptations and to solve conflicts. Characteristically, many delinquents describe their self-understanding in terms of "I am so confused," and "I don't know what it is all about." Well organized values should be accompanied by feeling of freedom based on ego strength and maturity. Healthy people are more confident in making decisions and undertaking responsibilities. Immaturity and weakness of personality are usually accompanied by anxiety, feelings of insecurity and a lack of energy. Development of an integrated system of values, as we have mentioned before, also depends on the

interaction of an individual with his social environment, his family and his community.

Drives, Motives and Incentives

Freud recognized the dominant role played in the personality by the desire for pleasure based on sexual instinct. He thought that from the earliest weeks of development, people have an essential desire for tender, pleasurable gratification, which makes them especially sensitive to love and other forms of affection. Through social learning, this basic biological desire is modified to meet the demands of social order and maturity, but basically the desire to love and to be loved provides a powerful motivating factor throughout the lifetime of an individual. Freud suggested that in order to understand normal or abnormal human behaviour, one should analyze early gratifications or frustrations in this important area of emotional adjustment.

Another prominent psychiatrist, Alfred Adler, advanced the theory that a "will for power" is the dominant motivating factor in human personality. He claimed that from earliest childhood a person is guided by the need to control his environment, to be centre of attention, to influence others and to dominate. He suggested also that a feeling of inferiority is one of the most painful human experiences, for which an individual will try to compensate either in reality, or if their ego is not strong enough, in fantasy or other forms of escape. The classic story of Cinderella, an abandoned beauty who magically attains pre-eminence, is found in legions of tales, books and films, in many cultures throughout the whole world. According to Adler, the desire for power underlies different forms of normal, abnormal or criminal behaviour.

More recently, Viktor Frankl[6] tried to replace the "will for pleasure" of Sigmund Freud[7] and the "will for power" of Alfred Adler[8] with his emphasis on the "will for meaning." According to his teaching, disturbed behaviour, or even mental disorders, result from the failure of many individuals to find or to recognize the significance of their existence. He believes that if people could be assisted to discover "what it is all about," they could organize their lives in a much happier and healthier manner. This may very well be illustrated by the above-mentioned references to delinquents or neurotic individuals who complain of being confused and lost. The school of existentialism, to which Frankl belongs, stresses also the danger of continuous brainwashing through different communication media, whereby people are influenced to respond to insidious social pressures and deprived of personal freedom. As an example, our culture seems to suffer from two forms of intense brainwashing: unscrupulous commercialism and the pressure of political systems that attempt to enslave the human mind, particularly those of young people, in order to achieve political goals. According to the existentialists, emotional disorders and antisocial behaviour are based on a lack of individual purpose and of an appreciation for the dignity of true freedom of choice.

Many sociologists are also trying to identify the most elementary human needs in our particular culture. As an example, W. I. Thomas[9] enumerated needs for security, response, recognition and new experience, all of them necessitating gratification from interpersonal experiences. Margaret Phillips[10] discussed the "need to be needed," which most likely has its root in the Freudian or Adlerian ideas of a person feeling unloved and unimportant if he is not needed. This need probably explains the prevalence of depression and even suicidal tendencies in people who grow older without having adequately defined the meaning of their existence.

Adjustment and Coping

In terms of the above discussion, it is clear that human actions, in order to be properly understood, should be analyzed in the context of an individual's dynamic needs. Most so-called well-adjusted people have adequately reconciled the discrepancy between their basic needs and the requirements and limitations set by their particular cultures and environments. Many others are not so successful; consequently, we tend to understand unhealthy, abnormal, antisocial or criminal behaviour as an attempt at adjustment that failed. One such necessary adjustment is between level of aspiration and level of attainment.

Biological drives and social motives may meet with different fates in different people. They may be gratified without producing a conflict with moral values or social order. Some people obtain adequate sexual gratification within the institution of marriage; some young people achieve independence and leave home without antagonizing their parents and developing severe guilt feelings, others obtain financial security and adequate comfort without compromising their honesty and self-respect.

Not infrequently, however, human drives, needs or appetites become frustrated. Some people can cope with frustration and adjust to painful experiences; others break down emotionally or act against the social order. Along with frustration, situations of severe conflict, usually based on the superego and the id pulling in opposite directions, may exhaust the personality and weaken the ego, leading to neurotic or delinquent behaviour. Healthy people are able to face life's difficulties, obstacles and limitations by employing healthy and successful defence mechanisms, working harder, and replacing unrealistic goals or ambitions with others that are easier to obtain and of equal value.

Learning and Style of Life

According to Adler, people differ from one another in their preference for different patterns of adjustment. He believed people attempt from early childhood to find out and select certain individual ways to control their social environment. He called this search the individual's "style of life." It is easy to observe how some children obtain popularity and recognition by being extremely sweet, polite or diligent in their work, while others control their environment by temper tantrums, belligerence and aggression, or by avoiding difficulties by being shy, withdrawn, and uninvolved faced with any obstacle or conflict. It is very likely that the social environment of the child and the spontaneous and instinctive responses of the parents fortify some patterns or weaken the others. One thing seems to be certain: that a "style of life" tends to persist throughout the life of an individual. In order to evaluate a particular personality, it is most important to investigate in detail his prevalent patterns of behaviour throughout his life from earliest childhood. The retraining of neurotic or antisocial styles of life may require considerable time and effort, through psychiatric treatment, correctional rehabilitation, and other therapeutic situations.

Stress and Mental Health

It may be also practically concluded from the above considerations that people differ from one another in their resistance to stress. Some are able to face a lot of frustrations, dangers and disappointments without breaking down; others feel limited in their freedom of behaviour by numerous fears and anxieties. Some people are afraid of taking an elevator, not to mention an airplane; others are propelled around the moon without undergoing excessive anxiety. Both types would be able to lead a reasonably normal existence, although they will display markedly different levels of mental health. It is, therefore, possible to define mental health as resistance to stress. Varying resistance to different types of stress significantly influences a person's feeling of freedom. Emotional and mental disorders, and even a number of antisocial behaviour patterns, sexual deviations and character disorders, would have one thing in common: the limitation of human freedom.

Inasmuch as the level of mental health differs among individuals, it may also differ in the same individual at different periods, depending on various circumstances. Physical illness, exhaustion, overwork, psychological difficulties, severe frustrations, disappointments

232 / The Police Function in Canada

and conflicts, lack of gratification of basic needs, confusion within the system of values, chaotic perception of the meaning of existence— all may result in significant drops in the level of mental health and undermine the ego strength of the individual. It is well known that in some systems of forceful interrogation (i.e., brainwashing), undermining of the ego strength and diminution of the level of mental health is deliberately intended.

Crisis Theory and Crisis Intervention

Our discussion of styles of life has stressed how firm behaviour patterns are and how difficult it may be to change them. The older a person becomes, the more difficult it is to change his established habits, whether good or bad. However, it has been observed that under certain circumstances the personality may be so disturbed that the old habits may be reorganized into new patterns of behaviour. It is common knowledge that when people move from place to place, change their jobs, go through some tragic experience, or are shaken up in some other way, their "frozen" system of adjustment mechanisms may be replaced with a new style of life. A change of homes is often successful in treating maladjusted children or young delinquents. In a crisis situation, an individual first becomes more childlike; he falls back to a more immature and highly emotional level from which he may recrystallize a new way of life. An extremely important point has been noted in observing people's behaviour in crises: whether after such experiences their new patterns of adjustment are either better or worse than those displayed before the crisis occurred largely depends on the amount of help provided during a crisis situation. People left to themselves often become more immature and antisocial. People assisted promptly may develop considerably higher levels of adjustment.

Assistance in crisis is known as "crisis intervention." It is different from the other aspects of psychiatric treatment. Quite often it is not done by mental health experts but by other people such as teachers, counsellors, clergymen, policemen, friends or relatives. Crisis intervention should be prompt and immediate. Waiting a few weeks for a psychiatric appointment often destroys the best chances of rehabilitation. All enlightened citizens, particularly those dealing with other people through different community services, should be prepared to offer crisis intervention.

It is customary to classify all crisis situations into developmental or accidental crises. Throughout life every individual is forced to change his environment, to face new life situations requiring a reorganization of his mechanisms of adjustment. A person enters kindergarten, then full-day school, perhaps later boarding school, goes to summer camp, to college, gets engaged, marries and has children, accepts various jobs, and assumes gradually more and more complex responsibilities.

Accidental crises may include illness, accidents, deaths of family members, loss of work, financial collapse, separation from significant individuals and various other disappointments—and even some unexpected successes. Many such accidents may require vigorous reorganization of a previous system of defences. Certainly, delinquent acts and criminal offences should be considered critical events in one's life history.

Mobility of the family has often been recognized as one of the important factors in juvenile delinquency. A child uprooted from his immediate environment and transferred to a strange school and unfamiliar social environment may be more easily attracted to the delinquent gang or other maladjusted individuals who have themselves been rejected. Any member of the armed services given a new assignment in a new community naturally goes through a crisis, together with the members of his family. It is of great importance to protect such people, their wives and children, from the adverse effect of crisis by organizing carefully their adjustment to the new community; this most likely should be the responsibility of their superiors and colleagues. Another classic example of crisis situation is the adjustment of immigrants to a new country. In this respect, Canada, with its high immigration rate, should do its utmost to salvage a considerable number of people from severe maladjustment and save money later spent on assisting them through severe crises.

Interpersonal Relations and Mental Health

It is evident from the above discussion that life is lived with people. Contact with other individuals may support an individual or undermine his adjustment. Ego strength is influenced by communication with others. Psychotherapeutic treatment depends essentially on supporting the ego of a sick person through a properly structured, new interpersonal experience. In crisis intervention, the ego weakened by unusual stress is also supported by friendly interpersonal relationships. It may be said that in any type of distress people have a tendency to "borrow" from the ego strength of other individuals. With this "loan," they more easily survive the crisis, until their ego strength improves through better adjustment. People who are members of closely knit families, who have many friends in their community, who communicate more easily with their social environment have better chances of facing stress than the lonely characters with poor abilities to communicate, who have been abandoned by their environments or who have moved to strange new places. Statistics on suicide suggest that the highest risks are lonely men in their forties with strong alcoholic tendencies. Quite recently, psychiatrists observed acute panic reactions in lonely individuals travelling for a number of days in foreign countries, unable to communicate due to the language barrier. Such "travel psychosis" may be prevented by establishing constructive communication with other individuals.

The "Telescopic Approach" to Human Personality

One of the practical conclusions from the above discussion consists of recognizing the value of understanding each human act as a signal from a particular personality with its special structure. Any human *act*, including antisocial, delinquent or criminal behaviour, may be properly understood in a "telescopic" way, by considering the *personality* behind the act, the *family* behind the personality, the *community* behind the family, and the *culture* behind the community. Particularly in the multicultural structure of Canada, consideration of various cultural traditions, different community structures, various family customs and different individual habits must be taken into account in understanding the reasons for certain behaviour patterns. At first such an approach may appear too involved and unwieldy for people used to facing definite situations and acting promptly in such circumstances. They find it difficult to think in terms of the total background of an individual who is committing a certain act. However, with proper orientation and additional training, one finds very fast that the telescopic approach is actually the most economical and time-saving in the great majority of situations.

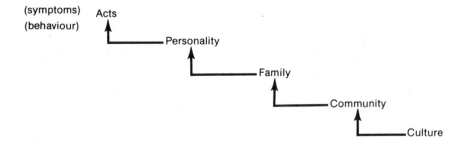

Figure 16 - 4
The telescopic approach to human personality.

Special Stress Areas and Life Problems Facing Members of the Police Force

Much of what has been said applies quite obviously to police officers. It is generally recognized that being a policeman exposes an individual to a considerable number of stressful situations; on the other hand, it should also be remembered that policemen are specially selected and through training and practical experience acquire greater skill in dealing with a number of stressful events. Another important factor to remember is that the occupation of a policeman not only involves the individual but also affects his family.

In dealing with stress among police officers, three basic steps should be undertaken: (1) to study and understand the particular aspects of stress affecting policemen; (2) to develop a system of preventive measures to increase resistance to stress and consequently diminish stress damage; (3) to develop a healing process for individuals affected by excess of stress. In reviewing stress-producing situations, different stages in a policeman's career may be briefly examined.

Selection of Candidates and Pre-induction Orientation

During this period, preventive measures are particularly important. In selecting candidates, the following factors should be considered:

—good physical and emotional health;
—adequate intelligence and special ability;
—clear goals in life and well-organized system of values;
—adequate self-acceptance and self-confidence;
—history of healthy growth and development throughout childhood and adolescence, with positive adjustment in the parental home, at school and in the community (this does not presuppose the ideal middle-class upbringing, but it implies that the candidates were able to cope satisfactorily and positively with any obstacles they encountered during their individual developments);
—proper motivation for police occupation, and realistic goals and ambitions.

At this stage, ample orientation and counselling are necessary. The candidate should be informed about the police function and its role in the contemporary community. In the case of married applicants, involving of the marital partner in such counselling is advisable; different aspects of police functioning should be presented, like different duties, areas of work (isolated postings, security, drug control, crime detection, etc.), possible transfers, promotions with broadening responsibilities, etc.

Preliminary Training Period

It seems advisable that such training should include a period spent at a training centre and a period "in the field," with assignment to one of the specially selected units, where new candidates would receive additional training and supervision by specially qualified and selected commanders. During this period, the training should be well grounded according to the AKS principle (developing of attitude, knowledge and skill), as discussed in the following section.

Among other factors, the importance of developing proper attitudes toward the "role conflict" inherent in modern police work, whereby a policeman appears either as a strict law enforcer, or as a helper and protector of citizens, should be carefully analyzed. It is also important to help the candidate understand the difficulties of communicating with individuals of different social classes, ethnic traditions, and ages. Most individuals working in the community find it difficult not to project onto others their own, usually North American middle-class values.

Special attention at this stage should be paid to marital or pre-marital counselling, with particular emphasis on the situations in which a policeman's wife and children may find themselves in our community. Learning to cope with marital problems and having positive attitudes to bringing up children may protect future policemen from many domestic stresses that can seriously affect their health and work.

In-service Training

No training is ever complete; all people learn throughout their lifetimes. The following points may be equally valuable during initial instruction at the training depots and throughout the professional life of a policeman.

It should be particularly underlined that the occupational life of a policeman is affected by two important factors. Most candidates enter the service with only an average level of general education; however, they will be dealing with many different people and often encounter quite complex situations and consequently they have to be willing to learn all the time. The second factor is the frequent change from one type of work to another. In other occupations, people tend to specialize and eventually stay within the rather narrow limits of their particular competence, which also gives them satisfaction and brings about recognition for being "experts." In police work, most people either remain "generalists" throughout their career or they are switched from one field to another, which generates the stressful need to acquire new knowledge and skills and deprives them of the gratification of established expertise.

Throughout in-service training, police officers should develop positive attitudes towards the self, associates and people in the community. They may be posted or transferred to special areas (isolated, Arctic, small remote villages or large, diverse metropolises); they encounter people from different subcultures and ghettos; when transferred, they go through crises of uprooting which involve themselves and their family. They cope with "developmental crises" of marriage, children, promotion, transfer, and retirement. They should be able to cope with such adjustment in their subordinates or associates and know how to identify symptoms of stress in others. They have to cope with different roles as colleagues, members of the team, subordinates, superiors and supervisors.

The policeman's family often participates in particular problems, including everyday dangers in the police profession, shift work, over-reacting of the public to any mistake by a policeman, hostility of some elements toward the policeman that may also spread to aggressive attitude toward his family, emergency situations and transfers.

In many occupational situations, the policeman has to control very forcibly his natural reactions, which results in the bottling-up of many strong feelings which may be later discharged at home, upsetting its harmony, and may undermine health.

Executive Development

Promotions with increased responsibilities generate stress and require adjustment. Some people find it particularly difficult to enlarge their scope of obligations; still others may display the "ceiling syndrome" whereby a new position exceeds their intelligence and abilities. This may be particularly harmful to conscientious individuals who function in a competent and efficient manner at lower positions but get lost when faced with more complex responsibilities. Problems of leadership and supervision, administration, budgets, new programs, etc. all create additional stress. A particularly important problem is empathy and communication across generations: a middle-aged executive has to find a common language with much younger subordinates. He must be adequately flexible and capable of examining, controlling and modifying his own reactions.

Retirement Preparations

Planning for retirement should begin a number of years before the critical date. It does not mean diverting attention from, or losing interest in, current activities; on the contrary, since better adjusted people suffer much less from possible complications of retirement, efforts to increase one's level of mental health and improve abilities to cope with stress would benefit both current work and future retirement.

The "AKS" Principle

Developing adequate stress preventive measures may be best explained by using the AKS principle (attitude, knowledge and skill). This principle applies to any type of training: as mentioned above, attitude may seriously change an individual's sensitivity to stress. People who undertake certain tasks with enthusiasm, keen interest, self-confidence, and conviction that such efforts are worthwhile would likely enjoy and benefit from such stress; many sportsmen do exactly that. On the other hand, individuals who consider the same activity useless, boring and distasteful, may bottle up a lot of resentment, with an ultimate damaging effect. The three elements in AKS are always interlinked: proper attitude helps in the acquisition of knowledge and skill; better knowledge improves the attitude and skill; and improved skill and greater experience provide higher motivation and increase understanding of a problem.

Attitude, as mentioned above, affects largely the reaction of the individual to a stressful situation. In treatment of stress-affected individuals, changing their attitude is obviously beneficial. Attitude may be influenced by factors operating from inside and outside the individual.

From inside, proper attitude is helped by:

—A good understanding of the meaning of life, work and other activities. The "right philosophy" of life helped many prisoners of war to protect themselves against stress. Well-organized life values, clear goals in every activity, positive interest, curiosity and ambition account for proper *motivation* toward work, however hard or frustrating it may be.

—Positive attitudes protect people from developing anxiety, insecurity, frustration, resentment, hostility and boredom. Proper attitudes underlie many important coping and defence mechanisms, which diminish the effects of frustration. Dr. Hans Selye,[11] an expert in stress management, recommends succinctly "fight always for the highest attainable aim, but never put up resistance in vain." This calls for good judgement with respect to different tasks, and if a certain project, challenge or situation is evaluated as worthwhile, an individual should be able to mobilize all his strength in pursuit of an ambitious but realistic goal. It also requires adequate flexibility to pull out of some situations and to withhold efforts from unrealistic dreams. Perseverance is not stubbornness!

—Other attitudinal *defences* include recognition of our limitations. People should avoid the "God Almighty" complex. Even top experts may encounter tasks beyond their proficiency. Accepting the possibility of limitations diminishes tension and adds mileage to our efforts. Everybody should try to do his best but not to work miracles. Such attitudes also help us to accept challenges in a cheerful way. An additional defence is curiosity: "how well can this task be accomplished?" is an attitude that may also be called sportsmanship. A sense of humour in encountering obstacles, and flexibility in changing attitudes toward them contribute to higher efficiency and prevent stress damage.

From outside: Having recognized the importance of our environment for proper life adjustment, it is obviously helpful to organize things around us in such a way as to obtain proper gratification, stimulation, encouragement, help and support. Certain guidelines to developing a supportive environment include:

—Feed-back: being surrounded by people who take keen interest in our work and accomplishments.

—Regular and appropriate recognition for work; lack of adequate recognition creates negative attitudes of boredom, laziness and procrastination.

—Success multiplies efforts; this is also largely dependent on reaction of people toward our accomplishments. Response from others counteracts feelings of isolation.

—The "need to be needed" is a powerful motivating factor. It is important to relate to the environment in such a way that people appreciate our competence and ask for assistance. This, however, should not be exaggerated. It is important to be able to say no to excessive demands.

—A feeling of freedom diminishes stress. People should remind themselves that many stressful situations are often the results of free choice. In counselling, analyzing and promoting such recognition helps many people change their attitudes toward stressful situations. As far as possible, opportunities to exercise freedom of choice should be taken: selecting an office, desk, secretary, associates, or even changing the placement of the furniture in the office or at home may bring about greater relaxation.

—Predictability of stressors increases security. Knowledge of schedules and periods of duty, predictable reactions of supervisors and of the members of one's family all remove uncertainty and anxiety.

—Job satisfaction is usually related to opportunity for success, recognition, adequate remuneration, fringe benefits, advancement, security, easy communication with supervisors, opportunity for ventilating grievances, etc.

—A "sympathetic ear" diminishes emotional tension. Ombudsmen, chaplains, counsellors, or simply friends are the important agents in lessening tension based on early infantile needs for love and fear of rejection.

—Close ties and healthy identification with a group, team, department or force is of positive value; in this there is mutual loyalty, support and assistance.

Knowledge and understanding help us to cope with life situations: to be informed is to be forewarned; the more one knows and understands, the less anxiety and panic are experienced and stress diminishes. In treatment of the fear of flying, explanation of the principles of aircraft operation has been found helpful. Many individuals become panicky when they experience some aches or pains but promptly relax when the doctor explains the innocent nature of their symptoms. No examination frightens students who know their material well.

In one experiment, two groups were given the same dose of mescaline, an hallucinogenic drug resembling LSD. One group was given a detailed description and explanation of the anticipated symptoms; the other was given just the drug. Not a single "bad trip" occurred among the forewarned, while in the other group many anxiety and panic reactions were observed.

Predictable stress is less harmful; knowledge of the nature of different stressors diminishes their damaging effects. Even taking a course on the nature of stress helps an individual to relax better under stressful situations through protective knowledge. Understanding the effect of crisis (transfer, promotion, change of work) diminishes its upsetting effect. Similarly, an understanding of unconscious processes, often responsible for marital conflicts, may save marriages and diminish marital stress.

Skill comes from direct practice and not from lectures and books. Mastering different tasks creates feelings of success and diminishes stress. People afraid of the water are often cured by learning to swim. Acquiring skill in using firearms, in car repairs or in techniques of interrogation diminishes the stress of such threatening and frustrating situations.

Skill increases self-confidence and flexibility. Even in many "hopeless" situations, there is often a satisfactory solution or escape if one is not "stiffened with fear" or "paralyzed with anxiety," and can rely on his own skill and experience. People who travel a lot may easily move from one place to another and visit foreign countries without excessive stress; for the inexperienced, even a short trip is a source of tension and anxiety. Being an "expert" gratifies human needs for success and recognition. A high level of skill and competence in some hobbies and favourite games and good physical fitness help many people to cope with tedious and boring everyday occupations. "The happiest and best adjusted society is the one where everybody is a top expert at something," one social analyst has said.

One should avoid factors that diminish skill: neglecting adequate training or regular practice, alcohol, smoking and drugs, overwork and inadequate rest, gaining weight and developing lazy life habits.

Adequate gratification of basic psychosocial needs has already been mentioned; in the work of police officers this is of particular importance. Such needs should be attended to in order to counteract feelings of frustration and isolation. The following needs may be identified:

—Need for *security* and for *recognition* (both within the police organization and in he police-community relations, where negative stereotypes of "cops," "hippies," etc. should be avoided or changed as far as possible);
—Need for *response*, counteracting feelings of isolation;
—Need for *new experience* in everyday functioning and in new areas of endeavour; avoidance of depressing monotony in life and work;
—*"Need to be needed,"* to be of importance to one's family and associates and to society, this is a very powerful area of positive (or negative) feedback;
—*Need for communication*: the "silent treatment," ignoring someone, depriving him of an opportunity to unburden his feelings—all have a devastating effect on mental health and stress tolerance. Many marriages collapse through deficient communication; adequate communication between supervisors and subordinates, representatives of different generations, etc. increases morale and efficiency. Counselling and psychotherapy are based on contact and communication with skilled professionals ("communicators").

NOTES

1. Stansfield Sargent and Kenneth R. Stafford. *Basic Teachings of the Great Psychologists*. Garden City, N.Y.: Doubleday and Co., 1965.
2. *Ibid.*
3. *Ibid.*
4. *Ibid.*
5. *Ibid.*
6. *Ibid.*
7. *Ibid.*
8. *Ibid.*
9. *Ibid.*
10. Margaret Philipps, *Education of the Emotions*, 1937.
11. Sargent and Stafford, *op.cit.*

FURTHER READINGS

Frankl, Viktor E. *The Doctor and the Soul*. Harmondsworth, Middlesex, England: Pelican Books.
_____. Man's *Search for Meaning*. New York, N.Y.: Pocket Books.
Philipps, Margaret. *Education of the Emotions*, 1937.
Szyrynski, Victor. *Human Personality and Principles of Communication*. Ottawa: RCMP Publications, 1969.
_____. *Understanding of Youth*. Ottawa: RCMP Publications, 1973.
_____. *Acute Family Conflicts and Helping Intervention*. Ottawa: RCMP Publications, 1975.
_____. *Understanding of Stress*. Ottawa: RCMP Publications and Canadian Police College, 1976.
_____. "Crisis Theory and Criminology." The Canadian Journal of Corrections. 10:239–251, 1968.

Chapter 17

The Future of Policing in Canada
W. J. Brown

Previous chapters present an historical and contemporary overview of the issues associated with policing in Canada. This final chapter seeks to identify future events at the global and Canadian levels and to outline ways in which the police may prepare for these events.

The Challenge: Scenarios for the Future

The Global Perspective

In order adequately to project future police roles and functions, it is desirable to identify and to understand the social, economic, technological and political forces that are likely to be in operation. It is impossible to predict with any certainty what life will be like in years to come, but various groups have attempted to set out the future global scenario.

The Institute of the Future (57) believes that there will be limits to growth and that the quality of life will be of greater importance. (11) In their opinion, there will be widespread citizen involvement and participation, a rejuvenation of urban centres, and increased emphasis on social welfare programs. Greater accountability of private- and public-sector programs will be required, as well as more understanding of the impact of technological change and the maintenance of the ecological balance between man and his environment. Many unresolved issues will still remain by 1994, such as the lack of an effective world order, laws and codes of behaviour for world peace-keeping and conflict resolution, and adequate mechanisms for allocating income among nations. Of equal importance will be the continued inability to structure institutions capable of self-renewal and adaptation to change, conflicts between the requirements of personal freedom and the demands of a collective society, and a lack of understanding of the policy and operational requirements for realizing social stability. In 1994, nuclear war will be a possible

W. J. Brown is currently Director of Research Studies, Edmonton Police Department and has been involved in many areas of the Canadian Criminal Justice System.

world threat, food will be a central issue, deterioration of the biosphere will continue, and imbalances in the distribution of wealth and material shortages will be of major concern (25).

Scenarios for the 1990s include a possible world energy shortage offset by drastic expansion of geothermal, coal, nuclear, tidal, and solar energy. However, efforts to resolve this problem will be severely hampered by a lack of international co-operation (50). Some believe that nuclear power cannot meet human requirements until 2020, and that because other energy sources are not sufficient, nations must concentrate research and development on coal. They imply that the energy crisis is due in part to a lack of government foresight and leadership; as a result, the private sector will be reluctant to invest large sums of money until government long-term energy policies stabilize (49).

The role of the family as an important component in society will be greatly diminished, its role usurped by the educational system, the media, and government social benefit programs. As a result of continued family disharmony and breakdown, new alternatives, such as the corporate family, will be found; this arrangement, defined as a legal entity, may provide stability, continuity, resources, and an infrastructure for the members to acquire education and access to technology (51). An alternative family arrangement of the future is termed the multi-adult household, in which a number of adults, often unrelated by blood or marriage, live together as a group. The benefits are thought to be an increased opportunity for human interaction and an enriched environment for children (48).

Unless understood and planned for, a new stage of technological civilization, a super-industrial stage with a transition period of twenty to fifty years, will be plagued by wars, insurrections, successionist movements, riots, revolutions, technological and ecological disasters, military outbreaks, and nuclear accidents. The impact of transition can be lessened if nation-states set out long-term democratic strategies concerned with the overhaul of industry, the reconstruction of cities, the creation of a rational energy base, a deescalation of military expenditures, and a rethinking of community structures. While there may be opportunities for freedom and self-realization, there will also be threats of serious stress caused by many demands for assimilation and control of change (57). In the period 1980 to 1985, increased social stress and tension may become more apparent if gross national product decreases. With reduced dollars for social welfare and people-oriented programs, redistribution of income will be more problematic. This could aggravate social and political conflict (3). Social and economic collapse is not imminent, but society must prepare to make numerous adjustments in the face of possible nuclear war and misunderstood technology (32).

In the leisure society predicted by futurists, 15 percent of the population will be able to provide all necessary goods and services. Should man abandon the idea that dignity and identity are derived primarily from a job, the question of life's purpose becomes crucial; in that event, educational structures will be required that stress interpersonal relations, human development, and man's intrinsic dignity (54).

The National Commission on the Causes and Prevention of Violence (62) in the United States concludes that unless drastic public action is taken, the following scenario may depict the environment of large cities of the future.

> Central business districts in the heart of the city, surrounded by mixed areas of accelerating deterioration, will be partially protected by large numbers of people shopping or working in commercial buildings during daytime hours, plus a substantial police presence, and will be largely deserted except for police patrols during nighttime hours.
>
> Highrise apartment buildings and residential compounds protected by private guards and security devices will be fortified cells for upper-middle and high-income populations living at prime locations in the city.
>
> Suburban neighbourhoods, geographically far removed from the central city, will be protected mainly by economic homogeneity and by distance from population groups with the highest propensity to commit crimes.
>
> Homes will be fortified by an array of devices, from window grills to electronic surveillance equipment, armed citizens in cars will supplement inadequate police patrols in neighbourhoods closer to the central city, and extreme left-wing and right-wing groups will have tremendous armouries of weapons which could be brought into play.
>
> High-speed patrolled expressways will be sanitized corridors connecting safe areas, and private autos, taxicabs, and commercial vehicles will be routinely equipped with unbreakable glass, light armour and other security features. Inside garage or valet parking will be available at safe buildings in or near the central city. Armed guards will ride on all forms of public transportation.
>
> Streets and residential neighbourhoods in the central city will be unsafe in different degrees and the ghetto slum neighbourhoods will be places of terror with widespread crime perhaps entirely out of control during nighttime hours. Armed guards will protect all public facilities such as schools, libraries and playgrounds in these areas (62).

The underground press suggests that, in future, riots will multiply—on the campuses, in the ghettoes, and in the jails. People will put more iron bars and locks on the windows of their homes; people will increasingly take fate into their own hands by beating up dope pushers, by sit-ins as an answer to unemployment and in support of wildcat strikes, and by looting stores in symbolic protest against price inflation (46).

The Canadian Perspective

Numerous commissions and task forces have discussed the current social, political, and economic state of Canadian affairs, in addition to developing national scenarios. Notable among these is a federal government position paper (12) outlining national direction, and policies and strategies for the years ahead. While focussing on inflation, it discusses possible national initiatives such as employment and social policies, labour/management relations, social responsibility, decentralization, growth and investment, and a policy of less direct intervention and increased reliance on the market economy.

Many are critical of the federal scenario. They suggest that the official paper omits any comprehensive and penetrating overview of national problems; in fact, it is suggested that Canada is faced with the possibility of Quebec's separation, deepening federal-provincial conflict, balkanization of the eastern, central, and western provinces, rising unemployment, high inflation rates, an energy crisis, declining ability to compete in world markets, rising balance of payments deficits, and sovereignty issues related to increasing foreign ownership and debt (56). Key issues left unidentified include the contribution of excessive government expenditures to the inflation rate, the percentage limits that government can spend of the gross national product, government's specific future priorities, and the funding of new programs. Future problem areas that require resolution are decreased productivity, the need to limit the expectations of society, the general lack of federal government goal direction, and increased government involvement in all aspects of society (45).

It is probable that inflation is the single largest problem facing this nation, and should productivity not increase, expectations for a certain standard of living and social services will not be fulfilled. Should inflation continue unchecked, the democratic free enterprise system will not survive because it is based on monetary stability. In future, governments must accept two factors: that people wish to have less government control and regulation, and that governments must operate more efficiently. The implications for public sector administrators is clear: there will be less money in the future than in the past. The environment will change from expansion to restriction and administrators must adapt to these new conditions (23).

A scenario (56) for Canada in 1984 may be projected as a result of present trends, forces and problems. It starts with the assumption that all major issues affecting individuals, groups, and organizations will be brought into the sphere of the political bargaining process, resulting in an immediate growth in government services. This leads to increased employment and welfare guarantees, and declining productivity; the result is a negative effect on profits, investment returns and business rewards. Private-sector income and wealth begin to decline, investment slows and private capital moves on to more attractive foreign opportunities. Unemployment rises and the standard of living declines. Major side effects develop such as increasing conflict over the redistribution of income and wealth. To prop up sagging employment figures, governments increase industrial loans, investments and development activities. Hard pressed to finance mushrooming operating and capital costs, the federal government prints money, raises taxes, and runs up deficits and foreign borrowings. Finally, funding limits are reached, capital and management leave the country, and foreign exchange restrictions are imposed.

Ultimately, the government cannot support welfare and pay back debt; recession develops and worsens to depression. Major government-union-business confrontations lead to chaos and to violence (56).

The Relationship: Future International and Domestic Issues, and the Role and Function of Canadian Policing

The previous section identified key issues at the national and global level. From these, it is possible to perceive three probable issues likely to affect the police role, function, and environment in a direct way at the national, provincial and municipal levels. These are: the requirement for increased accountability in the public sector; the necessity to change organizational structures to reflect changed roles and duties; and the need to counter increased social unrest, violence and criminal activity.

Increased Accountability in the Public Sector

The requirement for increased productivity and accountability in the public sector has been recognized. Traditionally, public-sector departments have been judged on system outputs rather than program outputs; that is, measurement based on the number of jobs finished rather than the degree of citizen satisfaction with the service. Measurement of performance is essential, because the knowledge derived provides essential information for planning and controlling the operations of an organization. Without a knowledge of an organization's performance, a manager cannot accurately calculate the resources required to meet a given workload. When resources are limited, the manager who knows the capabilities of an organization has the information needed to decide how far performance must be improved to cope with an increase in workload (11). For example, increased police productivity can occur in two general situations. The productivity ratio improves over time if resource needs diminish but police output remains constant; it improves if output increases but resource inputs remain constant (29). If new procedures are introduced to improve performance, the actual increase can be determined only by knowing what the performance was before and after the change. If performance is regularly monitored, significant deviations from plan can usually be detected in time to take corrective action (10).

One approach to developing the principles of effectiveness in service institutions is as follows:

1. Define "what our business is and what it should be."
2. Derive clear objectives and goals from the definition of function and mission.
3. Think through priorities of concentration, select targets, set standards of accomplishment and performance, set deadlines and begin work.
4. Define measurements of performance such as service satisfaction.
5. Use these measures as a feedback on efforts.
6. Develop an organized audit of objectives and results and eliminate programs that no longer serve the purpose or are unattainable (18).

Increasingly, the police community will be drawn into the process of performance measurement and evaluation for two reasons: policing is highly labour intensive and therefore increasingly costly; and police budgets constitute a major portion of public expenditures. Few municipal police forces have taken positive steps, however, to institute and appraise over-all operating efficiency; little work has been done to develop techniques that relate municipal police expenditures to results. It has been suggested, for example, that accountability and measurement of performance in future will not be the number of arrests made but the number of problems solved and the economic use of resources (16); consequently, it will become the responsibility of police administrators to use a systems approach to problem solving. As with other government ministries and agencies, it will be necessary to increase productivity in the face of sharply reduced annual increments; in future, police administrators will demand from staff members an account of the extent to which programs have reached target and are successful.

Traditional measures for evaluating police performance include crime rates, the number of arrests by crime category, the clearance rate, complaints from the public about police service, and activity measures of field operations. All of the above indicators are problematic. Crime rates are independent of police activity, and hence are not valid measures of performance. Arrest rates tell managers little in terms of how effective the police are in arresting the "right" person. Clearance rates do not correspond to police arrests made in the same time period. An analysis of complaints about the police often fails to discern whether it is an individual or a collective organization making the complaint; thus there is a very real danger of evaluating police performance on an inadequate and unrepresentative sample. Field activity measures record the amount of activity but fail to describe how well the job is done with available resources (63).

Presently an effort is underway to develop performance indicators and measurement techniques for municipal police forces that will begin to fulfill accountability requirements. One approach, the *patrol performance model* (6), as shown in Figure 17-1, seeks to determine the cost-effectiveness of patrol forces, and to determine the effect of changes in patrol deployment strategies on the quality of police service delivery. The model illustrates the interaction of system inputs and outputs.

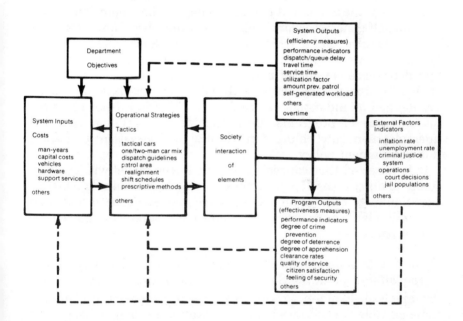

Figure 17 - 1
Patrol performance model.

System inputs have three parts: departmental objectives, internal inputs and strategies. Departmental objectives specify the resources and strategies to reach a department's goals. The broad objectives of a department may be to control crime, to protect lives and property, to maintain peace and good order, and to respond to community needs. Internal inputs are seen as costs incurred in funding an operation; in the case of patrol forces, these costs include man-years, capital costs (vehicles, hardware, etc.), support services and others. Strategies are the methods or approaches used by a department to produce the desired effect with the allotted resources. In the case of patrol forces, strategies consist of non-quantifiable procedures such as resource allocation practices and methods.

System outputs also have three parts: system outputs (measures of efficiency), program outputs (measures of effectiveness) and external factors. While the external factors tend to have an indirect influence upon patrol performance, system and program outputs play the most important role in the exercise. System outputs compare results with the resources committed to the activity; in the patrol environment, measures of efficiency include average dispatch or queue time delay, average service times, average travel times, average utilization factors, the amount of preventive patrol, the proportion of shift time for self-generated workload, and overtime. Program outputs are defined as the extent to which the stated objectives have been or are being met; examples of this include the degree of crime prevention and deterrence, quality of apprehension, and quality of service as shown by citizen satisfaction with police service. External factors are defined as indicators external to but having a bearing on the performance of programs; these include the inflation rate, the unemployment rate, changes in criminal justice system operations, and government policy.

It is expected that concepts inherent in the model will apply in future to other areas of police operations such as criminal investigation. Similarly, other approaches and techniques will be forthcoming that will advance the art of performance measurement and evaluation of police service.

Changing Organizational Structures to Reflect Changing Roles, Responsibilities and the Social and Political Environment

A major issue in planning will be the difficulty of structuring institutions capable of self-renewal and adaptation to change. Because of the responsibility to apply and to uphold a Criminal Code, statutes, regulations and bylaws, police agencies will find themselves increasingly buffeted by radical and reactionary forces, by the conflict between personal freedom and collective security. In future their position will become more difficult as opportunities for freedom and self-actualization clash with a concerted backlash of conservative forces. As society moves into and progresses through periods of rapid social and technological change, it is imperative that institutions such as the police recognize and understand the magnitude, complexity, and direction of change, and modify their organizational structures, philosophy and behaviour accordingly.

What are the major impediments to self-renewal of the policing institution? It is suggested that there are three major obstacles: the paramilitary structure, implementation problems and slippage, and police unions and associations.

The paramilitary structure. The paramilitary management style fails to recognize the reality of police operations (16). The police working model demonstrates that field personnel do act in an independent manner and do use discretion. However, because of the dilemma the police find themselves in—that is, the expectation that they will interact with the public at a professional level while operating within a hierarchical command structure built upon mistrust and negative sanctions—it is questionable whether the present system maximizes the potential of human resources or prepares and responds adequately to rapid social and political change. Present police organizations subordinate lower ranks through a rigid chain of command; this division of labour, with centralized command and direct accountability, results in an inability to innovate and to change. Contemporary police structures discourage independent behaviour and attitudes (27). Police departments were, and many still are, managed under a hard-line approach that shows little concern for human needs (55).

A considerable portion of the responsibility for the continuing state of apathy in Canadian policing must reside with chiefs and their management staff. Many police administrators have insufficient training or education, lack initiative, and consequently resist innovation. Middle-management personnel also resist change that threatens to upset the status quo and secure positions (27).

Implementation problems. In addition to structural constraints and human resistance to change, other influences act to limit the success of programs designed to improve the quality of police service. In broad terms, limits to success can be attributed to project slippage, that is, the disparity between the stated objectives and the end product. This can occur for several reasons. Program objectives may be vague or ill-defined, or project objectives and priorities can conflict or become inconsistent and incompatible as the number of agencies involved increases. An increase in regulatory bodies often slows the work. Institutional personalities are a major source of delay. For example, politicians and governments, concerned principally with short-term political expediencies, often provide inadequate support funding, or in the event that goals exceed the political means to achieve, introduce symbolic legislation without the means to enforce it. A further problem is the high turnover rate of politicians, which prevents continuity in the decision-making process. Finally, implementation problems often arise because project goals sometimes exceed the existing state of knowledge.

Police unions and associations. An important consideration in the change process will be the role played and the position taken by police unions and associations. These bodies will become increasingly important and are likely to have a strong impact on the development of the police service.

From an historical perspective, police unionism was caused by three factors: long suppressed job dissatisfaction; first-hand observation of gains made by minority groups through collective action; and an influx of young officers with radically different ideas toward authority and management (24). Generally, public servants in Canada did not become demanding until the example of private industry demonstrated to them that, if they exchanged the old notions about public service for the idea that a fair day's work deserves a fair day's pay, their lot would be greatly improved. Salaries in the public service were substantially below those in the private sector, working conditions were often poor, and all complaints were countered by the comments that there was job security. Grievance procedures, so essential to working out the normal frustrations and misunderstandings of any employment, were either non-existent or rusty from misuse (53). The net result is that the management function has come under close scrutiny of police associations; they are involved now in many areas that were formerly considered the exclusive responsibility of management (27). Termed "bureaucratic insurgency," police unions have found a mechanism that vetoes or alters the policies of an agency to meet the needs of the workers and, often, their perception of the public's needs (34). It is felt by some that the agency is being run for the convenience of its employees rather than for contribution and performance (18).

In the area of resource allocation, the status quo represents a series of hard-fought concessions from management (24). Because substantive changes in the nature of police service are often heavily dependent on management's ability to change working conditions, a fundamental change in operating policies and procedures may be blocked if a relatively minor change is challenged by the union. However, it is suggested that the rise of police unions and associations is a relatively new phenomenon. There is a lack of consensus about the extent of their role in the change process (24); some believe that the accomplishments of unions thus far can be seen as meeting the basic needs of members—wages, hours, and working conditions, with little over-all effect on the broader issues (31), while others view unions as a new and dynamic source for positive change. For the foreseeable future, it is unrealistic to expect union leadership to work entirely for dramatic change; rather, one can expect their position will be to further the short-term needs of the membership (24).

Countering Social Unrest, Violence and Criminal Activity

Scenarios described in the opening section suggest that rapid social, political and technological changes are likely to cause high levels of stress, uncertainty and frustration. It is probable that an increase in interpersonal hostility and group conflict will lead to greater anti-social and illegal behaviour in the form of disturbances and violent crime.

Police agencies will experience an increase in criminal activity broadly defined as crimes against persons and crimes against property. Murder, assault, robbery, rape and family trouble are examples of the former, while residential, commercial and industrial break and enter, arson and wilful damage illustrate the latter. It is suggested, however, that in future these common crime occurrences will be overshadowed by an emerging terrorism in the form of bombings, hostage taking, and irrational killings (22). In addition, there will be a shift to group rather than individual crime; criminal activity will become financially sophisticated and involve advanced technology (16).

A growing form of criminal activity is white-collar crime which can be described as an endeavour or practice involving the stifling of free enterprise or the promotion of unfair competition; a breach of trust against an individual or an institution; a violation of occupational conduct; or the jeopardizing of consumers and clientele (15). White-collar crime is normally committed without physical force, violence or threat, and may be an attack by an individual or conspiratorial group against an agency or large organization. White-collar crime includes such illegal activities as embezzlement, insurance fraud by arson, and trading in and the use of stolen credit cards. White-collar crime permeates society and ranges from industrial espionage to construction payoffs, from major frauds to bankruptcies, and from fraudulent stock market manipulations to the international marketing of stolen securities (13). For example, there have been more than 5,200 bank holdups in the past ten years, more than double the combined total for the previous twenty-five years; losses in 1975 exceeded $5 million. Total net fraud and forgery losses, exclusive of credit card crime, rose from $2.5 million in 1972 to $6 million in 1975; credit card fraud was in the order of $5 million. In an attempt to combat these trends, capital investment in bank security equipment was in excess of $850 million in 1975; annual maintenance charges and costs of related security services exceeded $14 million (39).

Of major importance in the future will be computer-related or computer-abuse crime. Computer abuse will occur if the return to the perpetrators is equal to or exceeds the returns from other functions in business and industry that were formerly mechanical or manual processes, and the criminal element must engage increasingly in computer abuse in order to carry on its illegal activity. Computer crime will occur in the area of electronic funds transfer and the extortion and kidnapping of financial and data processing personnel who have the skills and expertise required by the criminal element (44).

In light of increased probability for unrest, asocial behaviour, and criminal activity, it is prudent to consider the state of police preparedness to meet these challenges. This preparedness may be divided into two components: the direct and indirect approach.

The direct approach. In addition to the maintenance and expansion of direct crime prevention and detection measures such as direct intervention, high visibility, and a police omnipresence, public police forces will increasingly utilize technological advancements in resource allocation. The use of computer modelling is but one example of a more scientific approach. Modelling refers to a device or procedure that provides insight into the consequences of a decision. There are two basic types of models in use presently, the analytical and the computer simulation model.

Analytical models determine the outcome or solution from mathematical analysis by solving a set of equations. For example, the Hypercube Model (33) can be useful in aiding police planners to locate patrol units and to design response districts for a city. Another example of an analytical model is the Patrol Car Allocation Model (14), which allocates patrol units to patrol areas based on measures of performance related to the objectives of patrol operations. In this model, it is possible to predict the number and geographical distribution of patrol units to meet predetermined standards of performance.

Computer simulation models imitate the operations of a system so as to produce similar statistical behaviour as found in the real world; these models are descriptive in that they tell the policy maker what the consequences of a particular decision are likely to be. They do not, however, propose any alternatives to be considered. Examples of this work include the simulation and analysis of the patrol operations of police forces near Ottawa (35), Burnaby, British Columbia (36), and Red Deer, Alberta (37). These studies offer suggestions for improving patrol operations, such as patrol car and response time forecasting, as well as predicting future police manpower requirements. Closely associated with these studies have been projects that seek to determine accurately many simulation and operational variables. In a study of response speeds and response times (5), it was found that response times and distances travelled were frequently greater than simple calculations would suggest; this information is useful when patrol areas are being designed or patrol operations are being planned.

In addition to developing better procedures for the allocation of manpower, work has been done in the generation of work schedules. Examples of this in policing are computerized methods by Heller (1969) and Butler (1978), as well as a manual approach by Dalley (1977).

The indirect approach. In future, police agencies must be more vocal and accept the responsibility for informing the public that the police alone cannot stop social unrest and criminal activity; it is clear that all citizens must increase their level of responsibility for personal safety and security. The police thrust must be to raise the level of public awareness about criminal activity in the community. It will be the responsibility of police agencies to demonstrate that in any criminal attack there is an important interplay between the criminal and his victim; without a suitable victim, there would be no crime in the majority of cases. This new science, called victimology, suggests that victims contribute to the genesis of the crime. These victims may be classed in five ways: non-participating (victim of circumstances), latent (defenceless due to physical/mental handicap), provocative (incite criminal), participating (active or passive role) and false (victim yet no crime committed) (20).

In the resolution of any crime, it is essential to study more than the personality of the offender; rather one must study the interaction between the offender and the victim to determine the extent of the victim's contribution. This is not to condone criminal activity, but to recognize criminogenic situations and circumstances. From this, it is possible to transmit this general information to the public via innovative crime prevention programs.

Other crime counter-measures include rehabilitation of offenders, programs of instruction and education to promote defensive postures, and target-hardening such as improved locks, doors, fences, safes, and intruder-detection and crime-delaying devices (47). Unfortunately, no one has presented substantial evidence that one crime prevention activity is more effective than another, or that any of the general activities have shown signs of significantly reducing crime (26).

In the past two decades, Canada has undergone a vast migration of people from rural to urban environments. As a result, a marked trend away from single-family dwellings to medium- and high-density housing is evident. Because of the rapid increase in residence-related crime in the 1970s, social engineers began to discover certain relationships between housing density and criminal activity. As a result, crime control began to focus on the immediate environment. In a major study of the relationships of architectural design in housing projects to crime rates, it was discovered that proper building design can reduce crime. This theory, known as the concept of defensible space (42), is likely to provide further insight into the resolution of existing criminal problems in residential areas. Defensible space describes a residential environment whose physical characteristics function to allow inhabitants to become the key agents in ensuring their own security. A defensible housing complex has the appearance of being composed of small defined areas controlled by specific groups of residents.

It is imperative therefore that agents of change within the criminal justice system, particularly the police, begin a concerted drive to influence schools and students of urban architecture and planning in their orientation and philosophy. Incoming students are likely to be amenable and receptive to future design that eliminates many of the hazards inherent in present design technology.

An Approach: A Strategic Plan for Canadian Policing

The preceding description outlined several of the principal barriers to change within police organizations. While the private sector has developed and implemented innovative organizational designs, the police community has been somewhat less responsive to change; much original research and testing remains to be done. The following scenario is an attempt to advance the state of the art.

Redefinition of Objectives

The principal goal of a public service is to deliver a service to the taxpayer in the most efficient manner, just as in the private sector the goal is to maximize profits and to ensure the continuity of the organization by the efficient use of resources (23). While efficient and effective service delivery will continue to be the principal goal for the police, it is suggested that this is myopic and fails to recognize the socio-psychological needs of police personnel. As the tempo of social and technological change quickens, the philosophical base of the police service must of necessity be broadened to include innovation and change. Accordingly it is postulated that police administrators and resource persons will devote an increased proportion of their time and resources to the design and the development of organizational structures and management styles. Initial efforts to modify and to upgrade the paramilitary command structure may occur; however, as the magnitude and diversity of forces and demands made on the police magnify, the present style of management and organizational structure will prove inadequate. Police administrators will be charged not only with the responsibility for the development of new organizational models and structures, but also with the smooth and orderly transition from present structures to radically modified management styles and organizations.

The primary objective of alternative models will be to maximize the quality of police service at least cost. This mission must take precedence over all other factors and considerations, and must be a joint agreement of management, association and police membership. A second objective in the design will be the development of organizations that assimilate and maximize human resources, and provide a high degree of job satisfaction, recognition and meaning. Police administrators must develop structures to modify behaviour with respect to decision making and the expansion of responsibilities for subordinates. Lastly, the ideal organizational framework will maximize flexibility and speed, and permit a department to handle in a meaningful way necessary and inevitable contacts with social systems (40).

The Police Function and Organization Design

There are many who believe that police involvement in social problems should be restricted to immediate problem resolution, with disengagement as soon as possible and referral to the appropriate social agency for follow-up. This position is popular, it seems, because the police are not trained in counselling, and it is not possible to play the "enforcer" and "therapist" role at the same time (9). Others believe that the police role as defined by the public is seen as law enforcement and not as a social service. It is believed that if a social service function is implemented, there will be an increase in crime due to the reallocation of resources away from the detective work (64).

In spite of this current view of the police role, it is suggested that the role and function of police forces must and will change increasingly to that of public service departments with a wide diversity of responsibilities and obligations encompassing a myriad of social services (16). This change in role will come about for several reasons. It is a well-established fact that most community social service agencies fail to provide essential public assistance on a twenty-four hour basis. Because it is generally believed that an emergency service cannot be effective unless it is prompt and available at the time of need (59), police agencies will of necessity expand their roles

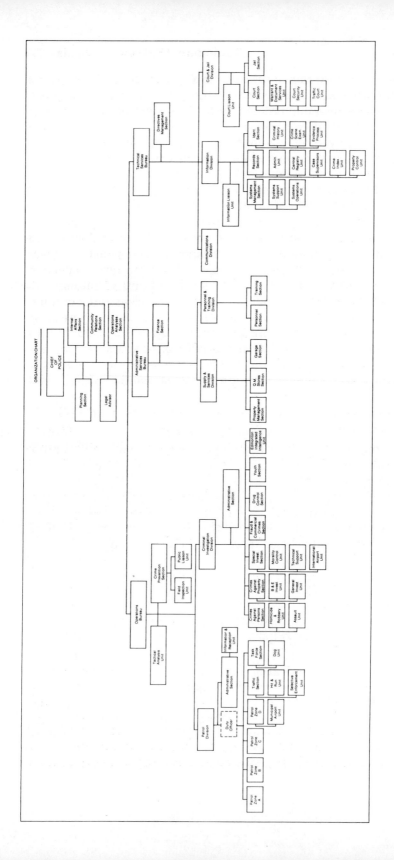

Figure 17 - 2
Organization chart.

and operational modes to meet this requirement. In addition, as the number of offences coming to police attention increases, there is a need to develop diversion processes to relieve court delay or collapse. One approach is to resolve promptly social problems whenever possible and divert people from the criminal justice system.

In order to reach these new objectives, it will be necessary to create new organizational structures. A major objective in organization design will be to broaden the span of control; that is, to increase the number of subordinates or functions that a supervisor is responsible for, and thus reduce the number of management "layers" or levels. Empirical evidence would suggest that contemporary police organizations are scalar or pyramidal in design; in this structure, great emphasis is placed on the need for many levels of authority as an inflexible rule of management. For example, Figure 17-2 illustrates the configuration for many police organizations. There is a minimum of six supervisory or management layers between street personnel and the chief of police. The resulting many-layered command structure precludes effective decentralization of services, and is dysfunctional from the point of view of attaining organizational goals (40). A current management axiom suggests that there is a set limit to the number of subordinates that a manager can adequately supervise, and that the efficiency and effectiveness of operations necessarily decrease as the number of men reporting to a supervisor increases (40). An alternative position suggests, however, that there are a variety of factors influencing the number of persons reporting to a supervisor, such as the type of co-ordination or control chosen, or the number and degree of job functions or types (38). It is difficult to say, therefore, that there is an "ideal" number in a police member-supervisor relationship; each situation must be studied in order to determine the optimum number.

A second major objective in police organization design will be to introduce decentralization; that is, to form a number of autonomous units, each with responsibility for performance, results and contribution to departmental objectives. One of the main purposes of decentralization is to strengthen top management, to allow it to carry out its principal responsibilities for setting organizational objectives, developing strategies to attain these, allocating resources, and setting the process in motion, rather than being forced to supervise, co-ordinate, and prop up organizational functions and tasks (18). The effect of decentralization is to restore two-way internal communication, to place decision-making processes at the lowest possible or optimum levels, and to prepare and test personnel for top management responsibility at an early stage. Important considerations include the need for participation, the impossibility of close supervision, and the increased responsibility of senior executives to develop subordinates (40).

An example of a non-scalar, decentralized organization design for a municipal police department is shown in Figure 17-3. This design broadens the span of control by increasing the number of assistant managers reporting to a general manager from three to seven (or more depending on the number of functions and the type of co-ordination); managers of increasingly autonomous field operations report directly to the general manager, as do assistant managers for centralized services such as technical support services, administrative services and special services.

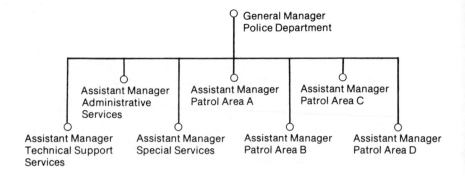

Figure 17 - 3
Non-Scalar Decentralized Management Design
for a Municipal Police Department.

At the operational level, the organizational structure consists of two major areas of specialization under one assistant manager: a Social Service Task Force (SSTF), and a Crime Prevention and Criminal Investigation Task Force (CPCITF) as shown in Figure 17-4. These functions are discussed in greater detail below.

The Social Service Task Force. The philosophy of the Social Service Task Force will be a reactive, multi-disciplinary, problem-solving approach to public service. The function of this group will be to respond to a multitude of social, civil and criminal problems and activities, such as family disputes, serious traffic accidents, armed robbery, assault, murder, lost children, youth problems and others. In an attempt to resolve problems quickly and on location, teams consisting of highly skilled police generalists, social service workers, and paralegal experts will be available in various groupings to meet the public need. There will be two positive spinoffs from this form of service delivery: each complaint that is resolved immediately reduces pressure on other social agencies and the criminal justice system; police personnel will begin to see some resolution of problems that before they could only read about reports. Insight into the resolution of complaints is a requirement for elevating the satisfaction level of police personnel.

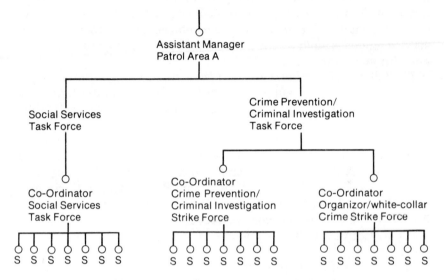

(S = squad of 7 to 9 members of multidisciplinary backgrounds with one member acting as a squad leader)

Figure 17 - 4
Non-Scalar Decentralized Organizational Design
for a Municipal Police Patrol Area.

The co-ordinator of the Social Service Task Force will be responsible for a number of multi-disciplinary squads; the number and size of squads will vary according to need and to priority, with one member acting as leader.

A concerted thrust must be made in two areas for successful implementation and operation of such a program. First, police personnel must be carefully selected and trained in this role; the techniques of crisis intervention and social mediation ought to form a large part of the training process. Candidates must possess certain physical and personality characteristics. Support staff must be prepared to rethink personal philosophies regarding the delivery process. The job will be of a non-routine nature and will require a high degree of stamina and commitment to change in the delivery of police service. The second major initiative will be the responsibility of police administrators; as greater demands for this service arise, a pool of resource workers will be required. It is recommended therefore that police administrators and agencies commence a long-range campaign to influence the current philosophy and orientation of university social service faculties. Because it is unlikely that the majority of incumbents are likely to alter present 9-to-5 counselling practices, it is imperative that the police community move to influence students and educators. Block placements with social and service agencies such as the police would promote awareness of the need for such a position.

The Crime Prevention/Criminal Investigation Task Force. While approximately 70 percent of all calls for police assistance tend to be of a service nature, it is important to realize that the general public will continue to hold the police accountable for the enforcement of laws, the prevention of crime, and the maintenance of peace, security and good order in the community. Consequently police agencies must intensify the quality of their activities to maximize productivity in this area. The philosophy of the Crime Prevention and Criminal Investigation Task Force (CPCITF) will be active preventive policing, with the express purpose of preventing, detecting, and where necessary, investigating all forms of street, organized and white-collar crime.

The organizational structure of the CPCITF will provide for two strike forces—street crime (the Crime Prevention/Criminal Investigation Strike Force, CPCISF), and organized/white-collar crime (the Organized/White-Collar Crime Strike Force, OWCCSF).

The Crime Prevention/Criminal Investigation Strike Force will consist primarily of highly trained police specialists whose purpose is to prevent, detect and suppress all forms of street crime. Taking an active position, random patrols will be abandoned in favour of directed patrols at specific targets, using decoy (member disguised as a potential crime victim), and blending (support team dressed to blend into the area) tactics, with the objective of effecting quality arrests (60). Operational methods will be supported by analysts whose function is to provide current data on criminal activity and patterns, such as shoplifting, armed robbery, sexual assaults, break and enters, and others. Plans to pursue specific targets can be formulated on the importance of suspects or groups and the intensity of criminal activity. The organizational structure will be sufficiently flexible to allow units to form and reform according to need and to priority using squads of varying size.

The Organized/White-Collar Crime Strike Force will consist of an operational and an intelligence gathering group. Principally active, the operations group will be a multi-disciplinary police specialist group, supported by resource persons such as criminologists, computer specialists, accountants and lawyers directed to sophisticated and technologically advanced white-collar/organized criminal activity. Because of resource limitations, productivity will be achieved through innovative tactical procedures and optimal allocation of personnel. Targeting—the concentration of resources at a specific suspect or group involved in criminal activity—will be based on the importance of the target in criminal activity and the degree of activity at a specific time. Such a procedure will mean a concerted and intensive round-the-clock operational style until the target has been apprehended and neutralized.

The intelligence system is to serve investigators as the single best source of accumulated information on specific offenders and their activities. As such, it will have three basic functions: to establish criteria by which information can be evaluated, to arrange a basic organization and analytical structure for information interpretation, and to develop a mechanism to reconcile or to purge conflicting information (61).

Flexibility will be a key component of this operation. Agencies need to be organized and managed so as to be alert to new variations of white-collar crime; each agency must provide a method for analyzing and detecting new schemes, and decide what resources to use in responding to a new threat (61).

The Change Process

The enlightened police administrator will be the key figure in the change process; his attitudes towards the necessity for change will set the tone within a police agency. In addition, he will invite resource persons with specialized skills and expertise in management science, operations research, budgeting and criminology to participate in the change process. These agents of change will, in consultation with management, define the short-term needs and long-range objectives of a police organization. Using specialized skills, change agents will set about to define the problem, specify the objectives, define criteria relating to the objectives, specify and analyze alternatives, present them to management for discussion and decision, and evaluate and present the results (33).

The planning process will be of increased importance; as uncertainties multiply, sophisticated and accurate planning will become vital. As society undergoes rapid social, political, economic and technological change, there will be increased need for flexibility in multiple contingency planning, and for speed in the review and revision of plans as conditions change. When predictions do not work out, the strategy will not be to abandon the planning process, but to abort that particular plan (52). The goal of a planner must be to remain flexible, and to avoid "firefighting" at all costs.

Three types of skills are required in the planning process. The first are program skills: the unit should employ one police generalist who knows the current state of the art, and in what direction policing is headed. The second skill is social analysis, drawn from a range of disciplines such as demography, urban planning and sociology. Administrative skill is also required to determine how the police structure operates and what organizational changes are needed to achieve department objectives (40). An awareness of the state of the art in the criminal justice, policing and urban service systems analysis will be mandatory for planning specialists. It will be the responsibility of all planning personnel to develop reference libraries and search systems for ongoing research (7).

A planner is not only someone who plans, but is also a person who creates and maintains a process by which plans are made by other people. He must be energetic, articulate, trustworthy and possess an interest in tomorrow's problems (4).

Attitude Shifts

In principle, it is safe to state that the main concern of most police management is the quality of police service delivery to the public. While this is the basic reason for the police service, the job enrichment needs of police personnel have taken secondary importance largely because of organizational constraints and failure to recognize that satisfying important needs of employees increases productivity. Police associations have stressed the improvement of factors such as wages and working conditions and regarded service to the public to be of secondary importance. This present relationship is shown in the upper half of Figure 17-5.

These attitudes display a high degree of short-term thinking on the part of both management and police associations. As external pressure on the police community increases, a shift in contemporary attitudes by management and labour will occur (bottom half, Figure 17-5) so that these concerns will be jointly endorsed and acted upon. There are two principal reasons for this. In order for police management to maximize the potential of each police member, present organizational structures and operating styles will develop a more participatory management style.

Secondly, as the police membership sees to needs being met and begins to subscribe to the philosophy of quality service delivery to the public, members of the force will display increasing concern for the issues and pressures confronting the organization, which will lead to the force developing a more united front.

ATTITUDE SHIFT

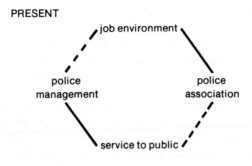

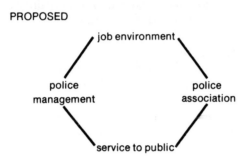

Figure 17 - 5
Required attitude shifts.

Mechanisms to Facilitate Joint Co-operation

In future, those responsible for the formation of police policy must create an environment of participatory management. This will depend increasingly on the talents of the chief of police and his ability to manage the police association's participation in the decision-making process. In future, police and association management will need to agree on which organizational objectives will maximize the quality of police service.

Present discussion arrangements will alter. For example, the present management-association consultation process, utilized in both the private and public sector to discuss issues and problems of common concern, will not only identify internal problems but will also consider external factors affecting the police organization. Because input from many levels will be encouraged by management, a greater awareness of and response to outside influences will be displayed by the police membership.

In the past, public servants such as the police could either submit their problems to binding arbitration or follow the normal route of conciliation and, in the event of failure, strike (53). In future a more formal and powerful instrument of negotiation is proposed. It is suggested that police administrators and police associations may jointly adopt the concept of mediation-arbitration as an alternative bargaining framework to compulsory arbitration in situations where strikes are illegal but where management and labour need not abrogate their collective bargaining responsibilities to the degree that they might under compulsory arbitration. Mediation-arbitration is seen as a superior form of negotiating by some in that one person, the mediator-arbitrator, serves initially as mediator, and subsequently as arbitrator if necessary. The skillful mediator-arbitrator, unlike the mediator, can use the threat or uncertainty of the binding arbitrated award to prod negotiations on. Hence collective bargaining need not atrophy to the same extent as it might under compulsory arbitration. If arbitration becomes necessary under the system of mediation-arbitration, the mediator-arbitrator is better prepared to bring forth a settlement that is satisfactory to both parties. There are problems, however, in that few skilled persons exist with these qualifications; also, few unions are prepared to relinquish the right to strike in order to invoke mediation-arbitration (21).

The Selection/Training Process

Successful decision making at lower levels is dependent upon three factors; police personnel at lower levels are competent to make decisions of greater importance within the framework of the organization's goals; personnel are given the authority to make decisions and the resources necessary to carry them out; and personnel at these levels have the desire and motivation to undertake additional responsibility. Underlying these assumptions is the necessity to select the "right" person and to educate that person properly. As the police role changes, selection criteria and training programs must adjust to changed realities.

There are two possible models for an ideal police officer. One model assumes that there is an ideal police profile and that matching this unique personality with job requirements will produce a new selection standard which, when validated, will predict on-the-job success. The other model assumes that there are several types of successful police officers with common profile areas; further research is required to identify and to validate instruments that will measure the qualities and characteristics of recruits and compare these with job specifications (9).

Training of recruits should be of a "generalist" nature, with subsequent education based on an integrated career development plan which reflects job needs and individual aspirations and abilities. In future, training curricula will emphasize the broader social and philosophical issues related to policing and the criminal justice system and also develop educational programs based on "learning by doing" techniques (9).

Summary

This chapter has attempted to link the traditional and contemporary issues in Canadian policing with projections about future possibilities and probabilities. Several global and national scenarios are provided to set the stage of events within which the police community will have to operate. The design for a decentralized organizational structure to meet probable future events has been proposed.

Social change on a vast scale will not be neat; it is a process that occurs at a million points at once. Futurists at all levels must identify new options, detect important situational variables, assign priorities to various future events, provide early warning services for the environment, the economy and society, and bring about an educational and cultural change focussing public attention on long-range problems and options through a multi-disciplinary approach (58).

In the society of the future, it is not possible or desirable to revert to former "truths," such as the divine right of kings, a revival of the church or the extended family as the solution to the problem. Rather, it is essential "to follow the challenges of new patterns of thought to see where they lead." It is suggested that such philosophies will include self-actualization, self-expression, interdependence, and a capacity for joy (65).

NOTES
1. Roy C. Amara. "Some Features of the World of 1994." *The Futurist*, June, 1974.
2. J. E. Angell. "Toward an Alternative to the Classic Police Organization." 9 Criminology, 185, 1975.
3. R. L. Ash. "The Outlook for the United States During the 1978–1985 Decade." *The Futurist*, August, 1974.
4. E. Brown. "A Planner Is Not Only Someone Who Plans." *Financial Post*, September 3, 1977.
5. W. J. Brown and F. R. Lipsett. "Response Speeds and Response Times of Urban Police Patrol Cars in Ottawa, Ontario." *Journal of Criminal Justice*, Vol. 4, No. 3, 1976.
6. _____, and D. B. Butler. "Patrol Operations: Performance Measurement and Improvement." *Canadian Police Chief*, Vol. 66, No. 3, 1977.
7. _____. "A Police Reference Library." *The Canadian Peace Officer*, October, 1975.

8. D. B. Butler. Computerized Manpower Scheduling. M.Sc. Thesis: University of Alberta (forthcoming).

9. Canada. "The Role of the Police in a Changing Society." Ottawa: Solicitor-General, 1972.

10. Canada. "Operational Performance Measurement." Ottawa, Treasury Board, Volumes 1 and 2, 1974.

11. Canada. "A Manager's Guide to Performance Measurement." Ottawa, Treasury Board, 1976.

12. Canada. "The Way Ahead: A Framework for Discussion." Ottawa: Anti-Inflation Board, 1976.

13. Canadian Association of Chiefs of Police. "Prevention of Crime in Industry." Secretariat. Ottawa, 1974.

14. J. M. Chaiken and P. Dormont. Patrol Car Allocation Model. Santa Monica: Rand Corp., 1975.

15. Chamber of Commerce of the United States. White Collar Crime. Washington, D.C.: Library of Congress, 1975.

16. V. Cizanckas. "The Role of the Police in the Year 2000." Santa Monica: Centre for the Study of Democratic Institutions, 1975.

17. A. F. Dalley. "A Systematic Approach to Shift Scheduling." RCMP Gazette, Vol. 38, No. 11, 1977.

18. P. F. Drucker. Management; tasks, responsibilities, practises. New York: Harper & Row, 1974.

19. J. F. Elliott. The New Police. Springfield, Ill.: Chas. C. Thomas, 1974.

20. E. A. Fattah. La Victime Est-Elle Coupable? Montreal: Presses de la Universite de Montreal, 1975.

21. E. G. Fisher and H. Starek. "Police Bargaining in Canada: Private Sector Bargaining, Compulsory Arbitration, and Mediation-Arbitration in Vancouver." Vancouver: University of British Columbia, 1977.

22. M. Fooner. "The Vulnerable Society." The Police Chief, Vol. 4, No. 2, 1974.

23. J. Gillies. "Managing in Times of Rapid Social Change." The Business Quarterly, Winter, 1976.

24. H. Goldstein. Policing in a Free Society. Cambridge: Ballinger Press, 1977.

25. T. J. Gordon. "Some Crises That Will Determine the World of 1994." The Futurist, June, 1974.

26. J. L. Grenough. "Crime Prevention: A New Approach." J. Pol. Sc. & Admin. Vol. 2, No. 3, 1974.

27. B. A. Grossman. Police Command, Decisions and Discretion. Toronto: MacMillan of Canada, 1975.

28. N. Heller. "Proportional Rotating Schedules." Ph.D. dissertation, University of Pennsylvania, 1976.

29. M. Holzer. "Police Productivity: A Conceptual Framework for Measurement and Improvement." J. Pol. Sci. & Admin., Vol. 1, No. 4, 1973.

30. C. R. Jeffery. Crime Prevention Through Environmental Design. London: Sage Publications, 1971.

31. H. A. Juris and P. Feville. Police Unionism. Lexington: Lexington Books, 1973.

32. H. Kahn. "Things Are Going Rather Well." The Futurist, December, 1975.

33. R. C. Larson. Urban Police Patrol Analysis. Cambridge: MIT Press, 1972.

34. M. A. Levi. Conflict and Collusion: Police Collective Bargaining. Cambridge: MIT Press, 1974.

35. F. R. Lipsett and J. G. Arnold. "Computer Simulations of Patrol Operations of a Semi-Rural Police Force." J. Pol. Sci. & Admin., Vol. 2, No. 2, 1974.

36. F. R. Lipsett, A. F. Dalley and J. G. Arnold. "Patrol Operations of Burnaby RCMP Detachment, Analysis and Simulation." Ottawa: National Research Council, Report ERB-887, 1975.

37. F. R. Lipsett, A. F. Dalley and J. G. Arnold. "Patrol Operations of Red Deer Rural RCMP Detachment." Ottawa: National Research Council, Report ERB-892, 1975.

38. J. A. Litterer. The Analysis of Organizations. New York: John Wiley and Sons, 1965.

39. R. A. McElwain. "Fighting the Cost of Crime." *The Canadian Banker and ICB Review*, Vol. 84, No. 3, 1977.
40. J. L. Munro. *Administrative Behavior and Police Organizations.* Cincinnati: W. H. Anderson Co., 1973.
41. National Institute of Law Enforcement and Criminal Justice. "Traditional Preventive Patrol." Washington: U.S. Department of Justice, 1976.
42. O. Newman. *Defensible Space: Crime Prevention Through Urban Design.* New York: MacMillan, 1972.
43. Ontario. Report of the Task Force on Policing in Ontario. Toronto: Solicitor-General, 1974.
44. D. B. Parker. *Crime by Computer.* New York: Charles Scribner's Sons, 1976.
45. D. A. Peach. "The Way Ahead—A Familiar Road." *The Business Quarterly*, Spring, 1977.
46. W. Powell. *The Anarchist's Cookbook.* New York: Lyle Stuart, Inc., 1971.
47. President's Commission on Law Enforcement and the Administration of Justice. *The Challenge of Crime in a Free Society.* Washington: U.S. Government Printing Office, 1967.
48. J. Ramey. "Multiadult Household." *The Futurist.* April, 1976.
49. L. Rocks and R. Runyon. *The Energy Crisis.* New York: Crown Publishers, 1972.
50. V. Smil. "Energy and the Environment." *The Futurist*, February, 1974.
51. D. P. Snyder. "The Corporate Family—A Look at a Proposed Social Invention." *The Futurist*, December, 1976.
52. Special Report. "Corporate Planning: Piercing Future Fog." *Business Week*, April 28, 1975.
53. W. Stewart. *Strike!.* Toronto: McClelland and Stewart, 1975.
54. R. Strom. "Education for a Leisure Society." *The Futurist*, April, 1975.
55. C. J. Swank. "The Police in 1980: Hypotheses for the Future." J. Pol. Sci. & Admin., Vol. 3, No. 3, 1975.
56. D. H. Thain and M. C. Baetz. "Canada's Way Ahead . . . On Course or Headed for Disaster." *The Business Quarterly*, Spring, 1977.
57. A. Toffler. *Future Shock.* New York: Random House, 1970.
58. _____. "The American Future is Being Bumbled Away." *The Futurist*, April, 1976.
59. H. Treger, D. Thomson and G. Jaeck. "A Police-Social Work Team." *Crime and Delinquency*, Vol. 20, No. 3, 1974.
60. *United States.* "Street Crime Unit." Washington: Department of Justice (LEAA), 1974.
61. *United States.* "The Investigation of White Collar Crime." Washington: Department of Justice (LEAA), 1977.
62. *United States National Commission on the Causes and Prevention of Violence*, Washington, 1969.
63. *United States National Commission on Productivity.* "Opportunities for Improving Productivity in Police Service." Washington, 1972.
64. *University of Toronto.* "Private Policing and Security in Canada: A Workshop." Toronto: Centre of Criminology, 1973.
65. L. T. Wilkins. "Crime in the 1990's." *Futures*, September, 1970.

Index